PROTESTORS AND THEIR TARGETS

PROTESTORS AND THEIR TARGETS

Edited by JAMES M. JASPER *and* BRAYDEN G KING

TEMPLE UNIVERSITY PRESS
Philadelphia • *Rome* • *Tokyo*

TEMPLE UNIVERSITY PRESS
Philadelphia, Pennsylvania 19122
tupress.temple.edu

Library of Congress Cataloging-in-Publication Data

Names: Jasper, James M., 1957– editor. | King, Brayden G, editor.
Title: Protestors and their targets / edited by James M. Jasper and Brayden G King.
Description: Philadelphia : Temple University Press, [2019] | Includes bibliographical
   references and index.
Identifiers: LCCN 2019015537 (print) | LCCN 2019014203 (ebook) | ISBN 9781439919118
   (cloth : alk. paper) | ISBN 9781439919125 (pbk. : alk. paper) | ISBN 9781439919132
   (E-book)
Subjects: LCSH: Social movements. | Political participation.
Classification: LCC HM881 .P7696 2019 (ebook) | LCC HM881 (print) |
   DDC 303.48/4—dc23
LC record available at https://lccn.loc.gov/2019015537

9 8 7 6 5 4 3 2 1

For Frances Fox Piven

Contents

Preface | James M. Jasper ix

Introduction: The Dance of Interaction | James M. Jasper
and Brayden G King 1

Part I: How Social Movements Select Targets

1 Disruptive Movements and the Play of Politics
| Frances Fox Piven 35

2 Why Did They Keep Quiet? Missing Protests against
School Closures in Sweden | Katrin Uba 49

Part II: Movement-Target Interactions

3 Protests, Precariousness, and Democracy: Cities and
"Service Delivery" in the Global South | Gay Seidman 69

4 Been Down So Long, It Looks Like Up to Me: Targets,
Repertoires, and Democracy in the U.S. Labor Movement
| Kim Voss and Pablo Gastón 91

5 Protest Episodes: Shifting Actors and Targets in Local
Movements | Kenneth T. Andrews and Sarah Gaby 124

Part III: Outcomes of Interactions

6   How Targets Influence the Influence of Movements:
    An Institutional Mediation Approach | Edwin Amenta
    and Nicole Shortt   145

7   Bolivian Water, Mexican Corn: State Response to Subsistence
    Protests | Erica S. Simmons   161

8   Missing Targets: Contemporary Slaveholder Responses to
    Human Rights Advocacy | Austin Choi-Fitzpatrick   191

    Contributors   213

    Index   217

Preface

This book is the result of a workshop sponsored by the Collective Behavior and Social Movements section of the American Sociological Association in Chicago in 2015. The first of these workshops was held in Ann Arbor in 1988, only a few years after the section was founded. The outcome was *Frontiers in Social Movement Theory*, one of the theoretically richest books ever published on social movements. We are still following the cultural and social-psychological paths that its authors blazed as a way out of the structural paradigm of resource mobilization and political process.

A 1992 workshop in San Diego propelled the field down the cultural path rather than the social-psychological trail. *Social Movements and Culture* found processes of meaning making in a number of places in social movements, helping confirm concepts like frames, narratives, collective identities, and rhetoric as unavoidable in the study of political action. The section's 1998 workshop in Davis then reinforced these trends, and by the end of the 1990s, purely structural theories that ignored the points of view of the players were no longer tenable.

A 2002 workshop at Notre Dame, "Authority in Contention," reasserted the centrality of conflict and strategy after the two workshops on culture. But as the title suggests, it revolved around images of challengers and elites, as influenced by structural notions of a movement in relation to its environment. A workshop at Hofstra in 2007 continued the theme of strategic engagement but with greater emphasis on actors and agency. As one of the editors of the resulting book, Rachel Kutz-Flamenbaum, wrote, *Strategies for Social Change* was intended to "create a model that reflects the processual and reiterative nature of strategy as a series of interactions between actors, targets, and opponents within specific cultural and structural frameworks" (2012, 285). Readers were encouraged to see the relationship between protestors and their environment in strategic terms rather than (or in addition to) the structural vocabulary that still permeated research.

Protestors and Their Targets follows this trajectory a step further. A more fully dynamic and interactionist framework examines all the players who engage one another across a number of strategic arenas. This book examines both the targets and the protestors as they feel and think about each other, do character work on each other, recruit new players, take advantage of shocks and opportunities, and try to win whatever is at stake in each arena. We are interested in understanding these long chains of interactions without losing a sense of institutional structures, cultural understandings, emotions, collective identities, tactical habits, and all the other theoretical accomplishments of recent decades.

Organizing a workshop is like organizing a demonstration. Chicago was no exception. We relied on our personal networks but also built new ones. Two of the organizers (Michelle Proctor and Wayne Santoro) had been elected to the CBSM Workshop Committee, another (Jasper) just started showing up uninvited (relying on his official position as the 2015 chair of the section), while yet another (King) offered necessary resources thanks to his official position at the Kellogg School of Management at Northwestern University. Austin Choi-Fitzpatrick contributed a frame, protestors and their targets, although we also faced the dilemma of how narrowly to focus on this rather than open the workshop to all suggestions (the extension dilemma). Our affluent elite ally, the Kellogg School, generously provided space for the meeting, technical support for the website, know-how about other things we needed to do, and food to keep us going each day. *Mobilization* sponsored a great party that allowed us all to toast Hank Johnston and the journal's twenty years of great scholarship on protest and social movements. Although Michelle and Wayne had commitments that prevented them from working on the book, we appreciate their efforts in making the workshop such a success. Thanks go, finally, to all who volunteered, organized sessions, presented papers, or simply attended.

Thanks go as well to Ryan Mulligan at Temple University Press, whose enthusiasm and suggestions kept us going during the long process of harassing contributors and refining arguments.

James M. Jasper

REFERENCE

Kutz-Flamenbaum, Rachel V. 2012. "Conclusion: Conceptualizing Strategy in an Interactive Processional Model." In *Strategies for Social Change*, edited by Gregory M. Maney, Rachel V. Kutz-Flamenbaum, Deana A. Rohlinger, and Jeff Goodwin, 285–300. Minneapolis: University of Minnesota Press.

PROTESTORS AND THEIR TARGETS

Introduction

The Dance of Interaction

JAMES M. JASPER AND BRAYDEN G KING

> Strategies are forged in a dance of conflict and cooperation between the parties to interdependent relations.
>
> —FRANCES FOX PIVEN, *Challenging Authority*

Protestors have purposes as well as passions. They threaten, persuade, spend money, and make claims on others, and these targets respond with their own dizzying array of tactics. These interactions between protestors and their targets shape the world around us in profound ways. This book takes a new look at these strategic interactions.

After decades of productive inquiry into the antecedents of collective action, intramovement dynamics, and the consequences of movement activity, the time has come for an emphasis on the targets that generate such contention and collective effort to better understand why movements do what they do and why their interactions with other societal actors turn out as they do.

Targets are part of the definition of social movements. As theories of social movements emerged out of crowd theories in the 1960s, one of their new, distinguishing ingredients was attention to "the appropriate agencies of control" that activists targeted in their efforts to spur change (Smelser 1962, 17). There were always other players in serious discussions of social movements; there had to be targets against which protest could be directed. Crowds might aimlessly express emotions; social movements, in contrast, aim their anger at targets—although not always the expected targets. It is now a truism that protestors are complaining about something—and to *someone*.[1]

Despite the central importance of targets to social movement activity, social movement theorists have not conceptualized movement targets as well as they could have. In the 1970s, the target was mostly assumed to be the state, especially in what came to be known as political process theory: Both the emergence of the movement and its influence were attributed directly to the structures of the state and the opportunities they provide or deny (McAdam 1982). Challengers battle members of the polity for admission, so that the state is both the arena and the central player making decisions about who can be citizens. Political process theory pointed to the importance of the "political environment" facing movements without always examining the full range of players that make up that environment.

As social movement theory developed, new perspectives offered alternative views of social movements' interactions with other players in the environment, but none of them captured the strategic importance of targets. For example, game theory offers a compelling depiction of individuals' choices and the recurrent trade-offs and dilemmas that these choices imply (Lichbach 1995), but the theory simplifies the social and political context of movement actors and fails to attend to the flows of interaction among a variety of players typical of a social movement or to explain why certain kinds of actors become the targets of a movement. John McCarthy's and Mayer Zald's (1977) theory of resource mobilization sought to explain how movement organizations emerge and thrive, depicting movements as interactive and strategic, but they focused—in their "partial theory"—on relatively friendly interactions with supporters rather than on conflictual engagements with opponents. Missing from this perspective were movements' short- and long-term strategic interactions with their targets. The cultural approaches that emerged in the 1990s also examined movements from the inside: the frames and moral shocks that help them recruit new members; the collective identities that offer solidarity for those members; and the narratives they develop to encourage participants. Less attention was given to the trade-offs between the cultural meanings that aid the movement internally and those that help them influence the external targets of the movement. When emotions were added to cultural theories, they too were almost always applied to movement participants and almost never to the police, government officials, corporations, and other players.[2]

These perspectives missed opportunities to flesh out our understanding of the targets of movements. Although resource mobilization theorists developed a framework of how movement organizations compete and mobilize donors and other resources, they did not simultaneously articulate how targets' use of resources influence *their* responses to movement players and shape their long-term strategies for gaining political advantages. Cultural approaches articulated a perspective on the internal workings of culture, emotions, and frames, but they ignored how the cultural meanings equally affect their targets' emotions and moral reactions. Movements, likewise, respond to the cultural expressions of their targets and often form cultural strategies that contest the symbols and discourse of their targets. The target remains a hollow creature in the social movement literature—largely lacking in strategy, motivation, and cultural tools.

This is a book about protestors *and* their targets, which includes how they view each other, how they interact, and how their strategies unfold. Their strategic interactions unfold over long periods, across many arenas, even as the players themselves are frequently transformed. In these interactions we see a variety of gains and losses for all the players involved; in almost no case is there a single big battle that determines everything. Even in cases where it seems that compromises have been reached, new issues and grievances emerge around which players strategize. Contestation never ends.

Our understanding improves—in the social as in the natural sciences—when our models replace vague entities with more precise ones. Our theories, which we discuss in more detail later, have sensitized us to the importance of the political and social context in which movements operate, but perhaps in doing so we have failed to develop a vocabulary for talking about the specific activities and interactions that occur between contending players operating in that context. Throughout the Introduction, we argue that our scholarly inattention to targets is a product of a theoretical orientation around movements operating within and against structures, institutions, and fields. These perspectives have masked the interactions between players operating strategically in different arenas and stunted our ability as scholars to theorize the nature of these interactions. Refocusing our attention on interactions between movements, targets, and other players helps us to see inside the structures that have dominated social movement theories and gives us a clearer view of the strategies and actions that both movements and targets deploy.

We believe the time has come to place equal emphasis on the various players in contentious settings so as to focus more on their interactions: to specify what populates "the environment" for social movements. What expectations do the players start with? What patterns can we discern in their engagements? How do gains and losses emerge along the way? How do the players themselves change during and due to their engagements?

Movements and Their Contexts

Much contemporary theory conceptualizes movements as operating within strong contexts that are both the sources of a movement's emergence and the forces against which the movement struggles to change. States and institutions figure heavily in these theories. Movement actors' views of what is possible are constrained or enlivened by shifts in the states and institutional alignments. Scholars' theorizing about these extramovement constraints have influenced how we think about what movements seek to accomplish and how they do it. We view these perspectives as problematic in that each fails to take seriously the idea that contexts are actually made up of many different types of interacting, strategic players, any of which can become the target of a movement. We now describe these theoretical oversights in more detail and highlight how they have led us to overlook the interactions between movements and their targets.

Political Opportunities

In the political process model, political opportunities are thought to allow or prevent protestors from mobilizing and obtaining their goals (Tilly 1978; McAdam 1982; Kriesi et al. 1995; McAdam, McCarthy, and Zald 1996). Opportunities, such as a government scandal or a squabble among elites, are thought to open or close, stirring movements to action inasmuch as actors consider the reduced costs of mobilizing or the increased potential for success. Scholars portrayed protestors as maneuvering within these structures and taking advantage of opportunities when they appear. Political opportunities are exogenous to collective action and strategies, and social movements have little chance of influencing them (cf. Kurzman 1996).

Inasmuch as political process theorists conceived of political opportunities as resting mostly with the state, movements are largely seen as ineffectual players, dependent on the state to change the norms and rules of society. Poor and oppressed people in particular find it hard to mobilize by themselves. In resource mobilization variants, they need the money that sympathetic elites can provide; in more political versions they require some decline in state repression, whether as a result of fiscal crisis, moral sympathy, or disagreements among elites.[3] Most of the time polities are stable orders that give little access to challengers. Only when those political structures become unstable do social movements have wiggle room to mobilize and generate any sort of influence.

This state-heavy conceptualization of movement behavior was, ironically, often quite devoid of the very actors that run governments, including the lawmakers, regulators, and state bureaucrats who implement policies (for exceptions, see Andrews 2001; King, Cornwall, and Dahlin 2005). The weakness of political process theory was in failing to characterize and even in masking the concrete interactions between these actors as well as the host of other players that move in and out of the state to accomplish their goals, including lobbyists, experts, and government contractors. By portraying political opportunities as fairly static structures, scholars failed to recognize the dynamic aspects of the political context (cf. Soule et al. 1999; McDonnell, King, and Soule 2015).

Conceptualizing states as made up of political opportunities led scholars to think of movement actors as highly reactive and one-dimensional. For example, many studies erroneously portrayed a social movement organization as existing solely to pursue the passage of a single law, which is undoubtedly a simplification of a more complex strategy for social change. But theorizing movements as reactants to opening and closing opportunities unintentionally leads us to simplify their actions and portray them as less strategic than they really are.

Once we consider the full range of players involved in any change process, we recognize that "political opportunities" are quite dynamic. Opportunities are what players make of them. An action (say, by elites or states) typically causes a reaction from other players (such as protestors). If that reaction leaves the second player in a better position, political opportunity theorists go back and call the first player's action an "opportunity" for the second player. This obviously underplays the causal impact of the second player's reaction, which could instead have been dumb rather than smart, further disadvantaging the second player. This truncated form of analysis also results from an image of movements and their environments, with the latter either generating or closing off opportunities. In this way, even clear setbacks, such as police repression, can be called opportunities, because the players attacked can turn their setbacks into public sympathy or anger and outrage. But this does not mean that the setback was actually a positive opportunity all along in any objective sense.

A similar problem in the political opportunity structure perspective is that many political opportunities are not identified a priori by researchers in a deductive fashion. Rather, scholars examine the conditions associated with a change in movement behavior (such as the founding of new organizations) and then subsequently label these conditions as an opportunity. A political opportunity became any environmental condition associated with changes in movements' actions. Even grievances were sometimes viewed, in a post hoc fashion, as opportunities, since movements would not appear without them (Smith and Jasper 2012).

Theoretical challenges mounted when scholars studied movements that do not operate in traditional political environments: movements that aim to change cultural understandings, often through art; those that attempt to establish alternative institutions; or those that promote religious views and conversions (Calhoun 1993; Goodwin and Jasper 2004). Attempts to fit the concept to different kinds of opportunities—exogenous changes in culture are just cultural opportunities—stretched the metaphor to the point of masking more than it reveals about certain contexts. Applying the language of political opportunity structure theory to corporations, for example, may unintentionally downplay the intentions of executives who run those companies or simplify the strategic intentions and actions of the corporation itself.

Corporations are vulnerable to the "disruptive power" of workers who can shut down key processes, such as dock and warehouse workers or truckers (Piven 2006, 38). Joseph Luders (2006) observes that targets weigh these disruption costs against the costs of concessions to movement demands. James Jasper and Jane Poulsen (1993) point out that in addition to these structural weaknesses, targets often create their own vulnerabilities, as occurs when they are caught in a lie. (Note that lying itself may give them an advantage, and it turns to a disadvantage only when discovered and revealed to the right audience.) The so-called paradox of state repression is similar: It may succeed in reducing protest, or it may instead inspire more, depending on how protestors (and bystanders) respond.[4]

Deconstructing political opportunities as interactions between players with sometimes conflicting goals and strategies helps us better understand the co-evolving patterns of protest and other movement tactics (Bosi 2008).[5] We must observe what occurs in specific arenas and not simply use the language of political opportunity to encase those interactions and relationships in structure. Once we dive into the context more deeply and explain the interactions between various players within that context, the concept of political opportunity loses its utility and we need more precise theoretical language to describe why players behave as they do.

Institutions

Social movements seek to change institutions, and for that reason institutional theory has informed our understanding of how movements operate. The power of institutional theory is to highlight the connection between norms, roles, and other ideas, on the one hand, and what people actually do, on the other hand, to enforce the norms, express roles, and spread ideas (Meyer and Rowan 1977; DiMaggio and Powell 1991; Jepperson 1991). Inasmuch as social movements seek to change institutions, scholars have seen their function as challenging or reconciling norms and values that are contradictory or obsolete (Smelser 1962; Clemens 1997; Armstrong 2002).

Much contemporary institutional theory has conceived of institutions as exogenous to action (and interaction) and as providing a template or set of operating principles by which actors behave. John Meyer and Brian Rowan (1977) even defined institutions as myth and ceremony, providing a general blueprint for individuals, who are thought to satisfy cultural expectations rather than technical ones. In many ways, the new institutionalism is a return to more of a consensus model than that of "old institutionalists" such as Philip Selznick and Alvin Gouldner, who believed that organizations evolve out of contestation over basic values (Stinchcombe 1997, 2).

One of the challenges for institutional theory is to explain how institutional structures change, given their tendency to reproduce themselves. In some theories, social movements have been assigned this social function of inventing new institutions, a source of creativity and agency in otherwise structural models (Smelser 1962; Habermas 1987, 391–399: Luhmann 1996, 397–404; Touraine 1981). This model of institutional change has become common in organizational theory, which frequently posits that movement-like activity is the force that underlies the creation of new markets and organizational forms (Hargrave and Van de Ven 2006; Hiatt, Sine, and Tolbert 2009; King and Pearce 2010). Such theories know in advance what a movement is "really" about, even if its participants do not.

The problem of change is linked to the question of who brings it about. Martin Kitchener complains that institutional analysts "have generally provided accounts of a new logic and archetype being imposed, top-down, by powerful actors (e.g., state agencies) relatively quickly, and with little reported *resistance to change*" (2010, 128; emphasis in original). Although it may be true that powerful actors initiate change most of the time (given our circular definitions of power, this is probably true by definition), institutional theory potentially hides the efforts of other players. It becomes unclear what norms are (and especially whose they are) or how they are distinct from the institutions that supposedly carry and enforce them (Finnemore 1996).

In the absence of a robust theory of change and its agents, institutionalist and other structural theories tend to exaggerate the coercive power of institutions and the agreement among those who participate in them. Institutions, as they have come to be defined, mask the boiling discontent and disagreement that often exist among those who contribute in some way to their reproduction.[6] Recent efforts to explain change have emphasized the complexity of institutions, including the overlapping, sometimes conflicting "institutional logics" that inform identities and norms of appropriateness for domain-specific behavior (Thornton, Ocasio, and Lounsbury 2012). Players take advantage of the multiplicity of institutional norms to assert their own values and interests and create opportunities for institutional innovation (Kraatz and Block 2008).

Yet institutional logics are still seen as exogenous to interactions. Players "interpret and respond to pressures emanating from wider field-level logics" (Lee and Lounsbury 2015, 850). The institutional-logics perspective can obscure the central role of interactions between different players as the basis for the institutional pressures, substituting logics for behavior and using actions as an indicator or expression of a particular logic (Lee and Lounsbury 2015). Not surprisingly, the actions of targets themselves are nearly irrelevant in institutional theory, inasmuch as targets are not purposeful or strategic actors in their own right but rather representatives or instantiations of an institution. Their motives are nearly as inscrutable as those of their movement counterparts.

In taking a closer look at the strategic interactions between players that overlap multiple institutions, we may discover that the institutions are more temporary, situational, and malleable than previously thought. Although we certainly recognize that any sound analysis of movements and their targets takes into account the surrounding institutional forces and norms that shape interactions, we believe that focusing on the strategic interactions between the various players also helps us better understand the changing dynamics of the institutions themselves.

Movements and Their Dynamic Interactions with Targets

Highlighting movements' targets requires that we think more carefully about the interactions between movement actors and other players in their environment, including those players that eventually turn into targets. Simply conceptualizing targets as part of a movement's context—either as part of a political opportunity structure or as a reflection of the institution—obscures the ways in which their actions influence what movements do and how movements' actions, in turn, shape targets.

Similarly, overly structural models do not account for changes of and within those structures, make structures appear more stable than they are, and do not allow dynamism in the relations between actors operating within structures, such as the state.[7] Not only innovation but any sort of dynamism in structural models typically comes from the outside, from exogenous shocks and other factors that are not part of the structures. Even endogenous models of institutional change assume that change tends to occur when a particular structural vulnerability arises (e.g., Clemens and Cook 1999), discounting the possibility that structural vulnerabilities are the products of interactions between various players in an arena.

In short, theorizing about movements and change has been weighed down by the heavily structural language that obscures and discounts the importance of strategic interactions among different types of actors. We offer two theoretical perspectives that could advance the way we conceptualize movement-target interactions and therefore potentially breathe life into our understanding of movement targets: field theory and a theory of arenas.

Field Theory

Pierre Bourdieu developed the concept of a field as a form of social structure in which we could map individuals, based especially on the amount and types of capital they bring to the field, the skills or habitus they demonstrate, or their relative success in the field. With this idea he could show the competition and latent conflict at the heart of institutions, for instance, academia, that are frequently viewed as consensual and cooperative.

The subjective element within fields is modest, as choices are made on the basis of a habitus typically internalized at a young age,[8] but recently scholars have adapted Bourdieu's theory of fields to conceptualize how players with varying levels of capital struggle for control over meaning and the "rules of the game" across a variety of domains (e.g., Goldstone 2004, 2015; Fligstein and McAdam 2012; King and Walker 2014). In these perspectives, fields are seen as relational and subject to bouts of stability and instability as players seek to exert influence and gain control over the field. In this view of fields, "social outcomes emerge from the multiple interactions of various actors and groups in highly non-linear fashion. Relationships move toward tipping points, coalitions build and expand, and security forces hold then suddenly divide and break" (Goldstone 2015, 236).

A common feature of these theories is that they seek to rethink institutions, including the state, as dynamic structures that transform and are transformed by interactions among actors. Neil Fligstein and Doug McAdam, for example, reject the view of the state as unified, hegemonic, and capable of imposing stability on fields from the outside. Instead, they usefully argue, "stability is relative and even when achieved is the result of actors working very hard to reproduce their local social order" (Fligstein and McAdam 2012, 7). Institutions, including corporations, are fields and therefore subject to contestation.

One benefit to seeing the world through the lens of field theory is to draw attention to players' relative positions and the access their positions give them to different kinds of resources, which in turn create power imbalances as they interact. In this way, field theory offered an improvement over other perspectives, because it brought more specificity to the players themselves and suggested that institutions and structures were ever changing, dynamic, and continually subject to contestation. One downside to the field metaphor is that it draws attention away from the interaction itself, focusing instead on the aggregate of interactions as represented in players' field positions (a problem similar to that of political opportunity structures). The elegance of field theory in representing players as distributed across unequal positions also tends to obscure the dynamic processes through which those positions are created and reinforced through interactions with other players.

At its worst, field theory relies on structural language and fuses several moving parts, sometimes to explain one of them but often on the assumption that they move together. In particular, as a structural model, it predicts what players will do based on their positions in the field or the habitus (or social skills) that they have brought with them to the field. By examining individuals' political careers, in and out of many organizations and movements, Olivier Fillieule (2010) shows that reducing players to mere positions in fields misrepresents the microlevel biographies of these players.

But at its best, field theory highlights the struggles between players as central to the creation, reproduction, and disruption of institutions, bringing greater attention to the strategic interactions between various types of players in this process. For instance, Sandra Levitsky and Jane Banaszak-Holl redefined institutions as fields in which "relations among a set of diverse actors all seeking to influence a common institution, whether that institution represents normative prescriptions for how social dynamics occur or is more rigidly embedded in legally sanctioned organizational forms" (2010, 11). In this view, actors are not heavily constrained in a top-down fashion by norms or rules, but instead we can see norms and rules as emerging out of the relations between actors. Similarly, Verta Taylor and Mayer Zald combine the concepts of institution and field, positing that the field is "driven by conflicting logics and beliefs about how practices and roles tied to the institution ought to be enacted" (2010, 307).

Moreover, field theory helps us reconceptualize structures, such as the state or a corporation, as a dynamic field of relations between different types of actors engaged in a struggle over meaning and control. Fields may vary between moments of stable cooperation and intense conflict and innovation, much as Donatella della Porta theorized that structural change often takes place during intense moments of "eventful protest" (2014, 17). Or as Mary-Hunter McDonnell, Brayden King, and Sarah Soule theorize, when we consider the strategic interactions between movements and players within a structure, we begin to see that political opportunities are "dynamic and responsive to social movement activities" (2015, 672). Movements are capable of creating their own opportunities inasmuch as they gain strategic advantages over their targets or develop cooperative relationships with former adversaries. If we wish to retain the most useful aspects of political opportunity theory then, as della Porta and McDonnell, King, and Soule suggest, we ought to refocus our attention on the ongoing interactions between movements and targets that lead to continual evolution in opportunities for influence.

Fligstein and McAdam (2012) contend that players are always trying to change structures and outcomes to their advantage, and we should never assume that we know when they can and cannot succeed. Quiet periods, like supposed equilibria in markets, are merely strategic stalemates until some player thinks up a new move or considers a strategic change that implies shifting to a new target. If used in this way, field theory has the potential to sensitize us to how targets move in and out of the vision of movements, depending on the particular struggle over rules or norms taking place at the time. Targets, in this sense, are dynamically constructed out of the relations between actors in a field (Bartley and Child 2014). While the institutional tradition emphasizes the stability brought by common understandings and practices, the field tradition highlights conflict (although that conflict is often seen as occurring within shared understandings). Targets emerge out of this conflict. Shifting analytic focus to the interactions of different players—including movements and their targets—gives us a more complete view of what constitutes a field and how fields evolve.[9]

Players and Arenas

In an effort to synthesize cultural and structural traditions, a group of scholars have explored the vocabulary of players and arenas (Duyvendak and Jasper 2015; Jabola-Carolus et al. 2018; Jasper and Duyvendak 2015; Verhoeven and Duyvendak 2017). Because it is intended to be fully dynamic and interactional, Jan Willem Duyvendak and Olivier Fillieule refer to it as the "strategic interaction perspective" and "dispositionalist interactionism" (2015, 295).

Arenas are physical settings—true structures in the nonmetaphorical sense—with rules and expectations of action in which decisions can be made (or avoided) with something at stake. They shape action by offering seats, lighting, entrances and exits, raised areas, cameras, decorations, guards, recording devices, and archives.[10] Players are individuals (simple players) and groups of individuals (compound players) with some (at least minimal) sense of identity and shared goals that they pursue in arenas through coordinated actions.

A language of players and arenas makes it clear who is interacting and where. Theories that incorporate the language of arenas attempt to address one weakness of structural models: the failure to combine agency and structure in ways that explain how structures change. Players can move from one arena to another, transform arenas, establish new arenas, but also act outside arenas. We can observe players and arenas, and the action of one in the other, without having to posit some mysterious additional level of reality— such as power, political opportunity structures, institutions, or fields—that we label *social facts* but that are actually our own analytic constructs (Latour 2005).

The strategic perspective embodied in arenas is parallel to recent discussions of assemblages or assemblies of heterogeneous raw materials, tools and other objects, places such as rooms and buildings, embodiments of symbols, and humans and other species. Sociologist Bruno Latour (e.g., 2005) uses his actor-network theory to criticize lazy conceptions of "the social" as something stable enough to cause effects in some mysterious, invisible way; philosopher Gilles Deleuze makes an ontological argument in his assemblage theory, similarly questioning the status of a "whole" or a "totality" that cannot be analyzed into its component parts (e.g., Deleuze and Guattari 1987, 88). Along these lines, players-and-arenas theory insists on microlevel observations without relying on "social" institutions, fields, opportunity structures, and other creations of the social scientist.

Like field theory, the players-and-arenas language leads us to break down the state conceptually into its many component players and the various domains in which they interact, often clashing with one another (Duyvendak and Jasper 2015). Armies disintegrate into different units, often at odds with civilian police (Roxborough 2015). Police follow their own rules and mistakes, which are not always those of the politicians who govern them (della Porta and Atak 2015); they pay informants who have their own agendas and play for both sides (Cunningham and Soto-Carrión 2015). Local and national units of government are notoriously at odds (O'Brien and Li 2006; Verhoeven and Bröer 2015). The language of players moves beyond a dichotomized model in which two sides struggle and emphasizes that there are many of them, including subplayers that do not always agree over what actions and priorities that larger player should adopt (Favre 1990; Armstrong and Bernstein 2008).[11]

The term "targets" covers many diverse players. An arenas perspective opens up the possibility of exploring targets that exist outside the state, players who are not merely open or closed, vulnerable or invulnerable, but who fight back. "We know relatively little," observes Edward Walker, "about how non-state organizations engage in forms of activist repression ranging from soft forms such as PR and grassroots campaigning all the way to more extreme measures" (2014, 194).

Scholars are beginning to fill these gaps, especially for corporate players (Dobbin and Jung 2015; King and Soule 2007) and the media (Amenta, Caren, and Tierney 2015; Sobieraj 2011). In some interactions corporate targets concede to movement demands (King 2008), but other interactions lead to counterperformances seeking to display the targets' morality or virtue (McDonnell and King 2013). Targets may even change their behavior in surprising ways to neutralize the influence of contentious interactions with movements. For example, Mary-Hunter McDonnell shows that corporations that have been frequent targets of activist boycotts become more likely to "voluntarily cooperate with [movements] to sponsor boycotts that protest the contested social practices of other companies and other entities" (2016, 53). McDonnell's research indicates that targets' repeated negative interactions with movements soften their stance toward those activists, even if only because they want to avoid the reputational damage that the attacks provoke.

Of course, not all actions occur in strategic arenas. Much action is preparatory for strategic interaction, as when movement actors hold meetings to plan a protest. Other actions are intended to influence internal members of a group, as when a protest movement holds a rally to bolster spirits of participants. And other actions have both strategic purposes and internal functions, leading to a greater level of strategic complexity. But one advantage of an arenas perspective is that it helps us analytically focus on the variety of purposes that actions have, including those taken by players that eventually become targets of a movement. In fact, as players move in and out of arenas, their actions may take on different meanings. In one arena an action may be quite clearly pointed at a target the player seeks to influence, whereas in an adjacent arena the same action may put the player squarely in the sights of another player and make it a target in its own right.

A protest rally may be intended to increase the commitment of members but also to influence politicians in advance of some decision in a legislative arena, as well as to reach media and—through them—bystander publics. But the same protest rally may actually make the movement a target of action by an ideologically conflicting movement and its associated media, as we have seen happen when far-right nationalists target protests sponsored by progressive students in an effort to draw attention to their nationalist cause and create a national media stir around freedom of speech on campus.

An arenas perspective also helps us see opportunities and contention between actors as, in fact, constituted by chains of strategic interactions among players and performances designed to elicit responses. Charles Tilly made the case that "contention involves making claims that bear on someone else's interests" and that actions are dramatizations of these claims (2008, 5). Actors continually engage in performances, seeking to create understanding with like-minded players and to distinguish themselves from those with whom they disagree. Moreover, performances evolve as a result of contentious interactions with other players. Rather than think about performances as fixed, Tilly argues that players draw from a rich repertory of performances that they alter through trial and error. What players do depends on the situation and interaction at hand. For example, consider an actor facing a reputational crisis, whose past actions have been called into question by other players who seek to make an example of them. In a defensive situation like this, the player might resort to a number of performances that demonstrate the player's innocence, draw attention away from the attack, potentially discredit the attackers, or highlight the actions' positive characteristics. The chosen performance is itself a product of past experiences (what we have learned how to do in the past), the nature of the attack, and the results of past interactions with the attackers (McDonnell and King 2013).

If one of the strengths of the players-and-arenas theory is to break down structures into sequences of interactions among players, the corresponding weakness is that it does not say much about other places in which action occurs or about metaphorical arenas such as public opinion. It is tempting to see opinions as a product in an arena, but the rules are amorphous and the places in which they are produced are numerous. It is not always clear how they add up to a single arena.

In addition, it is not always easy to distinguish players and arenas, especially for media and many components of states. Courts are easily analyzed as arenas, but judges and other court officials also pursue their interests as players and can easily be turned into targets by other players, as occurs when a federal judge is criticized by activists who disagree with a recent ruling. But the amorphousness of arena-player status reflects the reality of movement interactions and the evolving nature of arenas. As is true with field theory, a theory of arenas allows us to dynamically analyze these interactions and explain changes in arenas as a function of the interconnected, strategic actions taken by players.

To summarize, a healthy conversation about movements and targets would shift our analytic focus to the strategic interactions between various players in their arenas. Understanding those interactions would require greater sensitivity to the particularities of their situations, including how players understand their goals and interests and the various actions and performances that players are capable of using to accomplish them. Movements' and targets' interactions evolve over time, and one promising object of future study is to examine how and why these interactions change to produce a variety of strategic responses.

Studying Movements and Their Targets

We begin this Introduction with the premise that social movement research would benefit from an increased focus on the targets of mobilization. The chapters of this book provide different views about how movements and their targets ought to be studied and suggest the kinds of questions we should ask as we examine movement targets. We do not claim that the book offers a comprehensive outline of how movement scholars ought to incorporate targets more fully into our analyses, but we hope its chapters are a step in the right direction.

Three broad topics of inquiry emerge in the book: (1) how movements choose particular targets, (2) the dynamics of movement and target interactions, and (3) the outcomes of movement and target interactions. In the following sections, we address each of these topics and discuss them in the context of the chapters.

How Movements Choose Targets

In a struggle for political or social change, there are more potential targets than actual targets. Some players may, for a time, appear as inconsequential to a movement only to become seen at a later point as having important political consequences. Movements choose their targets selectively, sometimes ignoring the candidates that do the most harm and instead focusing on those that are vulnerable or that help them draw greater attention to their cause (McDonnell and King 2013; McDonnell, King, and Soule 2015). As Tim Bartley and Curtis Child argue, "The public identification of particular actors as responsible for injustice" is a product of a movement's strategic intent and results in the social construction of what types of actors and behaviors deserve condemnation (2014, 654).

The selection of one type of target over another may reflect a more general strategy for social change. For example, environmentalists may switch from a legislative strategy to a more direct approach in which they appeal to the interests of businesses that produce excessive carbon (or they may decide to pursue a multifaceted strategy that encompasses legislation, lawsuits, and direct action). This strategic choice and shift in arena shape which players become targets and subsequently the types of tactics and discourse that activists may use; they also influence the movement's own identity and hence recruitment.

Targeting is not always a calculated decision, and new targets can appear as a result of accidents, scandals, political controversies, or mere association with other movement targets (Molotch 1970; Jasper and Poulsen 1993). Legislators, businesses, or other elites can draw the attention of activists if they are associated with others who are previously targeted. For example, in the Red Scare, individuals became targets merely because they were associated through business relationships with people previously accused of being communist agitators (Pontikes, Negro, and Rao 2010). Analyzing the relationships among various types of players in an arena ought to help us better understand why certain players become targets and others are ignored.

Frances Fox Piven, in Chapter 1, provides a vivid example of how social movements interact with other key players in the highly contested arena of voting rights, thereby shifting the types of players that become targets. Social movements have long understood the need to secure voting rights to build power and influence in the United States, yet over the course of the country's history certain groups have been systematically deprived of those rights. For that reason, voting rights have been at the center of the civil rights movement. The balance of power between civil rights activists and their political adversaries depended on the extension or repression of voting rights to Black Americans.

Piven illustrates how the movement's targets changed over the course of the struggle for voting rights and depended greatly on the strategies the civil rights leaders chose to pursue. During the early 1960s, the targets were political leaders within the Democratic Party, like John Kennedy and Lyndon Johnson, whom civil rights leaders hoped to convince to promote voting rights legislation. But as electoral politics changed and southern Democrats switched to the Republican Party, the targets became state legislators who sought to redraw district boundaries and dilute Democratic—and by association, Black—votes. At various times business interests became targets as they sought to demobilize the Black voting bloc and push policies that took entitlements away from the poor. Piven's story demonstrates that targets shift as a movement's strategy changes and as loyalties and alliances within the political arena change.

In Chapter 2, Katrin Uba takes a unique approach to an important question in social movement research: When does protest *not* materialize around a potential target? She recognizes that not all potential targets become actual targets and offers a case in which activists chose to target certain actors but not others: protests around Swedish school closures. Although not nearly as politicized as closures in the United States, Swedish school closures are still quite contentious in that they require families to move their children to new schools. Despite being controversial, closures do not always result in protest. Uba finds that schools are more likely to become the target of protest if the closure is partial, which increases the perceived deprivation among members of the school who feel they are losing valued services. Schools are less likely to become targets if there is a broad coalition supporting the closure and when other options for "exit" exist. She shows that schools are most likely to become targets of protest when they remain the only option on which neighborhood families depend and exit is not possible.

Uba's analysis demonstrates the importance of considering the relations between other players and other strategic options that movements have when considering whether an organization becomes a target. As Bartley and Child (2014) have argued, not all potential targets become targets, so we must examine the various other options for action that movement participants have, including exiting from the contentious situation entirely. If protest never occurs, potential targets slide into obscurity without becoming the focus of conflict. Target choice, of course, ultimately shapes the movement as much as (or maybe even more than) the target itself, which makes this initial selection quite important for the trajectory and fate of a social movement.

Movement-Target Dynamics

As movement players and their targets interact, they change one another. Once movement players select a target and begin interacting with it, the movement itself may begin to adapt its strategies, tactical repertory, and perhaps even its identity (Bob 2012; Fetner 2008; McDonnell 2015). Interactions imply actions and responses. An activist group may decide to protest outside a rally of a sitting president, which may in turn elicit a response from the president. The president's reaction may further inflame the activists, especially if the president tries to denigrate their behavior or demonize them in some way. The activists likely respond with further protests or other tactics, such as online trolling, to damage the president's reputation and draw attention to their cause. This may continue for some time, creating greater polarization between the president, the president's supporters, and the activist agitators.

Targets may instead choose to ignore movement activists, in which case activists will seek other tactics that they believe will be more effective at drawing the target into an interaction. Targets may also seek to negotiate with a social movement and potentially concede to particular demands (King 2008). Or a target may seek other ways to neutralize the movement's tactical influence (McDonnell and King 2013). Each target response requires movement actors to respond in turn and potentially to draw on a different set of tactics than they used in the past. The possibilities of action/reaction are numerous and do not always fit into the stylized conceptual boxes that social movement scholars have created to understand movement tactics.

By focusing more explicitly on the interactions between movements and their targets, we believe there is great potential to understand why and how movements and targets act as they do and how social movements contribute to social and political change. Although past research on tactical innovation (McAdam 1983), collective action frames and cycles of protest (Snow and Benford 1992), and tactical diffusion (Soule 1997) all touch on the interactions between movements and targets, targets are usually of secondary concern. Moreover, the variety of ways in which targets influence internal dynamics of social movements has been largely ignored. It is as if our theories perceive targets as outside the landscape in which movements form and evolve.

In Chapter 3, Gay Seidman shows how targeting new types of actors can change the conditions of mobilization and coalition formation within movements. She examines urban movements in postcolonial cities, where distinctions between poor and elite are amplified by a lack of citizenship and social rights. She tracks the evolution of these urban movements from those focused explicitly on pro-democratization to new protests in which middle-class citizens are equally likely to participate and the focus of which is highly localized.

In the past, the targets of urban protest movements in postcolonial cities were often the ruling elites—descendants of colonial landholders and power holders in democratic institutions—whereas increasingly protestors target local administrators who promote market liberalization policies such as state retrenchment and currency devaluation. Liberalization policies have wreaked havoc on urban infrastructure, further debilitating the well-being of the poor but also creating dissatisfaction among middle-class constituents who depend on basic services such as water or electricity.

Seidman is interested in the potential for broad urban movements that unite the middle class and the poor. She notes recent examples of protests centered around the failure of local municipalities to provide basic services. These protests are far less macro-oriented than previous protest movements in postcolonial countries, but Seidman believes that in shifting to local, bureaucratic targets, there is still potential to create a real democratic movement. The localization of movement targets allows collective action that cuts across economic classes, political parties, or other traditional group boundaries. She illustrates that targeting has a direct impact, for better or worse, on the ability of protestors to form cohesive movements among otherwise disconnected groups.

Kim Voss and Pablo Gastón, in Chapter 4, offer a similar view of how shifts in movement targets change the internal dynamics of a movement. Examining the relationship between businesses and unions, they argue that American unions faced internal strategic conflict inasmuch as they transformed their repertoires of contention to keep pace with changes in their corporate targets and the evolving political landscape. In previous eras, when manufacturing was dominant, unions organized primarily in the workplace, using tactics like strikes to wield collective power. But as service jobs replaced manufacturing jobs, unions had to change their strategy, increasingly relying on externally focused anticorporate campaigns. This strategic shift moved unions closer to other social movements, such as the human rights movement, in creating coalitions with other social justice activists and using discursive tactics to build public support for their causes.

As unions' strategies have become more community oriented, their targets have expanded to include local city and state governments, which have been at the center of right-to-work and other controversial employment laws. External campaigns, of course, require different skills and deemphasize workplace organizing and the accompanying efforts toward union democratization. Thus, one negative consequence of the externalization of union tactics has been a deemphasis on democratic decision-making as an ideal. One of Voss and Gastón's insights is that the transformation of targets can create internal, cultural tensions in movements that formed around a specific tactical repertoire. If movement participants come to associate the movement with a particular style or repertoire of contention, changes in tactics to keep up with the targets' own development may lead to decreased participation and weaken the movement's ability to mobilize in the future. This trend is evident in the labor movement.

Voss and Gastón conclude that when targets are vulnerable to tactics that require direct action by movement participants, the movements are more democratic, but when targets are more vulnerable to tactics that do not require direct action, movements will become less democratic and face internal struggles.

In Chapter 5, Kenneth Andrews and Sarah Gaby delve into the episodic and disjointed nature of social movements. Rather than think of movements as continuous, linear flows of collective action, they argue that movements occur episodically and are far more locally oriented than we think. Movement targets are also episodic; even in the same communities, local movement leaders may shift their focus considerably, initially targeting a local business, switching to a municipality, and then targeting a political party.

Andrews and Gaby's episodic analysis allows us to explore the dynamic interactions between movements, targets, and other actors in a delimited time period. Episodes combine multiple events and are driven by the strategic interactions of the various players involved in a conflict. Narrowing in on a particular episode allows us to specify the particular historical, political, and social context that drives the particular interactions.

Why do episodes begin and eventually end? This is the central question that motivates a study of episodes rather than a broader analysis of a movement's life course. Consider the primary example offered in the chapter: episodes of civil rights demonstrations in Durham, North Carolina, in the early 1960s. Episodes typically began with the introduction of a new tactic by civil rights leaders (e.g., sit-ins at lunch counters), accompanied by shifting to a new target, followed by ongoing interactions between the activists and the target, possibly negotiations, and ultimately a resolution of some sort. The conclusion of one episode typically feeds into another by shaping the strategic context in which targets and movement actors make future decisions.

These chapters all demonstrate that interactions between movements and targets may transform the political and social environments in which they operate. Focusing on the dynamic interactions between movements and targets reveals that environments are not static or completely exogenous;

rather, movements play a role in shaping their environment, not least because they can provoke targets to respond (McDonnell, King, and Soule 2015). Actions and responses between targets and movements transform the very environment and create the conditions for future mobilization.

Outcomes of Interactions

A central concern of social movement theorists over the past few decades has been whether social movements matter. Do they achieve their goals, and if so, when and how? Studying how social movements influence change presents a window into studying movement targets. Inevitably, if we are to understand how movements do or do not obtain their desired goals, we need theories about how movements influence their targets.

Much research in this vein emphasizes general strategic approaches. For example, Frances Fox Piven and Richard Cloward (1977) stressed institutional disruption as a mechanism for building collective power and influence (see also Chapter 1 in this book). Other studies have found that disruption, at least in certain contexts, is effective for influencing a target's behavior (e.g., Luders 2006; Rojas 2006; King 2011; Young and Schwartz 2014). Scholars who have studied movements' roles in the legislative process have demonstrated the importance of social movements in shaping policy and issue agendas (King, Cornwall, and Dahlin 2005; Soule and King 2006; Agnone 2007; Olzak and Soule 2009).

Research on movement outcomes has begun to shift to the targets themselves, highlighting the importance of understanding targets' motivations and interests and thinking through the various reasons that targets might consider the objectives of social movement actors. To understand how movements can achieve their objectives, we need theories about the targets' own goals and motivations.

In Chapter 6, Edwin Amenta and Nicole Shortt offer an institutional approach to understanding the influence of targets on movement outcomes. Like others in the book, they point out that much social movement research, even that which has studied outcomes, has been too inward looking and movement focused. Scholars should pay attention, they say, to the institutional processes through which political outcomes are achieved and then figure out how movements fit into these processes. In other words, our analysis should begin by theorizing the targets and how collective decisions and policy changes are made by those targets and then situate movements within those processes. For example, if we are to understand how movements affect legislative change, the starting point should be theories that explain how legislation is accomplished.

The advantage of this institutional approach is to deemphasize any one type of player and instead focus on the processes through which outcomes are achieved. Movements may or may not matter to the ultimate outcomes, depending on how they adapt to the institutional context. If our entry point to studying movement outcomes is the targets and the institutional processes of decision-making, we will be able to compare the influence of movements to that of other competing players in the arena of interaction.

An institutional mediation approach, of course, entails a deeper knowledge of the contexts in which movements operate. Social movement scholars studying legislative outcomes need a deeper engagement with theories of legislation in political science. Cultural sociology and economic sociology are relevant when considering cultural or business outcomes, just as organizational theory helps us comprehend a wide range of strategic players. To understand movements' interactions with various types of targets, we need better theories of the targets themselves.

Erica Simmons, in Chapter 7, offers a complementary perspective by highlighting the importance of culture in shaping the outcomes of movement and target interactions. She seeks to better understand the reasons that targets respond as they do to movement activists. Through two case studies—Bolivian protest against the government's privatization of water and Mexican protest against rising corn prices—she suggests that we look to the targets' perceptions of activists' claims and the potential threats these claims pose.

Targets' and activists' perceptions of the others' actions are shaped by deeper cultural meanings. Targets that understand the cultural significance of the activists' claims (and how these claims would be interpreted by the larger community) will take the activists more seriously and respond accordingly. Failure to understand activists' claims may trigger even deeper resistance to policies and weaken a target's ability to respond effectively.

Simmons shows how a failure by local elites to understand the symbolic value of certain resources held by local communities creates seeds of discontent that may eventually blossom into mass mobilization. Even if they are not targeted initially, political elites can become additional targets when they fail to respond appropriately to mobilization or to demonstrate an appreciation for the community's culture—a case of "procedural grievances" (Gordon and Jasper 1996). Simmons also shows the importance of culture in creating divides between movements and their targets. Ultimately, she suggests that to enrich our scholarship on movement targets, we need to contextualize grievances and strategic calculations in local cultures. Along with Amenta's and Shortt's chapter, we believe this is a strong call to study the rich contexts—political, social, economic, and cultural—of the targets themselves.

Finally, in Chapter 8, Austin Choi-Fitzpatrick offers a rich theorization of how interactions between movements and their targets (or as he calls them, incumbents) lead to different types of outcomes. Choi-Fitzpatrick moves beyond simple dyadic outcomes to a typology of targets' responses. He conceptualizes four types of responses that vary by the motive and ability of the target to respond to a movement's demands. Targets may be more or less willing to respond, and some are more or less capable of responding. A response that is less receptive may result from a target that lacks the power or resources to respond. Consider, for example, a politician who is facing an onslaught of controversies around issues completely unrelated to movement actors' demands. The weak response may not signify a lack of willingness at all but may be the result of a lack of attention and a redirection of resources to other, seemingly more urgent matters.

One of the strengths of Choi-Fitzpatrick's analysis is that he turns to the nature of the interaction between the movement and targets to theorize how these responses might evolve. He notes that targets possess different cultural resources, including ideologies, that shape what kinds of responses are even possible. Notably, he emphasizes the power differential between movements and targets. His view is that incumbent targets are almost always more powerful than their adversarial movements. Nevertheless, some of the more interesting and potentially transformative movement-target interactions occur between those movements and targets where the movement has resources that the target wants. The ability of a burgeoning populist movement to shape electoral outcomes is one such example. In those cases, the targets—politicians and policy makers—may succumb quickly to movements' demands and seek to make them allies in their efforts to secure power. Authentic identity movements are another example of movements that often have power over their targets because of their cultural cachet. Such movements, of course, are in danger of being co-opted and losing their authenticity as incumbent targets seek to appropriate their symbolic resources for their own use. Choi-Fitzpatrick's typology gives us the resources, as movement scholars, to better conceptualize the unintended, sometimes surprising consequences of movement-target interactions.

How to Study Protestors and Their Targets

The study of social movements and their interactions with their targets (and potential targets) reflects a broad shift in the field of social movements, away from grand narratives about social change and macrostructural conditions that prevent or facilitate mobilization and toward the cultural expectations, decision-making processes, strategic trade-offs, and dynamic responses of the various players involved. In other words, the study of social movements and targets requires theories of action and interaction (Jasper 2012). Although the authors in this book bring distinct analytic perspectives, they each in their own way bring a more dynamic, more interaction-focused lens to the study of movements, tracing the processes that led (or did not lead) from conditions to outcomes and evolving strategies.

We suggest that studying these processes, which consist of long chains of interactions among various sorts of players, ought to be at the center of an analysis of movements and their targets. Rather than assume that social movements begin with clear objectives and targets in mind, we ought to instead embrace the idea that both of these are in flux and a product of the interactions between various players as they make decisions, reform themselves, create and revamp strategic arenas, and react with passion to the actions of other players.

We believe that a focus on the interactive context will rejuvenate the field of social movement research, which at times has become myopically focused on particular social movements or specific policy goals. Intense interest in a single movement and its particular manifestations in a given place and time leads scholars to miss the broader interactive context, including the range of players in the movements' arenas and the interdependencies that have developed between these different actors. Case studies, for example, that fail to account for the historical and ecological arenas in which the movement operates may offer overly simplistic accounts of movement behavior. This becomes particularly problematic when interactions with a movement's targets are absent from discussion, but the same criticism could be made of studies that do not consider a movement's interactions and interdependencies with other movements. In some ways, we are making a similar criticism of movement analyses as scholars in the 1970s did of their predecessors: Movement analyses that do not take into account the interactions with other players in their arenas, including targets, may fail to understand the subjective and strategic aspects of their behavior.

To move beyond broad macroanalyses of social change and myopic analyses devoid of analysis of the broader arena, we may need new methods and new theoretical lenses for thinking about how interactions between movements and their targets unfold at a local level. In Chapter 5, Andrews and Gaby suggest episodes, and elsewhere Jasper and colleagues (2019) recommend player-arena matrices, for cataloging both actions (what each player does in each relevant arena) and outcomes (for each player in each arena). These matrices can either summarize the output of an arena or list a series of moves and outcomes in the same arena over time. Episodes are a more granular level of arenas, and to study arenas effectively, we might focus on the various episodes that make up a larger arena of interaction. Historians have always woven strategic interactions into compelling narratives, but we need better visual representations to help us look for patterns in those episodes and engagements.

Episodes create opportunities for the targets as well as for activists. Community leaders may use an episode as a chance to build more power if they are able to handle the episode effectively, just as for movements episodes create windows to create new coalitions and activate new constituents. Viewing interactions between movements and their targets as episodes helps us understand the historical links between movements' actions and their relationships to a variety of players, including potential allies and collaborators. Episodes build on one another, creating streams of interactions that constitute the historical narrative of a social movement. When analyzing the macrohistorical changes associated with movements, we would benefit from deconstructing those changes into episodic interactions between movements and targets that build on one another.

Conceptually, we need to move beyond a simple linear narrative of movement and target interaction that leads to clear, dyadic consequences. Much of the past research on movement outcomes has viewed social movements as being either successful or not at convincing targets to change a particular policy. As the chapters in this book suggest, such interactions rarely proceed in such a linear fashion. Movement actors frequently change strategy in the middle of an interaction with a target, the targets themselves have numerous ways they can respond to movement actors' demands, and interactions between a movement and its target occur simultaneously with interactions with other actors. Moreover, strategic interactions between movement actors and their targets are ongoing and rarely end with a single outcome.

For example, consider that Greenpeace is always engaged in multiple campaigns, some targeting the international whaling community with others going after specific petroleum companies in the Arctic. Greenpeace, like other environmental movement organizations, has a variety of goals and may change its emphasis at any time, depending on which issues are most salient and motivating to its members and supporters. Moreover, the responses of its targets will affect how and where it deploys its resources. The international political arena in which Greenpeace plays a part also involves a variety of government lawmaking bodies and regulators, as well as nongovernmental private regulators. The complexity of Greenpeace's arenas of interaction, as well as the various responses it elicits in its targets, leads to an ongoing evolution of its tactical repertoire and strategic emphasis. A sensible methodological approach to studying Greenpeace would take into account the matrix of activities it participates in relative to these various targets, considering the interdependencies between those actions and the variety of consequences they produce.

Movement researchers would be wise to pay attention to the complex ways in which movements and targets change in the midst of interactions that go beyond simple, dyadic outcomes. "Outcomes" may no longer be the best term to use when describing the consequences of movements. Instead, we ought to theorize the interactions themselves and the myriad consequences they produce.

Our hope, with this book, is to encourage more research that embraces an interactional approach. In doing so, we can begin to draw a more rigorous understanding of not just the nature of movements but also of their targets. By understanding what motivates targets, how they strategically respond to movements, and what the consequences are of these responses, we will also gain a greater understanding of why social movements behave as they do. Movements and their targets cannot be understood in isolation. Movements' actions are always outgrowths of interactions with other players in their arenas. We cannot understand the character of the civil rights movement without also developing a sophisticated theoretical perspective on the motives and actions of the southern segregationists they sought to overcome. The same idea applies to any analysis of contemporary movements, whether the #MeToo movement or radically conservative movements such as white nationalism.

A richer methodological and theoretical toolkit for understanding these interactions will highlight new problems in the study of social movements and ensure that we are neither too broadly macro-oriented nor too myopic in our empirical and theoretical focus. The promise of a social movement perspective that embraces both movements and targets is that it leads us to analyze the details of interactions and their connection to historical changes in a social movement's context. Social movement scholarship is ready for this kind of theorizing.

NOTES

Acknowledgment: Thanks go to Fran Piven for comments on an earlier draft.

1. To be fair, Herbert Blumer distinguished acting crowds, with external goals, from expressive crowds that were content to express excitement such as in dancing (1939, 239).

2. The critique of supposedly movement-centric theories has been a staple of political process models since Doug McAdam (1982), who has recently worked to fill this gap by examining the influence of social movements within U.S. political parties (McAdam and Kloos 2014; also see McAdam and Boudet 2012).

3. Frances Fox Piven and Richard Cloward (1977) dissented. Although they accepted that some form of breakdown spurs insurgency, they suspected that elite resources mostly co-opt protest rather than meet its demands. And in contrast to structuralists, they insisted on the importance of the intentions of opponents, especially the violence of corporations against labor.

4. State players also make decisions about repression. Structural models can explain whether a state has the capacity to repress protestors (tanks, tear gas, loyal

troops) but not whether state players will decide to use it or not. See Steedly and Foley 1979.

5. Jack Goldstone complains that although political opportunity structures "may describe simple macro conditions relevant to aggregate patterns of protest (e.g. democratization, political crises, and national patterns of authority), a more detailed analysis of the specific context of individual movements is required to understand their dynamics, and for that, I believe it is essential to map out the full range of relationships with other actors and groups that affects their activity" (2004, 356). Relatedly, Edwin Amenta's (2006) political mediation model conceptualizes the political environment in which a movement's strategy is matched to the actions and strategies of its adversaries.

6. The classic critique of structural functionalism was that there is often coercion behind what looks like consensus; people can cooperate without embracing the dominant norms and values (Dahrendorf 1958; Gouldner 1970; Mann 1970).

7. In addition to explicit critics like Jeff Goodwin and James Jasper (2004), several creators of the political opportunity paradigm recognized this problem and turned to mechanisms to insert some dynamism into their theories (McAdam, Tarrow, and Tilly 2001). Mechanisms were supposed to be causal regularities that could be concatenated together into longer causal chains to explain political processes and outcomes. But rather than adopt the usual definition of mechanisms as a lower level of reality (usually individuals instead of organizations and institutions), they adopted Robert Merton's view in which mechanisms are miniature middle-range theories. In this "mousetrap" view of mechanisms, they are sitting there waiting to be flipped from state A to state B, almost inexorably once they are triggered. There is change, to be sure, but of a billiard-ball sort of certainty rather than one including any agency, choice, or indeterminism. The structuralism of political process theory is reproduced at a more local level.

8. A large number of French researchers have analyzed the field dynamics of protest, such as Olivier Fillieule (1997) and Cécile Péchu (2006). Lilian Mathieu (2012) criticizes fields and prefers the term "space," but this seems to share many of the former's limitations. Cyril Lemieux (2011) sharply criticizes fields.

9. For example, Wooseok Jung, Brayden King, and Sarah Soule (2014) examine how cooperative interactions between different protest groups reconfigured the field of the entire social movement sector over a thirty-year period. One can also imagine looking at the evolution of the field as a consequence of movement actors shifting between different types of targets.

10. An arena need not be a single room; it may be a set of linked places, such as polling locations, whose actions are aggregated into the outcome. Even when voting occurs through the mail, with less face-to-face interaction, it is part of the electoral arena.

11. In an exemplary book on the Occupy movement, Michael Gould-Wartofsky (2015) includes succinct tables of relevant players: for example, allies such as unions, targets such as banks, and state agencies.

REFERENCES

Agnone, Jon. 2007. "Amplifying Public Opinion: The Policy Impact of the US Environmental Movement." *Social Forces* 85:1593–1620.

Amenta, Edwin. 2006. *When Movements Matter: The Townsend Plan and the Rise of Social Security*. Princeton, NJ: Princeton University Press.

Amenta, Edwin, Neal Caren, and Amber Celina Tierney. 2015. "Put Me In, Coach? Referee? Owner? Security? Why the News Media Rarely Cover Movements as Political Players." In *Players and Arenas*, edited by James M. Jasper and Jan Willem Duyvendak, 229–250. Amsterdam: Amsterdam University Press.

Andrews, Kenneth T. 2001. "Social Movements and Policy Implementation: The Mississippi Civil Rights Movement and the War on Poverty, 1965 to 1971." *American Sociological Review* 66:71–95.

Armstrong, Elizabeth A. 2002. *Forging Gay Identities: Organizing Sexuality in San Francisco, 1950–1994*. Chicago: University of Chicago Press.

Armstrong, Elizabeth A., and Mary C. Bernstein. 2008. "Culture, Power, and Institutions: A Multi-institutional Politics Approach to Social Movements." *Sociological Theory* 26:74–99.

Bartley, Tim, and Curtis Child. 2014. "Shaming the Corporation: The Social Production of Targets and the Anti-sweatshop Movement." *American Sociological Review* 79:653–679.

Blumer, Herbert. 1939. "Collective Behavior." In *An Outline of the Principles of Sociology*, edited by Robert E. Park, 219–288. New York: Barnes and Noble.

Bob, Clifford. 2012. *The Global Right Wing and the Clash of World Politics*. New York: Cambridge University Press.

Bosi, Lorenzo. 2008. "Explaining the Emergence Process of the Civil Rights Protest in Northern Ireland (1945–1968): Insights from a Relational Social Movement Approach." *Journal of Historical Sociology* 21:242–271.

Calhoun, Craig. 1993. "'New Social Movements' of the Early Nineteenth Century." *Social Science History* 17:385–427.

Clemens, Elisabeth S. 1997. *The People's Lobby*. Chicago: University of Chicago Press.

Clemens, Elisabeth S., and James M. Cook. 1999. "Politics and Institutionalism." *Annual Review of Sociology* 25:441–166.

Cunningham, David, and Roberto Soto-Carrión. 2015. "Infiltrators." In *Breaking Down the State: Protestors Engaged*, edited by Jan Willem Duyvendak and James M. Jasper, 157–178. Amsterdam: Amsterdam University Press.

Dahrendorf, Ralf. 1958. "Out of Utopia." *American Journal of Sociology* 64:115–127.

Deleuze, Gilles, and Felix Guattari. 1987. *A Thousand Plateaus*. Minneapolis: University of Minnesota Press.

della Porta, Donatella. 2014. *Mobilizing for Democracy*. Oxford: Oxford University Press.

della Porta, Donatella, and Kivanç Atak. 2015. "The Police." In *Breaking Down the State: Protestors Engaged*, edited by Jan Willem Duyvendak and James M. Jasper, 113–132. Amsterdam: Amsterdam University Press.

DiMaggio, Paul J., and Walter W. Powell. 1991. "Introduction." In *The New Institutionalism in Organizational Analysis*, edited by Walter W. Powell and Paul J. DiMaggio, 1–40. Chicago: University of Chicago Press.

Dobbin, Frank, and Jiwook Jung. 2015. "Professions, Social Movements, and the Sovereign Corporation." In *Players and Arenas*, edited by James M. Jasper and Jan Willem Duyvendak, 141–168. Amsterdam: Amsterdam University Press.

Duyvendak, Jan Willem, and Olivier Fillieule. 2015. "Conclusion: Patterned Fluidity." In *Players and Arenas*, edited by James M. Jasper and Jan Willem Duyvendak, 295–318. Amsterdam: Amsterdam University Press.

Duyvendak, Jan Willem, and James M. Jasper, eds. 2015. *Breaking Down the State: Protestors Engaged*. Amsterdam: Amsterdam University Press.

Favre, Pierre. 1990. *La manifestation* [The demonstration]. Paris: Presses de la Fondation Nationale des Sciences Politiques.

Fetner, Tina. 2008. *How the Religious Right Shaped Lesbian and Gay Activism*. Minneapolis: University of Minnesota Press.

Fillieule, Olivier. 1997. *Stratégies de la rue* [Street strategies]. Paris: Presses de Sciences Po.

———. 2010. "Some Elements of an Interactionist Approach to Political Disengagement." *Social Movement Studies* 9:1–15.

Finnemore, Martha. 1996. "Norms, Culture, and World Politics." *International Organization* 50:325–347.

Fligstein, Neil, and Doug McAdam. 2012. *A Theory of Fields*. New York: Oxford University Press.

Goldstone, Jack A. 2004. "More Social Movements or Fewer? Beyond Political Opportunity Structures to Relational Fields." *Theory and Society* 33:333–365.

———. 2015. "Conclusion: Simplicity vs. Complexity in the Analysis of Social Movements." In *Breaking Down the State: Protestors Engaged*, edited by Jan Willem Duyvendak and James M. Jasper, 225–238. Amsterdam: Amsterdam University Press.

Goodwin, Jeff, and James M. Jasper. 2004. "Caught in a Winding, Snarling Vine." In *Rethinking Social Movements*, edited by Jeff Goodwin and James M. Jasper, 3–30. Lanham, MD: Rowman and Littlefield.

Gordon, Cynthia, and James M. Jasper. 1996. "Overcoming the NIMBY Label." *Research in Social Movements, Conflict, and Change* 19:159–181.

Gouldner, Alvin W. 1970. *The Coming Crisis of Western Sociology*. New York: Basic Books.

Gould-Wartofsky, Michael A. 2015. *The Occupiers: The Making of the 99 Percent Movement*. New York: Oxford University Press.

Habermas, Jürgen. 1987. *Theory of Communicative Action*. Vol. 2, *Lifeworld and System*. Boston: Beacon.

Hargrave, Timothy J., and Andrew H. Van de Ven. 2006. "A Collective Action Model of Institutional Innovation." *Academy of Management Review* 31:864–888.

Hiatt, Shon R., Wesley D. Sine, and Pamela S. Tolbert. 2009. "From Pabst to Pepsi: The Deinstitutionalization of Social Practices and the Creation of Entrepreneurial Opportunities." *Administrative Science Quarterly* 54:635–667.

Jabola-Carolus, Isaac, Luke Elliott-Negri, James M. Jasper, Jessica Mahlbacher, Manès Weisskircher, and Anna Zhelnina. 2018. "Strategic Interaction Sequences: The Institutionalization of Participatory Budgeting in New York City." *Social Movement Studies*, August 6. Available at https://doi.org/10.1080/14742837.2018.1505488.

Jasper, James M. 2012. "Introduction: From Political Opportunity Structures to Strategic Interaction." In *Contention in Context*, edited by Jeff Goodwin and James M. Jasper, 1–34. Stanford, CA: Stanford University Press.

Jasper, James M., and Jan Willem Duyvendak, eds. 2015. *Players and Arenas*. Amsterdam: Amsterdam University Press.

Jasper, James M., Luke Elliot-Negri, Isaac Jabola-Carolus, Marc Kagan, Jessica Mahlbacher, Manès Weisskircher, and Anna Zhelnina. 2019. "Gains and Losses." Unpublished manuscript.

Jasper, James M., and Jane Poulsen. 1993. "Fighting Back: Vulnerabilities, Blunders, and Countermobilization by the Targets of Three Animal Rights Campaigns." *Sociological Forum* 8:639–657.

Jepperson, Ronald L. 1991. "Institutions, Institutional Effects, and Institutionalism." In *The New Institutionalism in Organizational Analysis*, edited by Paul J. DiMaggio and Walter W. Powell, 143–163. Chicago: University of Chicago Press.

Jung, Wooseok, Brayden G King, and Sarah A. Soule. 2014. "Issue Bricolage: Explaining the Configuration of the Social Movement Sector, 1960–1995." *American Journal of Sociology* 120:187–225.

King, Brayden G. 2008. "A Political Mediation Model of Corporate Response to Social Movement Activism." *Administrative Science Quarterly* 53:395–421.

———. 2011. "The Tactical Disruptiveness of Social Movements: Sources of Market and Mediated Disruption in Corporate Boycotts." *Social Problems* 58:491–517.

King, Brayden G, Marie Cornwall, and Eric C. Dahlin. 2005. "Winning Woman Suffrage One Step at a Time: Social Movements and the Logic of the Legislative Process." *Social Forces* 83:1211–1234.

King, Brayden G, and Nicholas Pearce. 2010. "The Contentiousness of Markets: Politics, Social Movements and Institutional Change in Markets." *Annual Review of Sociology* 36:249–267.

King, Brayden G, and Sarah A. Soule. 2007. "Social Movements as Extra-institutional Entrepreneurs: The Effect of Protest on Stock Price Returns." *Administrative Science Quarterly* 52:413–442.

King, Brayden G, and Edward T. Walker. 2014. "Winning Hearts and Minds: Field Theory and the Three Dimensions of Strategy." *Strategic Organization* 12:134–141.

Kitchener, Martin. 2010. "Social Movement Challenges to Structural Archetypes." In *Social Movements and the Transformation of American Health Care*, edited by Jane C. Banaszak-Holl, Sandra R. Levitsky, and Mayer N. Zald, 128–143. New York: Oxford University Press.

Kraatz, Matthew S., and Emily S. Block. 2008. "Organizational Implications of Institutional Pluralism." In *The Handbook of Organizational Institutionalism*, edited by Royston Greenwood, Christine Oliver, Kristen Sahlin-Andersson, and Roy Suddaby, 243–275. London: Sage.

Kriesi, Hanspeter, Ruud Koopmans, Jan Willem Duyvendak, and Marco G. Giugni. 1995. *New Social Movements in Western Europe*. Minneapolis: University of Minnesota Press.

Kurzman, Charles. 1996. "Structural Opportunity and Perceived Opportunity in Social Movement Theory." *American Sociological Review* 61:153–170.

Latour, Bruno. 2005. *Reassembling the Social*. Oxford: Oxford University Press.

Lee, Min-Dong Paul, and Michael Lounsbury. 2015. "Filtering Institutional Logics: Community Logic Variation and Differential Responses to the Institutional Complexity of Toxic Waste." *Organization Science* 26:847–866.

Lemieux, Cyril. 2011. "Le crépuscule des champs" [The twilight of the fields]. In *Bourdieu, théoricien de la pratique* [Bourdieu, theorist of the practice], edited by Michel de Fornel and Albert Ogien, 75–100. Paris: Editions de l'EHESS.

Levitsky, Sandra R., and Jane Banaszak-Holl. 2010. "Introduction." In *Social Movements and the Transformation of American Health Care*, edited by Jane C. Banaszak-Holl, Sandra R. Levitsky, and Mayer N. Zald, 3–21. New York: Oxford University Press.

Lichbach, Mark. 1995. *The Rebel's Dilemma*. Ann Arbor: University of Michigan Press.

Luders, Joseph. 2006. "The Economics of Movement Success." *American Journal of Sociology* 111:963–998.

Luhmann, Niklas. 1996. *Social Systems*. Stanford, CA: Stanford University Press.

Mann, Michael. 1970. "The Social Cohesion of Liberal Democracy." *American Sociological Review* 35:423–439.

Mathieu, Lilian. 2012. *L'espace des mouvements sociaux* [The space of social movements]. Paris: Le Croquant.

McAdam, Doug. 1982. *Political Process and the Development of Black Insurgency.* Chicago: University of Chicago Press.

———. 1983. "Tactical Innovation and the Pace of Insurgency." *American Sociological Review* 48:735–754.

McAdam, Doug, and Hilary Boudet. 2012. *Putting Social Movements in Their Place.* New York: Cambridge University Press.

McAdam, Doug, and Karina Kloos. 2014. *Deeply Divided.* New York: Oxford University Press.

McAdam, Doug, John D. McCarthy, and Mayer N. Zald, eds. 1996. *Comparative Perspectives on Social Movements.* Cambridge: Cambridge University Press.

McAdam, Doug, Sidney Tarrow, and Charles Tilly. 2001. *Dynamics of Contention.* New York: Cambridge University Press.

McCarthy, John D., and Mayer N. Zald. 1977. "Resource Mobilization and Social Movements: A Partial Theory." *American Journal of Sociology* 82:1212–1241.

McDonnell, Mary-Hunter. 2016. "Radical Repertoires: The Incidence and Impact of Corporate-Sponsored Social Activism." *Organization Science* 27:53–71.

McDonnell, Mary-Hunter, and Brayden King. 2013. "Keeping Up Appearances: Reputational Threat and Impression Management after Social Movement Boycotts." *Administrative Science Quarterly* 58:387–419.

McDonnell, Mary-Hunter, Brayden G King, and Sarah A. Soule. 2015. "A Dynamic Process Model of Private Politics: Activist Targeting and Corporate Receptivity to Social Challenges." *American Sociological Review* 80:654–678.

Meyer, John W., and Brian Rowan. 1977. "Institutionalized Organizations: Formal Structure as Myth and Ceremony." *American Journal of Sociology* 83:340–363.

Molotch, Harvey. 1970. "Oil in Santa Barbara and Power in America." *Sociological Inquiry* 40:131–144.

O'Brien, Kevin J., and Lianjiang Li. 2006. *Rightful Resistance in Rural China.* Cambridge: Cambridge University Press.

Olzak, Susan, and Sarah A. Soule. 2009. "Cross-cutting Influences of Environmental Protest and Legislation." *Social Forces* 88:201–225.

Péchu, Cécile. 2006. *Droit au logement* [The right to housing]. Paris: Dalloz.

Piven, Frances Fox. 2006. *Challenging Authority.* Lanham, MD: Rowman and Littlefield.

Piven, Frances Fox, and Richard A. Cloward. 1977. *Poor People's Movements.* New York: Random House.

Pontikes, Elizabeth G., Giacomo Negro, and Hayagreeva Rao. 2010. "Stained Red: A Study of Stigma by Association to Blacklisted Artists during the 'Red Scare' in Hollywood, 1945 to 1960." *American Sociological Review* 75:456–478.

Rojas, Fabio. 2006. "Social Movement Tactics, Organizational Change, and the Spread of African-American Studies." *Social Forces* 84:2147–2166.

Roxborough, Ian. 2015. "The Military." In *Breaking Down the State*, edited by Jan Willem Duyvendak and James M. Jasper, 133–156. Amsterdam: Amsterdam University Press.

Smelser, Neil J. 1962. *Theory of Collective Behavior.* New York: Free Press.

Smith, Christian, and James M. Jasper. 2012. "The U.S. Movement for Peace in Central America." In *Contention in Context*, edited by Jeff Goodwin and James M. Jasper, 203–223. Stanford, CA: Stanford University Press.

Snow, David A., and Robert D. Benford. 1992. "Master Frames and Cycles of Protest." In *Frontiers in Social Movement Theory*, edited by Aldon D. Morris and Carol McClurg Mueller, 133–155. New Haven, CT: Yale University Press.

Sobieraj, Sarah. 2011. *Soundbitten: The Perils of Media-Centered Political Activism*. New York: New York University Press.

Soule, Sarah A. 1997. "The Student Divestment Movement in the United States and Tactical Diffusion: The Shantytown Movement." *Social Forces* 75:855–882.

Soule, Sarah A., and Brayden G King. 2006. "The Stages of the Policy Process and the Equal Rights Amendment, 1972–1982." *American Journal of Sociology* 111:1871–1909.

Soule, Sarah A., Doug McAdam, John McCarthy, and Yang Su. 1999. "Protest Events: Cause or Consequence of State Action? The U.S. Women's Movement and Federal Congressional Activities, 1956–1979." *Mobilization* 4:239–256.

Steedly, Homer R., and John W. Foley. 1979. "The Success of Protest Groups." *Social Science Research* 8:1–15.

Stinchcombe, Arthur L. 1997. "On the Virtues of the Old Institutionalism." *Annual Review of Sociology* 23:1–18.

Taylor, Verta, and Mayer N. Zald. 2010. "Conclusion." In *Social Movements and the Transformation of American Health Care*, edited by Jane C. Banaszak-Holl, Sandra R. Levitsky, and Mayer N. Zald, 300–318. New York: Oxford University Press.

Thornton, Patricia H., William Ocasio, and Michael Lounsbury. 2012. *The Institutional Logics Perspective: A New Approach to Culture, Structure, and Process*. Oxford: Oxford University Press.

Tilly, Charles. 1978. *From Mobilization to Revolution*. Reading, MA: Addison-Wesley.

———. 2008. *Contentious Performances*. New York: Cambridge University Press.

Touraine, Alain. 1981. *The Voice and the Eye*. Cambridge: Cambridge University Press.

Verhoeven, Imrat, and Christian Bröer. 2015. "Contentious Governance: Local Governmental Players as Social Movement Actors." In *Breaking Down the State: Protestors Engaged*, edited by Jan Willem Duyvendak and James M. Jasper, 95–111. Amsterdam: Amsterdam University Press.

Verhoeven, Imrat, and Jan Willem Duyvendak. 2017. "Understanding Governmental Activism." *Social Movement Studies* 16:564–577.

Walker, Edward T. 2014. *Grassroots for Hire*. Cambridge: Cambridge University Press.

Young, Kevin, and Michael Schwartz. 2014. "A Neglected Mechanism of Social Movement Political Influence: The Role of Anticorporate and Anti-institutional Protest in Changing Government Policy." *Mobilization* 19:239–260.

PART I

How Social Movements Select Targets

1

Disruptive Movements and the Play of Politics

FRANCES FOX PIVEN

In this chapter, I offer a definition of the distinctive source of power tapped by protest movements and then describe the complex ways that movement power interacts with the power deployed by other political actors. These interactions inevitably change over time and unfold in different arenas with different actors, to borrow James Jasper's terminology (Jasper and Duyvendak 2015). In the process, movement power may cease to be significant, and the movement is represented if at all by the social movement organizations that arise in its wake. The main case I draw on is the civil rights movement in the United States and its demand for voting rights for Black Americans.

There can be little question that protest movements have sometimes exerted power in American politics.[1] From the radical Democrats in the revolutionary era, to the abolitionists, to the strike movement of the Great Depression, to the civil rights movement, masses of defiant people have changed the course of U.S. politics. But the path through which movements exert an impact remains unclear. After all, few of the participants in these movements commanded the assets or attributes that we usually call power resources.

One answer to the puzzle about why movements sometimes exert power, offered with growing frequency, is that movements are influential because they are disruptive. But "disruption" itself remains an ambiguous term. We say, for example, that entrepreneurs offering new products disrupt markets (see Christensen 1997). Or that academics proposing new paradigms disrupt established approaches (see, e.g., Forrest 2016). Alternatively, movement scholars seem to suggest that disruption means the noisy, raucous, and even violent behavior of movement participants. But just how do noise and unruliness come to overwhelm the money, prestige, coercive forces, electoral influence, or organizational capacities that we ordinarily consider power resources?

My own answer to that question is that the collective actions we call disruption can threaten to upset the complex interdependencies that constitute institutional life. People in motion refuse to perform their normal roles, and when they do, the impact of their refusal reverberates through the webs of cooperation of a functioning society. Inevitably, severe disruption in one institutional sphere affects other institutional spheres, as disruption in production can affect family life, for example.

Moreover, disruptive (or interdependent) power does not necessarily follow the pattern of hierarchical accumulation and concentration that characterizes the deployment of other sources of power, as, for example, when wealth buys prestige and political influence, so that those who have some resources acquire more resources, and the rich get richer and the poor, poorer. In fact, people at the bottom also have disruptive or interdependent power—the kind of power that movements sometimes exercise.

Thus, while poor people are sometimes said to be "excluded," that is not quite right. They may be excluded from material benefits and honorifics, but in other ways they usually are very much included, albeit as subjugated and exploited partners. They are nannies or cleaners or trash collectors or fast-food or retail workers. The jobs are demeaning and the wages bad. But these workers are not in fact excluded, and therefore they are not powerless. Even the chronically unemployed poor can block highways or riot in the streets and disrupt the routines of civic life.

Think of the domestic workers in the global cities of New York, London, San Francisco, or Boston. They mind the children, clean the apartments, and cook the dinners in place of their employers, often better-off and better-educated women who now work as professionals or midlevel managers in firms that keep the global economy humming. If the maids and nannies stop, the repercussions spread through the ranks of the lawyers, accountants, administrators, and bankers who run an increasingly complex and far-flung economy.

So domestic workers in fact have a kind of power, contingent on their ability to refuse their normal roles (Sharp 2012; see also Engler and Engler 2016). Refusal means ceasing to cooperate in an intricate system of interdependencies. It is in effect a strike, sand in the gears of a complex division of labor. To be sure, some disrupters are more important; some, less. A strike by capital will have far more serious repercussions than a walkout by university students. Nevertheless, collective action by the less important can also disrupt the system. That is what I mean by movement power.[2]

Thus, protest movements tap a kind of power that is not usually recognized. It is not the kind of power that flows from the accumulation of resources such as money or prestige or organizational clout. And it is not the kind of power that sometimes results from the mobilization of voters. Rather, I think movement power is rooted in the occasional ability of people to interrupt, or disrupt, the fundamental interdependencies that constitute social life. Moreover, while the roots of movements may be deep, long, and tangled, and the repercussions may extend over time, the actual exercise of disruptive movement power is typically relatively short-lived, if only because disruption provokes elites to roll out both the repressive and concessionary measures necessary to restore order.

Ordinarily, however, when we think of popular power, we do not think of movements. Rather, we think first of the electoral representative arrangements that we equate with democracy. And electoral conditions are important influences on the life course of movements. Movements are encouraged or discouraged by the political discourse generated by politicians competing for election. If movements become large, they inevitably become entwined with electoral politics for the simple reason that politicians running for office will try to win the support of people who are drawn to the movement. And the victories of movements in electoral democracies, particularly when they score big victories, are usually a result of their impact or threatened impact on electoral coalitions. In fact, I think movement outcomes are best analyzed as the result of the interplay between the movement and the electoral dynamics to which the movement contributes.

The idea of electoral democracy has been the most inspirational idea of the modern era. It is the idea that widely and equally distributed votes are the key element in a system of governance.[3] If ordinary people have the right to vote, they will be able to exert influence on a potentially coercive state apparatus. And since that state apparatus has always been critical to the protection of property, democratic arrangements also provide a path to improve the economic well-being of common people. This was the dream that inspired the radical democrats of the American revolutionary era, and it also inspired the remarkable Chartist movement that arose in England a few decades later. A poem by Percy Bysshe Shelley, telling the story of the Peterloo massacre of 1819 at a time of terrible hardship in England, became a kind of anthem for the Chartists, and it expressed the core of their democratic dream:

Rise, like lions after slumber,
In unvanquishable number,
Shake your chains to earth like dew
Which in sleep had fallen on you—
Ye are many—they are few— (Shelley 2003, 404)

But of course, if the idea of government by the many inspired ordinary people, so did it inevitably evoke fierce resistance by the propertied. Indeed, the astute proposals for democratic reforms championed by the Chartists were generally ignored (Thompson 1984). Not until 1884 with the passage of the Third Reform Act did England extend the franchise to men without property.

The American Constitution, written by slaveholders, merchants, and financiers in the wake of the tumultuous revolutionary era and in the immediate aftermath of Shays' Rebellion of indebted farmers in Massachusetts, was intended to curb the democratic aspirations that the revolution had unleashed. Put another way, the strategic ploy was to create a new arena with new rules and different players. Thus, the Constitution assigned influence to the new federal government over policies of key importance to the landholding and commercial elites of the time, including trade, currency, and war making, and this when ordinary people were active only in local or state politics. Moreover, the aspirations of the radical democrats were blunted by arrangements for popular representation in the new national government that were sharply skewed to favor the propertied, especially the large landholders of the rich southern states.

Once electoral representative arrangements are institutionalized, the life course of a big movement becomes closely entwined with these arrangements. For one thing movements sometimes spring up because they are inspired by electoral contests that give hope to otherwise hopeless people. Competing political elites need supporters, and in the process of recruiting support they are often led to name the issues that come to inspire popular insurgency. Electoral arrangements may also map the strategic opportunities of the movement. Movements raise issues and press them with their disruptive power, and by doing so they can reveal the potential cleavages in the voter coalitions that political leaders need to hold together.

The revolutionary era provides an example of the inspirational impact of elites in need of popular support. The colonial elites who are usually named as the fathers of the American Revolution had issues with Britain. But elite or not, they could hardly fight a war with Britain without the support of the artisans, sailors, laborers, and farmers who made up the bulk of the population of the colonies. Seeking to win the support of a restless populace sometimes given to "pulling down" the houses of the rich, they began to speak the rhetoric of radical democracy. The strength of that development and its impact on popular insurgency are evidenced in the extraordinary state constitutions that were adopted during the revolution. The Pennsylvania Constitution of 1776, for example, established a unicameral legislature whose members were elected annually and abandoned property qualifications for voters, central precepts of the radical democrats. Not surprisingly, the revolutionary-era constitutions were quickly revised once the emergency of war had passed (see Wood 1969).

Meanwhile, the new federal Constitution said nothing about the right to vote, except perhaps for specifying that slaves were to count as three-fifths of a man in allocating representation, thus simply ensuring the overrepresentation of the slaveholding South. There was good reason for Gordon Wood to characterize the constitution as a counterrevolutionary document. The devices it contained for limiting voter power by delimiting the authority of elected politicians (think of the Supreme Court) and by skewing representation toward landed property instead of people (think of the Senate) set the pattern for the next two centuries. Indeed, American history can be read as a series of deep and extended conflicts, usually confused and muffled by the sheer complexity of electoral representative arrangements, over the rights and ensuing power of voters, and voters did not always win.

The passage of the Voting Rights Act of 1965 was the culminating triumph of the civil rights movement. The political process that led to this momentous event illustrates the dynamic interplay of movement and electoral arenas and also transformed those arenas.

The roots of the Black dream of voting rights go back at least as far as the Civil War,[4] which was followed by the emancipatory politics of Reconstruction and what Abraham Lincoln imagined in his Gettysburg Address would be a "new birth of freedom," presumably to be guaranteed by the postwar constitutional amendments that granted Blacks personal freedom and, in principle at least, the right to vote. As the southern states were reincorporated into the Union, and as northern capital became increasingly invested in the South, federal troops were removed from the rebel states, Reconstruction came to an end, and Blacks were then effectively stripped of the right to vote by southern state governments.

This was much more than an exercise in symbolic politics. The disfranchisement of Blacks was a key element in the caste system that was being developed to force newly freed Blacks back into subjugated labor, now as serfs rather than slaves. The terror of the lynch mob was the enforcer; an enfranchised population that elected local sheriffs would inhibit if not prevent the ritual lynchings that came to characterize the South.

The Jim Crow caste system persisted for a century. No wonder that southern Blacks, especially older southern Blacks whose lives were shaped by Jim Crow, bring so much passion to the issue of voting rights (see Berman 2015). But after the violent suppression that ended Reconstruction, the fight for Black voting rights did not become a mass movement again until the mid-twentieth century. When it did, national electoral politics played a large role in giving southern Blacks a reason to hope.

Broad economic and demographic changes in the country were creating a new political actor, the northern Black voter. As southern agriculture mechanized, Black tenants, laborers, and sharecroppers were being pushed off the plantations where they were no longer needed. Like other dispossessed people before them, they made their way to the cities in search of employment, including the cities of the North and West, where they did have the right to vote.

In the presidential election of 1948, Harry Truman was running a close race with Thomas E. Dewey, the Republican contender. He also faced a third-party challenger on his left, Henry Wallace, who was bidding for labor and Black votes. Truman exerted himself to appeal to northern Blacks by delivering a strong civil rights speech to the Congress that called for outlawing the poll tax and making lynching a federal crime, and he pushed a strong civil rights plank through at the Democratic convention. (He appealed for labor votes with a veto of the antiunion Taft-Hartley bill. The bill was passed over his veto, and once he was reelected, Truman did not hesitate to use it.) Die-hard southerners rebelled, walking out of the convention and forming a States' Rights Party, a reaction that prefigured the movement/electoral dynamics generated by the subsequent civil rights movement and its disruptive tactics, although at this early stage Truman's strategists apparently still took southern loyalty for granted and did not anticipate the southern defections that ensued.[5]

The 1948 Democratic platform, like all party platforms, was of course a campaign document, but rhetoric can be informative and encouraging, and in this case the rhetorical support of historic civil rights demands seems to have transmitted the message that Democrats in the federal government might be pushed to support civil rights for southern Blacks, including voting rights.

At this point, the players in the electoral arena were in motion and the pattern that would emerge was not yet clear. The Republicans were also contemplating a bid for the northern Black vote. Northern Blacks had shifted to Franklin D. Roosevelt in the 1930s, but in the South, Democrats were the enemy of racial advance, and southern Republican parties had provided something of a haven for Blacks in the decades between Reconstruction and the 1950s. In the run-up to the 1960 election, both parties actually contemplated the possibility of championing civil rights issues to win northern Black votes (Yarnell 1974, 44).

In other words, changes in the electoral arena were creating an opening for the emergence of a Black protest movement in the 1950s, a movement that gained courage because its demands were being echoed by national politicians. The decade that followed was tumultuous with movement boycotts, freedom rides, and riots by southern Blacks countered by escalating mob violence by southern whites. And the impact of tumult in the South on the electoral arena and ultimately on federal policies was heightened by the fact that the southern civil rights movement had northern Black voters and their allies at its back.

By the mid-1960s a Democratic regime in Washington had made much of the civil rights program national law, and the crowning feature was the Voting Rights Act of 1965. The drama of the struggle for voting rights had drawn in a penumbra of supporters, including liberal lawyers and advocacy organizations, some old, some brought to life by the civil rights movement. As a result of the litigation and lobbying of these social movement organizations, and also the iconic status that the civil rights movement had quickly acquired, the act was vigorously implemented, and it proved remarkably successful in enfranchising southern Blacks. These developments set other changes in motion in the electoral arena, as new actors emerged and older ones repositioned themselves.

The Democratic majority formed in the election of 1932 had been a peculiar coalition of the one-party white South and the northern white working class, led by big-city machines and the unions and the growing numbers of Blacks who had migrated to the cities. As time went on, the regional cleavages in the coalition were expressed mainly in the emergence of a bipartisan congressional coalition of business-oriented Republicans and southern Democrats who together successfully blocked legislative expansion of many New Deal policies. But in national elections, the Democratic coalition held firm and the South remained loyal to the national ticket. In return, national Democratic leaders refrained from civil rights initiatives that would interfere with the southern caste system.

The civil rights movement upset that accommodation. The tumult generated by the movement not only disrupted local civic life, but the attention it generated activated the increasing numbers of Black voters in the North. When Adlai Stevenson, the Democratic presidential candidate in 1952 and 1956, wary of another southern rebellion against the national Democratic ticket, hesitated to support desegregation, his margins among Black voters fell, and this in the big industrial states that loomed large in the electoral college. The lesson was learned, and both John F. Kennedy and Lyndon Baines Johnson endorsed the main civil rights demands in their campaigns.

In response, the white southern wing of the Democratic Party, which had been critical to the huge majorities of the party during the New Deal and afterward, gradually but steadily moved to the Republican column. (The shift might have been more rapid, but changing party labels was costly to congressional representatives who lost seniority in committee assignments as a result.) In less than two decades, the South became the bulwark of support for Barry Goldwater, the (losing) Republican presidential candidate in 1964.

The new electoral configuration that emerged from this period of flux was soon evident. The South became reliably Republican, although newly enfranchised Blacks entered the southern state-level Democratic parties, thus compensating to some extent for the massive defection of white voters. Northern Blacks were also firmly Democratic, but as they became more numerous and as the movement spirit of the South ignited Black militancy in the North, race and race issues began to create cleavages in the state and local northern Democratic parties. National Republicans took advantage of that sore spot by nationalizing the race-based appeals of southern politics, a strategy pioneered by the maverick politician George Wallace but quickly adopted by Republican contenders. The strategy worked, and in the decades following the civil rights victories, white Democratic voter defections increased. When Ronald Reagan ran for president in 1980 and again in 1984, his only slightly shrouded racist appeals attracted a rush of "Reagan Democrats" to Republican columns.

Meanwhile, in what Jasper would call another "arena" (James Jasper, pers. comm., 2015), with its own players and their distinctive goals and distinctive political resources, the lions of American business were beginning to pay more attention to American domestic politics. Of course, business had always paid attention, but mainly to the politics and policies that affected its specific industries. We usually call this interest group politics. In the several decades after the New Deal business had become more or less reconciled to broad government regulation and probably even saw its advantages.[6] There were multiple reasons for the business turn in the 1970s against domestic government programs,[7] but perhaps the most salient was simply that the post–World War II period of uncontested American international market domination was coming to a close as recovering West German and Japanese industries became more competitive. Competition of course created new pressures on profit margins, something that American business had largely been spared during the quarter of a century that other industrial nations needed to recover from World War II. Recurrent oil embargoes from 1969 to 1974 by the Arab petroleum-producing nations also added to the costs of production and to business anxieties.

The short-term solution was to shore up profit margins by reducing costs, which from the business perspective meant reducing the costs of the New Deal, including the costs of unionized labor, New Deal and Great Society social programs, increased government regulation, and taxes.[8]

There were formidable political obstacles, including the organized opponents that would have to be overcome if the business program was to succeed. The big unions quickly became a target, and the decades-long campaign to destroy them began in earnest early in the 1970s. The event that came to symbolize the turn occurred when Lane Kirkland, seemingly astonished and indignant at the demands of business representatives in Jimmy Carter's Cost of Living Council, announced that business had declared war on American unions. But the full impact of business influence was to depend on its success in the electoral arena.

And then there was the Democratic Party. However ambivalently, the Democrats were the party of labor and also now the party of Blacks. No surprise therefore that the Republican Party became the main (but not exclusive) party vehicle for a business political offensive that played out in both interest group and electoral arenas. The electoral shifts set in motion by the civil rights movement gave the White House to the Republicans from 1968 until 1992, with the brief interregnum of the presidency of Jimmy Carter. Carter's election was made possible by the Watergate scandal and President Richard Nixon's resignation. But also, despite the ongoing realignment of the South, Carter as the former governor of Georgia did relatively well among white southerners, as did Bill Clinton, the former governor of Arkansas, in 1992.

Then in 1994, the House of Representatives, which had remained a Democratic bastion, also became Republican. As money and expertise flowed into electoral politics from enlarging business profits, the business legislative agenda made steady progress, in tax cuts, rollbacks of financial and business regulation, and the revamping of social programs, including dramatic cuts in 1996 to cash assistance to poor families. Moreover, business money and expertise were also directed to nurturing a changing array of right-wing populist groups, from the John Birch Society to the patriots to the militias to the Tea Party, developments in which business money and right-wing Republican political operatives were closely involved.[9]

The electoral arena became tangled and, in many places, closely competitive. Blacks were Democrats, but the race issue was causing the party to bleed white voters, especially white male voters, making some Democratic candidates ready to borrow from the southern strategy. Moreover, Democrats were also competing for the political largesse of corporate America. It was Bill Clinton, a Democratic president from the center-right Democratic Leadership Council, who championed the Violent Crime Control and Law

Enforcement Act of 1994, which resulted in expanded police forces and the growth of the prison population. Clinton, with his slogan of "End welfare as we know it," also played a large role in the 1996 legislation that slashed cash assistance to poor women and their children. As the Democrats fell more and more under the influence of corporate money and influence, they also became the champions of the trade agreements and business and banking deregulation that were decimating working-class communities.

To be sure, voters also matter in party calculations. There were voter constituencies on the Democratic side of the arena that stood in the way of the business agenda, and there was reason to think those actors were becoming more numerous, and at least potentially more influential. As Martin Gilens (2012) has shown, while affluent voters are far more likely to see their preferences prevail in policy making, Democratic majorities in government matter. When Democrats are in control, the poor do significantly better.[10] No wonder therefore that voters, especially minority and less well-off voters, also became the focus of political calculation.

The electoral arena not only has adjacent arenas, but it has multiple levels. Federal elections, especially presidential elections, loom large in public awareness. But the states have large powers in the American electoral system.[11] Except when federal legislation explicitly says otherwise, state laws and practices determine who has the effective right to vote, the procedures through which that right is exercised, and how votes are translated into representation. Moreover, because many state governments are elected in low-turnout, off-year elections that are not dramatized by the media, poorer, younger, and minority voters are more likely to stay home, and older and more conservative voters who do turn out more regularly determine outcomes. No wonder that in the past decade and more, key policy issues, including union rights and voting rights, have been moved downstairs to state legislatures.

In 2008 when Barack Obama ran for president the first time, a surge of minority, poorer, and young voters brought him victory, and they reelected him in 2012. That surge seemed to many observers to presage a "new electorate."[12] Not only would the new electorate be majority minority, but it would be stamped with the emancipatory culture of the young, especially with the preoccupation with growing inequality that the Occupy Wall Street protests had injected into contemporary political discourse. The prospect of such a new electorate, brought inexorably into being by demography, helped provoke the Republican right into action in the state legislatures with complex voter-suppression schemes designed to reduce voting among minorities, the poor, and the young, thus potentially reversing the liberalization of voting rights that was the achievement of the civil rights movement.[13]

Moreover, it is state governments that draw district lines for congressional and Electoral College representation. And as I note earlier, the translation of votes into representation is a key determinant of the actual weight of different voter blocs. Guided by the corporate-funded American Legislative Exchange Council and enabled by Republican victories in 2010,[14] the states have introduced conditions to make voter registration and balloting more difficult, often targeting voting practices such as early voting or mail-in voting that Black voters and organizers have come to rely on.

Meanwhile, in another adjacent arena, the resurgent business-dominated right was developing a strategy for using the federal courts to advance its electoral fortunes by shrinking the electoral constituencies that were likely to stand in its way. Two decisions bear directly and importantly on this argument. In 2000, the Supreme Court effectively shut down a recount of the vote in a number of Florida counties that had been ordered by the Florida Supreme Court. The result was to give the presidency to Republican George W. Bush, who, assisted by the jingoism of war, held the office until 2008. The second decision in 2013, *Shelby County v. Holder*, struck down Section 4(b) of the Voting Rights Act, which contained the formula determining that jurisdictions with histories of discrimination in voting must seek federal preclearance before changing voting law or practices. Republican state legislatures moved rapidly to take advantage of the new ruling by introducing legislation requiring government-issued identification, or proof of citizenship; eliminating same-day registration that allowed people to register and vote on Election Day; shortening the period of early voting; or placing onerous requirements on voter registration campaigns. As the election of 2016 approached, ten states had introduced voter-suppression laws for the first time in a presidential election, including the swing states of Ohio and Wisconsin.

These several political trends contributed to the 2016 election of Donald J. Trump as president, both directly by affecting turnout and the vote count and indirectly by helping shape a socioeconomic landscape that was crucial to that outcome.[15] The uncertainties and hardships created by globalization and industrialization left the working-class base of the Democrats increasingly deracinated, their communities ravaged, their future radically uncertain, and their customary political guides of union and party weakened or compromised. Inevitably they were susceptible to the strongman appeals of Donald Trump.

But politics, the efforts of people big and small to use collective efforts to shape the future, continues, revealing new constituencies and new possibilities. The reemergence of the women's movement; the vigor of Black Lives

Matter; spreading strikes by teachers, service workers, and even prisoners; and the rush of energy and enthusiasm for reviving and transforming the Democratic Party all argue that our limited and crippled political democracy will survive and may even thrive.

NOTES

1. For the extended argument, see Piven 2006.

2. For an interesting analysis comparing the impact of disruptive and conventional contention over welfare policy reform, see Bailey 2015.

3. As V. O. Key put it, "The electorate occupies, at least in the mystique of [democratic] orders, the position of the principal organ of governance" (1955, 3).

4. And arguably, at least in the North, these roots go back to the decades after the American Revolution. See Malone 2008.

5. For more on the uncertainties that figured into these calculations, see Piven and Cloward 1977, chap. 4.

6. This question of whether business is actually both the proponent and beneficiary of much government regulation and social spending is much debated. See, for example, Domhoff 1990; Ferguson 1984; Gordon 1991; and Swenson 2002.

7. For more on the business political mobilization, see, for example, Phillips-Fein 2009; Hacker and Pierson 2005, 2010; and Perlstein 2008.

8. The business program was laid out in a memorandum to the U.S. Chamber of Commerce written by Lewis Powell, soon to be nominated to the Supreme Court.

9. For a chilling account of the activities of David and Charles Koch, who built a network that penetrates and supplants the Republican Party, see Skocpol and Hertel-Fernandez 2016.

10. See also Gilens and Page 2014; and Manza 2015, a review essay. I should note that the thrust of Gilens's argument is that neither interest groups nor the preferences of most voters matter much compared to the preferences of the most affluent.

11. State legislative action to weaken unions has also been important and successful. For a discussion, see Lafer 2013.

12. For recent data on the divergent policy preferences of new voters and potential voters, see McElwee 2015.

13. Much of this effort took place in the courts. See, for example, Keck 2004; Southworth 2009; Teles 2010; and Hollis-Brusky 2015.

14. Republicans succeeded in winning a "trifecta," control of all three branches of government, in a majority of state governments in 2010.

15. Trump's narrow win in the Electoral College, although he had three million fewer votes in the popular vote, was the result of the role of the Electoral College in modifying the popular vote in presidential elections. The Electoral College itself was the result of a constitutional maneuver by merchant and landed elites who, in the aftermath of the American Revolution, were anxious to limit the impact of electoral democracy.

REFERENCES

Bailey, David J. 2015. "Resistance Is Futile? The Impact of Disruptive Protest in the 'Silver Age of Permanent Austerity.'" *Socio-Economic Review* 13:5–32.

Berman, Ari. 2015. *Give Us the Ballot: The Modern Struggle for Voting Rights in America.* New York: Macmillan.

Christensen, Clayton M. 1997. *The Innovator's Dilemma*. New York: HarperCollins.

Domhoff, G. William. 1990. *The Power Elite and the State: How Policy Is Made in America*. New York: Transaction.

Engler, Mark, and Paul Engler. 2016. *This Is an Uprising: How Nonviolent Revolt Is Shaping the Twenty-First Century*. New York: Nation Books.

Ferguson, Thomas. 1984. "From Normalcy to New Deal: Industrial Structure, Party Competition, and American Public Policy in the Great Depression." *International Organization* 38:41–94.

Forrest, Michael. 2016. "For a Ruthless Criticism of U.S. Politics." *Polity* 48:5–28.

Gilens, Martin. 2012. *Affluence and Influence: Economic Inequality and Political Power in America*. Princeton, NJ: Princeton University Press.

Gilens, Martin, and Benjamin I. Page. 2014. "Testing Theories of American Politics: Elites, Interest Groups, and Average Citizens." *Perspectives on Politics* 12:564–581.

Gordon, Colin. 1991. "New Deal, Old Deck: Business and the Origins of Social Security, 1920–1935." *Politics and Society* 19:165–207.

Hacker, Jacob S., and Paul Pierson. 2005. *Off Center: The Republican Revolution and the Erosion of American Democracy*. New Haven, CT: Yale University Press.

———. 2010. *Winner-Take-All Politics: How Washington Made the Rich Richer—and Turned Its Back on the Middle Class*. New York: Simon and Schuster.

Hollis-Brusky, Amanda. 2015. *Ideas with Consequences: The Federalist Society and the Conservative Counterrevolution*. Oxford: Oxford University Press.

Jasper, James M., and Jan Willem Duyvendak, eds. 2015. *Players and Arenas*. Amsterdam: Amsterdam University Press.

Keck, Thomas M. 2004. *The Most Activist Supreme Court in History: The Road to Modern Judicial Conservatism*. Chicago: University of Chicago Press.

Key, V. O., Jr. 1955. "A Theory of Critical Elections." *Journal of Politics* 17:3–18.

Lafer, Gordon. 2013. "The Legislative Attack on American Wages and Labor Standards, 2011–2012." Economic Policy Institute, October 31. Available at https://www.epi.org/publication/attack-on-american-labor-standards.

Malone, Christopher. 2008. *Between Freedom and Bondage: Race, Party, and Voting Rights in the Antebellum North*. New York: Routledge.

Manza, Jeff. 2015. "Reconnecting the Political and the Economic in the New Gilded Age." *Contemporary Sociology: A Journal of Reviews* 44:449–462.

McElwee, Sean. 2015. "Why Voting Matters: Large Disparities in Turnout Benefit the Donor Class." Demos, September 16. Available at https://www.demos.org/research/why-voting-matters-large-disparities-turnout-benefit-donor-class.

Perlstein, Rick. 2008. *Nixonland: The Rise of a President and the Fracturing of America*. New York: Scribner.

Phillips-Fein, Kim. 2009. *Invisible Hands: The Making of the Conservative Movement from the New Deal to Reagan*. New York: W. W. Norton.

Piven, Frances Fox. 2006. *Challenging Authority: How Ordinary People Change America*. Lanham, MD: Rowman and Littlefield.

Piven, Frances Fox, and Richard A. Cloward. 1977. *Poor People's Movements: Why They Succeed, How They Fail*. New York: Pantheon.

Sharp, Gene. 2012. *From Dictatorship to Democracy: A Conceptual Framework for Liberation*. New York: New Press.

Shelley, Percy Bysshe. 2003. *The Major Works*. Oxford: Oxford University Press.

Skocpol, Theda, and Alexander Hertel-Fernandez. 2016. "The Koch Effect: The Impact of a Cadre-Led Network on American Politics." Paper presented at the Southern

Political Science Association annual conference, San Juan, Puerto Rico, January 7–9.

Southworth, Ann. 2009. *Lawyers of the Right: Professionalizing the Conservative Coalition*. Chicago: University of Chicago Press.

Swenson, Peter. 2002. *Capitalists against Markets: The Making of Labor Markets and Welfare States in the United States and Sweden*. Oxford: Oxford University Press.

Teles, Steven M. 2010. *The Rise of the Conservative Legal Movement: The Battle for Control of the Law*. Princeton, NJ: Princeton University Press.

Thompson, Dorothy. 1984. *The Chartists: Popular Politics in the Industrial Revolution*. New York: Pantheon.

Wood, Gordon. 1969. *The Creation of the American Republic, 1776–1787*. New York: W. W. Norton.

Yarnell, Allen. 1974. *Democrats and Progressives: The 1948 Presidential Election as a Test of Postwar Liberalism*. Berkeley: University of California Press.

2

Why Did They Keep Quiet?

Missing Protests against School Closures in Sweden

KATRIN UBA

> It is very remarkable. Before the closure of this school [Brikegårdens]
> I did not hear of any protests, neither via email nor phone.
>
> —A POLITICIAN IN KARLSKOGA MUNICIPALITY,
> quoted in *Nerikes Allehanda*, April 9, 2000

Swedish local authorities have closed more than six hundred and threat-ened to close more than one thousand primary schools since the early 1990s. These threats have often faced fierce opposition from pupils, par-ents, teachers, and local communities; more than fifteen hundred protests were mobilized from 1991 to 2010. Sometimes these demonstrations, strikes, petitions, or letter campaigns achieved a concession, and authorities post-poned or stopped the planned closure. Sometimes the protests had no such political impact, and the schools were nevertheless closed, with their pupils sent to other schools and the school facilities sold, used for other purposes (e.g., kindergarten, housing), or just demolished. Considering this emotional process—the closure of a school is known to strongly affect pupils, parents, and teachers in Sweden as well as in the United States, Canada, and New Zealand—it is surprising that 363 of the Swedish schools were threatened and closed without any reports of public protests. There were no petitions, no angry letters in the local media, and no demonstrations or school strikes. Why this quiescence—especially as protests against school closures some-times do achieve their goals? Was it related to the lack of resources or moti-vation for mobilization in the community, the low perceived efficacy of pro-tests and significant power of the targets to suppress the protests, or the general lack of opportunities for influencing the decision-making? This chapter aims to provide some answers to this relatively rare question in so-cial movement research.

Studies on contentious politics and on political participation usually ask why and when protests are mobilized (Andrews and Biggs 2006; Kitschelt

1986; Kriesi 1995; Soule et al. 1999; Koopmans 2005) or who participates in protest actions and why (Van Aelst and Walgrave 2001; Barnes and Kaase 1979; Brady 1999; Van Deth, Montero, and Westholm 2007; Fatke and Freitag 2013; Verba, Schlozman, and Brady 1995). The results of these studies are relatively coherent and argue that specific micro-, meso-, and macrolevel factors explain mobilization and participation (see reviews in Opp 2009 and Van Stekelenburg and Klandermans 2013). At the micro- or individual level, participation is often related to incentives such as perceived relative deprivation and injustice, resources (knowledge, civic skills, time, networks), and emotions (Bäck, Teorell, and Westholm 2011; Van Deth, Montero, and Westholm 2007; Trousset et al. 2015; Van Stekelenburg and Klandermans 2013). At the meso- or group level, social movements and/or political parties are seen to have an important mobilizing role in building the identity of the "activist," recruiting new activists, cooperating with each other, or opting for countermobilization (Koopmans 2005; Tarrow 2011; Verba, Schlozman, and Brady 1995; Van Zomeren, Postmes, and Spears 2008). Finally, at the macrolevel, there is a need for open political, discursive, and economic opportunity structures or simply a context where contention is not directly repressed or covertly hindered by the targets (Kriesi 1995; McAdam, Tarrow, and Tilly 2001; Meyer and Minkoff 2004; Kousis and Tilly 2015).

The question of "missing protests" or individuals defecting from a protest is seldom discussed in the literature because it is often assumed to be just the flip side of participation (see Klandermans and Van Stekelenburg 2014). There are, however, a few excellent accounts, such as John Gaventa's *Power and Powerlessness: Quiescence and Rebellion in an Appalachian Valley* (1980), which argue and demonstrate empirically that in the context of significant inequalities the lack of protests should be understood in the framework of use and misuse of power by the authorities (i.e., the targets of the potential protest). I follow Gaventa's design of studying outliers—that is, studying cases where according to prior research we expect to find public protests but cannot find any despite the use of various sources of information and applying this on a wealthier and more egalitarian context than the Appalachian Valley—Sweden. More specifically, I use the case of missing protests in the Swedish municipal school-closure process as an empirical example. Similar cases of school closures can be found in Canada, Denmark, New Zealand, and the United Kingdom (Basu 2007; Bondi 1988; Egelund and Laustsen 2006; Witten et al. 2003). In this chapter I first use prior research on protest mobilization to construct a framework to explain the unexpected quiescence in this example; then I describe the importance of triangulation in the data-collection process in a study of missing protests; and finally I combine a quantitative large-N analysis of protests against school closures in Sweden with an analysis of a few outliers to show that the unexpected quiescence is often related to the actions of the targets.

Precipitating Protest? State of the Art

While high electoral turnout and citizens' participation in electoral politics are often seen as desirable for democracy, citizens' engagement in protests has not always been seen as inherently good or rational (Teorell 2006; Koopmans 2005; Rucht 2007). Therefore, it is not surprising that protest actions are sometimes viewed as unacceptable by the general public (Crozat 1998) or political elite (Uba 2016b) or that many people would not mobilize or participate in such actions. For example, according to the 2010–2014 World Values Survey, 25 percent of Swedish respondents said that they would never attend a peaceful demonstration (compared with 54 percent in neighboring Estonia and 30 percent in the United States).[1] However, protest mobilization is not unusual in Europe, in the United States, or elsewhere (Atak et al. 2014; Béjar and Moraes 2016; Hutter 2014). Perhaps, therefore, scholarly works focus more on explaining the presence of protests rather than on discussing the lack of contentious gatherings (Tilly 1978).

At the microlevel, a somewhat similar question was recently asked and answered by Bert Klandermans and Jaquelien van Stekelenburg in an article titled "Why People Don't Participate in Collective Action" (2014). Their article assumes that a mobilization is already occurring and can be joined; but what if no mobilization is occurring? Spontaneous protests do sometimes arise (Piven and Cloward 1979; Opp 2009), but most protests involve a careful mobilizing process. The reasons for protest mobilizations are many. In general, however, they can be explained by the presence of specific incentives (e.g., real or perceived grievances), the availability of resources, and open political opportunity structures. The grievances emerge or are perceived to emerge as a result of some macrolevel critical event (Opp 2009), such as an announcement by a municipal government that it plans to close one or more primary schools. The few systematic analyses of the long-term consequences of school closures do not find many negative effects of the closures (Egelund and Laustsen 2006). However, in the short term, the closures increase insecurity for pupils, parents, and teachers; increase traffic insecurity; and prolong the distance and time required for everyday travel between home and school (Witten et al. 2003). Schools provide employment and social-service opportunities and help strengthen local identity via cultural events that take place on school premises (Kilpatrick et al. 2002). The threat of closing a primary school is therefore perceived as a grievance, which should increase the probability of protest mobilization, according to theories of relative deprivation (see reviews in Edwards and McCarthy 2004 and Opp 2009). If this grievance is combined with general feelings of injustice and spreads as a result of grievance extension (Gordon and Jasper 1996), the mobilization might also involve a broader group of people than those who are directly affected by the closure. This approach indirectly hints that the quiescence means consent; if the affected groups do not react to a threatened closure, they do not perceive any grievances. Gaventa (1980) shows that this does not have to be a case and the reasons for missing protests should be looked for in the power relations in the community.

Others argue that mobilization requires the availability of resources such as preexisting networks and leadership, which help increase social incentives for mobilization. Many discontented people fail to mobilize because they lack resources and organization (Snyder and Tilly 1972). Primary school pupils, especially younger ones, are usually picked up by their parents after a school day, increasing the "meeting points" for parents. Thus, these parents should show a development of tighter networks that become useful for mobilization of protests. This networking obviously varies with the socioeconomic resources of the parents, the school, and the community. However, it is likely that networks in small rural communities are tighter than those in urban settings. Discontented pupils and parents can persuade a local village community to support their action by arguing that a threat to the school is actually a threat to the future of the village. Schools tend to be the center of a village community, and a closed school might mean fewer work opportunities and fewer newcomers, thereby escalating the process of a dying village (Åberg-Bengtsson 2009; Lind and Stjernström 2015). Small rural communities have a strong politicized collective identity, which helps them overcome the lack of human resources and benefits protest mobilization (Van Zomeren, Postmes, and Spears 2008; Gamson 1996). Many such examples exist all over Scandinavia (Lind and Stjernström 2015), suggesting that missing protests against school closures are more likely to occur in small urban communities than in rural communities.

In urban communities, especially in those with a higher degree of segregation, tight parents' or pupils' networks are often missing and political activism is generally low (Strömblad and Myrberg 2013). Immigrant populations often lack the resources necessary for mobilization (Verba, Schlozman, and Brady 1995); for example, writing a protest letter requires some knowledge of Swedish and an understanding of the ways in which the political system works at the municipal level. However, for mobilizing at least one public protest, it might suffice to have a few active families that can initiate a mobilization. While it is likely that protests more frequently take place in the municipalities with a large proportion of educated and well-off citizens, this might not explain the missing protests. Therefore, it is particularly important to combine the large-N analysis of protest mobilization with the detailed analysis of outliers.

Finally, it is well known that incentives and resources are not enough to explain protest mobilization; a specific window of political opportunity is also required (Kitschelt 1986; Kriesi 1995; Meyer 2004). Gaventa (1980) even suggests that the long-term lack of institutional and symbolic opportunities for mobilization are important for explaining the quiescence. Activists' expectations for success—in this case, their expectations for influencing the decision on school closure—depend on political context (Soule et al. 1999). While protest mobilization sometimes involves the risk of repression (McPhail and McCarthy 2005), this is seldom the case for small-scale local protests in democratic welfare states such as Sweden. Here, opportunities to protest are related to disagreements among political parties and to the availability of powerful political allies (Meyer and Minkoff 2004). It is likely that activists have a higher expectation of success in times of electoral campaign or when ruling parties have some disagreement in relation to a school-closure proposal.[2]

The closure of school facilities in Sweden is not as much an ideological issue as it is a choice between publicly or privately funded education, where the difference between the standpoints of political parties is clear. The decision for closure is framed as an inevitable solution to the problem of decreasing numbers of pupils and increasing economic costs of school premises (Amcoff 2012; Åberg-Bengtsson 2009). The situation is the same elsewhere (Basu 2007; Kearns et al. 2009; Witten et al. 2003). The Swedish Left Party is the only political party that clearly opposes the establishment of the new independent schools (*friskola*) that are sometimes opened as a reaction to closed public schools.[3] A recent analysis demonstrated that left-wing governments—that is, the coalitions run by the Social Democratic Party, the Left Party, and/or the Green Party—are significantly less prone than right-wing governments to allow independent primary schools (Elinder and Jordahl 2013). Although outsourcing public services is not the same as closing public schools, and although incumbent politicians—regardless of their political color—disapprove of protests against school closures (Uba 2016a), the following analysis takes into account the type of government in power. With regard to instability among elites (Meyer 2004), the analysis also accounts for the timing of elections, as one might expect protests against school closures to be more common during election periods.

It is also likely that the authorities, which anticipate protests, do not propose many school closures just before elections even though it has been shown that closure of a school does not have much effect on municipal election results (Wänström and Karlsson 2011). Anticipating protests is also relevant for other factors (e.g., the resources), as one could assume that targets of the potential protests (e.g., local politicians) would not threaten a large school in a well-off area with a closure as eagerly as they would a small school in a poor neighborhood. But the argument of saving the public money works more in the case of small rather than large schools, and it is also known that municipalities tend to threaten and close smaller rather than larger schools (Larsson-Taghizadeh 2016).

In sum, prior research on contentious politics suggests that if certain conditions (i.e., grievances, resources, opportunities) are present, then protest mobilization is also likely to take place. If these conditions are not present, we expect quiescence. I test this argument by combining a conventional comparison of threatened schools both with and without protests against the proposed closure with an analysis of some outliers—that is, schools that were closed without protests.

Data about Protests against School Closures in Sweden

Any discussion of missing protests requires an important methodological note about protest definition and data collection, as it is possible that we, the scholars, have in fact overlooked an event that actually took place. This study opts for the conventional definition of "protest" as a collective contentious action that targets the authorities with specific claims (see, e.g., Earl et al. 2004). "Collective" refers to three or more people, and the "claims" are in this case related to school closures. Those "targeted" are the local municipal authorities, especially the politicians and bureaucrats in charge of education and school politics at the local level. "Contentious actions" range from demonstrations, petitions, and letters in local newspapers to illegal school strikes, in which parents refuse to send their children to school. All the data for this chapter were collected using conventional methods of protest event analysis (Earl et al. 2004; Hutter 2014) and rely mainly on the media—national and local newspapers, social media, and the internet.

To minimize a typical bias of newspaper data—overrepresentation of large, newsworthy events that take place in the central arena and target national actors (Earl et al. 2004; Oliver and Maney 2000; Ortiz et al. 2005; Smith et al. 2001)—a specific triangulation process was applied. First, all 290 Swedish municipalities were contacted and asked to send information about the primary schools that they have threatened to close and have closed since 1991. About 60 percent of contacted municipalities responded; many of those that did not respond were experiencing ongoing conflicts over school closures (e.g., Botkyrka). Second, the lists of threatened and closed schools were compared with a list of all primary schools in Sweden in 2000–2006. This list was obtained from the database of the Swedish School Board (SIRIS) and from Statistics Sweden. Third, the names of schools were used

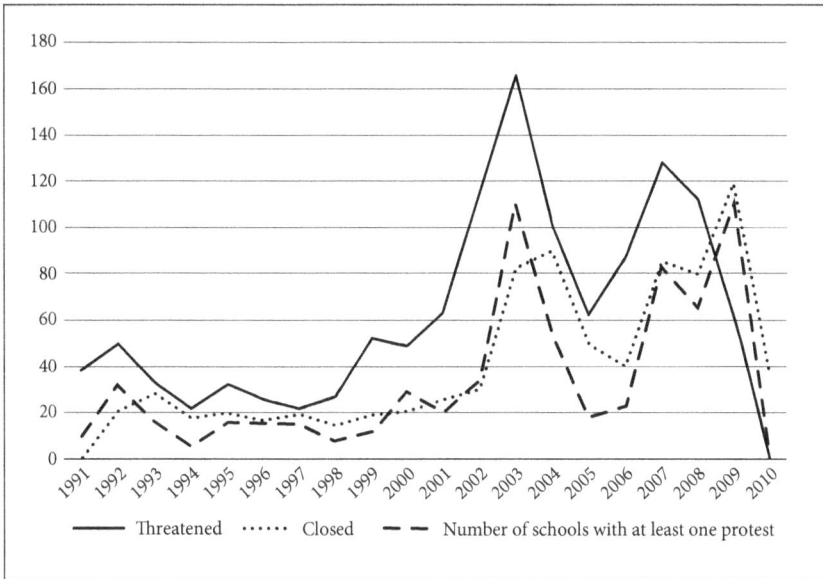

Figure 2.1. School closures and protests against closures in Sweden, 1991–2010

as keywords while searching the digital newspapers' archive (Retriver), as well as the digital archives of Swedish Radio and TV. Fourth, the names of schools that had no records of protests by the end of the media search were then used in a regular Google search. In the end, information was obtained on 1,245 school facilities that had been threatened with closure during the period 1991–2010; of these, 600 schools had been closed.[4] Reports were found on more than thirteen hundred protest events; in the case of some schools, there were many protest events (e.g., the Gustav Adolf school in Helsingborg), while in other cases there was only a single public letter in a newspaper (e.g., the Djursdala school in Vimmerby).

Figure 2.1 presents the trends of threats, closures, and protests over time and demonstrates that the number of schools with at least one protest against a proposed closure correlates relatively well with the number of closed schools per year. Still, in the case of 363 schools that were threatened by closure, no protests were registered. Although it is likely that the media coverage of events taking place in the early 1990s was not as good as that in the early 2000s, Figure 2.1 does not indicate such a problem, as the number of schools with at least one protest forms a similar proportion of the number of threatened schools all across the examined time frame.

As citizens often contact municipalities through direct channels such as phone calls, letters, or emails, it is likely that such a small-scale mobilization went unnoticed. To test this premise, eleven relatively populous and heterogeneous municipalities were contacted and asked to provide all the documents they had from school-closure processes since 2002.[5] There were 118 threatened schools in these municipalities, but authorities had received a total of 324 letters, postcards, emails, and petitions in relation to the proposed closures of only 55 different schools (for further information about these letters, see Uba 2016a). This check revealed 10 more schools with protests. In the end, only 28 of the studied schools (24 percent) in these eleven municipalities remained without any protest information. The majority of these schools were in the same municipality—Hagfors. In this municipality, politicians proposed to close all 10 existing smaller schools and build a big new central school in 2005. Parents started a petition campaign to initiate a local referendum over the question of constructing this new school, but no clear opposition to the proposed closures was formulated in the text of this petition.[6] The petition was eventually signed by one thousand people,[7] but as it was not directly about school closures, our media search did not catch it. This discovery suggests that the protest data for all 1,135 schools in this study might indeed have omitted several protests, perhaps about 10 percent of the events. However, the information obtained directly from the municipalities was not infallible, since municipal bureaucrats had not received (or archived) any protest letters from 34 schools that did have (media-based) records about protests.

In sum, similar to any studies of quiescence or lack of protests, it is important to be aware that we measure only visible public protests and that it is likely that some actions were missed during the data-collection process. However, these actions are probably randomly distributed and would not systematically affect our analysis of the conditions that explain the lack of protests against proposed school closures.

How Can the Missing Protests Be Explained?

To explain the unexpected quiescence in respect to threatened school closures in Sweden, two different analyses were conducted. First, a quantitative analysis tests whether the incentives, resources, and opportunities have any significant effect on the mobilization of the first anti-school-closure protest. Second, we performed an analysis of a few outliers—that is, the schools that should have experienced some protests according to the results of the first analysis but did not.

The first analysis assumes that as soon the threat of closure becomes public, there is an incentive for protest, since a closed school is an objective grievance. It is likely that if politicians propose to close only some classes or only part of a school, the perceived relative deprivation will be more severe. Parents might ask authorities why they are closing their child's class and not some other. Pupils might understand that they but not others will have to leave their friends and join a new school. This perceived deprivation is expected to increase the incentives for mobilization, and therefore our analysis considers how the type of closure—partial or not—influences the risk of protesting.

Community resources are more difficult to measure, as we do not have access to information about the socioeconomic background of the pupils or their parents. The closest possible proxy is the number of pupils in the school in the year the threat became public (or the most recent available number of pupils). Data from SIRIS were not available for all 1,245 threatened schools, so the quantitative analysis uses only 1,135 schools. Large schools mean that there is a higher probability of having active pupils or parents; there should also be more networks in place, which allow solidarity-based mobilization. Among the threatened schools in our sample, smaller schools dominate, as half of the schools have fewer than 65 pupils and the largest had 855 pupils. Although smaller schools are threatened more frequently than larger schools and our results should be interpreted with this preselection bias in mind, it is expected that if a school is threatened, then larger schools are more likely than smaller schools to mobilize protests against the proposed closure. In addition to the size of the school, the analysis accounts for the distance from the closed school to the remaining school (in kilometers). It is a proxy for rural schools. Rural communities are likely to have stronger networks, and therefore there should be some positive effect of this variable on mobilization.

Political opportunities were measured by accounting for whether a school was threatened with closure during an election year, when it is more likely for elites to disagree over the process of a school closure and the opportunity for protest mobilization should open up. To denote the political party or coalition in power, three categories—left, right, and the coalition across party lines—was used since it is likely that protests will be more common under the rule of broad coalitions.

Finally, the quantitative analysis also uses the percentage of highly educated people in the municipality (measured in 2000, data from Statistics Sweden) as a control variable. This value is a kind of proxy for wealthier municipalities, where people are expected to be more politically active in general. Ideally, it would be preferable to use the percentage of the non-Swedish population in the municipality as a control variable as well, but the data available for the entire period of interest (1991–2010) do not differentiate between immigrants on the basis of their country of origin. This is problematic, as there are several border municipalities close to Finland and Norway (e.g., Eda, Haparanta, Årjäng, Övertårneå) with historically high proportions of non-Swedish inhabitants. Authorities have threatened and closed many schools in all of these municipalities, despite significant protest campaigns. In the municipalities where immigration has significantly increased since the 1970s (e.g., Botkyrka, Malmö, Södertälje), there are fewer threatened schools and fewer protests against school-closure processes.[8]

Statistical Analysis

The analysis uses a setup of the survival (discrete event history) analysis, which allows an examination of how different factors affect the likelihood (risk) of protest mobilization. The method comes from medical studies, in which one examines the extent to which the specific treatment prolongs the life of the patient or increases her or his survival rate. In our case, every threatened school is a patient; the previously listed factors, which prior studies relate to protest mobilization, are treatment; and the analysis calculates the risk of the first protest. There is a clear difference from medical studies as protests can be mobilized more than once, but frequency of protests is beyond the interest of this study. All threatened schools have some risk of protest mobilization. The clock starts when the school is threatened and stops when the first protest appears or when our period of observation ends. The analysis also accounts for the fact that the examined 1,135 schools are nested in 239 municipalities. While the measures of partial closure and distance from the remaining school are time invariant, the number of pupils in every school varies over time. Several municipality-specific variables, such as the ideological leaning of the ruling coalition and the occurrence of an election year, also vary over time.

The results of this analysis demonstrate several interesting patterns (see Table 2.1): First, the likelihood (risk) of protest mobilization is larger when a part of the school is proposed to be closed, but this effect disappears when we account for different political opportunities in examined municipalities. As partial closures are proxies for perceived relative deprivation, the results suggest that relative deprivation is not as important as opportunities. Second, resources (at least, when measured in terms of the size of a school) do not have any significant effect on protest mobilization, and schools that are farther away from other schools have only a slightly increased risk of protests. Partially, the size of the school and distance from other schools might decrease the incentives for community protests because targets are already aware of the costs of relocating many pupils. Another possibility is that there was no clear perceived deprivation as a result of closure because the premises of the threatened schools were in very poor shape (e.g., Järnbrottskolan in Gothenburg, Talldalsskolan in Kristianstad, Gunillaskolan in Gällivare). Such information was not available for all the schools, and therefore it was not tested in the large-N study. However, three larger schools without

TABLE 2.1 THE RISK OF ANTI-SCHOOL-CLOSURE PROTESTS IN SWEDEN (MULTILEVEL MODEL)

	Model 1	Model 2
Partial closure	1.27 (.17)*	1.23 (.17)
Number of pupils (log)	1.02 (.06)	1.02 (.06)
Distance from closest remaining school (km)	1.01 (.00)*	1.01 (.00)*
Municipal rule (Right wing = baseline)		
Left-wing parties		0.86 (.14)
Coalition across party lines		0.86 (.24)
Elections		0.43 (.07)**
Percentage of highly educated people in municipality	1.25 (1.57)	0.89 (1.7)
Wald chi^2	789.12	672.51
Log likelihood	−1,483.56	−1,431.46
N	3,349	3,349
Number of schools (municipalities)	1,135 (239)	1,135 (239)

Note: The hazard ratio greater than 1 indicates the growing likelihood of protests, while the hazard ratio less than 1 indicates that the likelihood of protests is decreasing. I have tested the robustness of the models with various methods of estimation, and the ones in the table come from the random intercept conditional logit (cloglog) model. The estimates do not differ significantly from other possible methods of estimation. *$p < 0.1$, **$p < 0.001$; the coefficients for time intervals are omitted.

protests did have problems with facilities, and pupils were moved to more modern school facilities as a result of the closures. Third, the factor that affects the likelihood of protest mobilization most is election time—the indicator of open political opportunities; and this factor has an unexpected negative effect. That is, protests are *less* likely to take place during election years. Other political opportunity indicators, such as the coalition in power, did not have a significant effect on risk of protest mobilization, probably because incumbent governments tend to be negative toward protests against school closures regardless of their ideological leaning (Uba 2016b). Such an attitude, especially if some former protests have been ineffective, could lead to a sense of powerlessness among protestors and dampen their willingness to mobilize (see Gaventa 1980).

There are two explanations for the unexpected negative effect of elections. First, several politicians have noted that they will not make any proposals concerning school closures during election years, suggesting that politicians perceive the general public as being negative toward the school-closure process, even without protests. Second, and a more likely explanation, is that elections provide an alternative channel for expressing public opposition to school closures. If the issue (of school closures) is already on the agenda, protests might be considered to be a less efficient channel for influencing the targets than the traditional channel of representative democracy.

Outliers: Schools Closed without Protests

The quantitative large-N analysis suggested that protests are less likely to happen during election years, and the effect of partial closures and distance from other schools on protest mobilization was less robust. Hence, we still do not know what explains the quiescence and need to look at the outliers. Of the 1,135 schools in the large-N study, 469 schools had no protests. If we assume that there is more incentive to protest if the threat of closure is greater, then it is reasonable to look at the schools that were eventually closed—we are left with 305 schools without any registered protest event. Of these, 66 closures were threatened during an electoral year, and because elections were shown to decrease the risk of protesting, we exclude all schools whose closure process took place during an election year. Thus, 153 schools remain in the set of outliers.

If we exclude the schools where only one or more classes were threatened—that is, partial closures, which were shown to slightly increase the likelihood of mobilization—then we are left with 125 schools with an average duration of the school-closure process of 1.14 years (86 percent of these schools had a process that lasted one year). This suggests that the authorities managed to close the school so fast that it is not surprising that people did not manage to mobilize any protests. When examining the 101 similar schools (full closures not during an election year) with at least one protest, these did experience only a slightly longer closure process (an average of 1.2 years, with 80 percent lasting one year). So the duration of the process does not seem to explain the missing protests.

Although the 125 outliers are dispersed between fifty municipalities, there is a clear trend: 50 percent were threatened and closed by left-wing governments, 29 percent by center-right governments, and 21 percent by governments run by coalitions across blocks. The respective percentages for similar schools where protests did occur were 55 percent (left), 31 percent (center-right), and 14 percent (coalitions across blocks). Although the large-N study did not show the statistical effect of the party in power, government coalitions across blocks can demonstrate greater political support for a closure and might be a reason for fewer protests because of lower perceived effectiveness and fewer potential allies.

This was also the case with three outliers that came from the same municipality: Mark. Even though the government in Mark was run by the left-wing coalition, its proposal on school closures was also supported by the conservatives (*Moderaterna*). Hence, targets' behavior probably decreased the incentives for protest mobilization in this municipality. In the case of another outlier, Hacklinge school in Gävle, all parties voted in favor of the closure, although some politicians (e.g., from the Green Party) initially opposed the plan and lobbied against it. In this case, several parents opted to "exit" instead of choosing a "voice" strategy (Hirschman 1970) and moved their children to surrounding independent schools just after the plans for closure became public. Although similar information is unavailable for all the schools in this study, it should be noted that such an exit strategy was very frequent among schools without protests (at least ten schools). This action could be considered an indirect form of protest, especially as the targets, that is, the municipal politicians, will not save any money when pupils move from a public school to an independent school.

Conclusion

This chapter examines the reasons for a lack of protest mobilization in cases where the conventional theories of contentious politics would predict them to take place. First, I tested the common arguments about grievances, incentives, resources, and political opportunities for the case of protests against school closures in Swedish municipalities. Because of a lack of data, all aspects of incentives and resources could not be measured as well as might be desired; however, the analysis of more than one thousand cases showed that the risk of protests is higher when authorities propose closing only a part of the school (some classes), which should increase the perceived injustice and deprivation. However, the risk of protest mobilization was shown to be smaller during election years. This unexpected result could be explained by the specifics of the issue, as school closures in Sweden are rarely a matter of ideological differences between political parties and therefore also not so important for elections.

As the large-N analysis was insufficiently informative, I further examined the cases where one expects but does not find any protests—the outliers. This analysis revealed three interesting patterns that could explain the missing protests. First, the targets matter. The political opportunity was not open despite the rule of the left-wing parties, which are usually seen as allies for the activists. When all or the majority of the political parties agreed to close the school, few allies were available and no protest was mobilized. Second, the choice of exit in terms of moving pupils to independent schools decreased the incentive to protest. This factor is probably more common for urban schools, since in rural areas, parents often started their mobilization with a threat to open an independent school. Third, often there was a real lack of incentive such that the closure was probably not perceived as a loss because of the problematic state of the school premises. It is not surprising for pupils and parents not to protest against the closure of a "bad" school.

The first two findings encourage further research into protest mobilization, as studies on contentious politics often focus on the parties in power and not directly on the parties in favor of particular decisions. This narrow focus on targets might be misleading: The large-N analysis in this study did not show a significant role for the party in power; rather, the analysis of outliers demonstrates that it was the size of the coalition supporting the decision that mattered for the quiescence. Obviously, these data might be affected by a certain selection bias, as municipalities that have no majority support for school closures in the first place might not propose any schools for closure. Considering that almost all Swedish municipalities (273 of 290) have proposed at least one school for closure, this bias is probably very small. Hence, a more detailed measurement of where the targets stand in regard to the issue at stake would be useful in future studies of protest mobilization.

Finally, the parents' option to choose another school instead of mobilizing a protest to keep the old one open is an interesting process that requires further analysis: Which kinds of social groups are more likely to opt for exit instead of voice, and in what context? Considering that the option to choose an independent school instead of a public one is available in other countries besides Sweden, this issue would also be interesting from a comparative perspective. Moreover, the process is relevant for other types of contentious issues (e.g., siting various energy projects) as well—those in which we usually examine the probability of protest (voice) or loyalty (quiescence) and only rarely look at the exit.

NOTES

1. World Values Survey data are available at http://www.worldvaluessurvey.org/WVSDocumentationWV6.jsp.

2. The probability of mobilization and expected success are also affected by prior protest experiences and perceived procedural injustice (Tyler and Smith 1998). Without microlevel survey data or interviews, I am unfortunately unable to examine this question here.

3. These schools are funded by municipalities but not controlled by the municipality in the same way as the municipal (public) schools.

4. Here, "closure" does not mean the implementation of a closure but the decision made by politicians in the municipal parliament. The school often remained open for some months or even a year after the decision, as the practical process of closure might require preparations (e.g., finding places for all pupils in new schools).

5. According to Swedish law (*offentlighetsprincipen*), authorities must make such information available, and all municipalities cooperated. The details about these municipalities (Boras, Borlänge, Botkyrka, Falun, Gävle, Göteborg, Helsingborg, Kal-

mar, Lund, Örebro, and Uppsala) are described in Larsson-Tagizadeh 2016 and Uba 2016a.

6. Local referenda over school organization have become more common recently, but the results of such referenda are not obligatory for decision makers to follow. Even though 70 percent of the participants voted against the closures in Strängnäs municipality in 2018 (turnout was 59 percent), the ruling local politicians decided to ignore the vox populi. See "Så röstade Strängnäsborna i folkomröstningen" 2018.

7. See also "Hagfors Nya Skola" [The new Hagfors school], 2005, previously available at http://lokalt.folkpartiet.se/lokalt/varmlands-lan/kommuner/hagfors/skolfragor/hagfors-nya-skola (printout in the author's possession).

8. Another potentially relevant control variable would be the quality of education provided in the threatened school; however, appropriate data are unavailable for many of the primary schools in this study.

REFERENCES
Åberg-Bengtsson, Lisbeth. 2009. "The Smaller the Better? A Review of Research on Small Rural Schools in Sweden." *International Journal of Educational Research* 48:100–108.
Amcoff, Jan. 2012. "Do Rural Districts Die When Their Schools Close? Evidence from Sweden around 2000." *Educational Planning* 20:47–60.
Andrews, Kenneth, and Michael Biggs. 2006. "The Dynamics of Protest Diffusion: Movement Organizations, Social Networks, and News Media in the 1960 Sit-Ins." *American Sociological Review* 71:752–777.
Atak, Kivanç, Ondřej Císař, Priska Daphi, Cristina Flesher Fominaya, Ari-Elmeri Hyvönen, Maria Kousis, and Antonio Montañés Jimenez. 2014. *Spreading Protest: Social Movements in Times of Crisis*. London: ECPR Press.
Bäck, Hanna, Jan Teorell, and Anders Westholm. 2011. "Explaining Modes of Participation: A Dynamic Test of Alternative Rational Choice Models." *Scandinavian Political Studies* 34:74–97.
Barnes, Samuel, and Max Kaase. 1979. *Political Action*. Beverly Hills, CA: Sage.
Basu, Ranu. 2007. "Negotiating Acts of Citizenship in an Era of Neoliberal Reform: The Game of School Closures." *International Journal of Urban and Regional Research* 3:109–127.
Béjar, Sergio, and Juan Andrés Moraes. 2016. "The International Monetary Fund, Party System Institutionalization, and Protest in Latin America." *Latin American Politics and Society* 58:26–48.
Bondi, Liz. 1988. "Political Participation and School Closures: An Investigation of Bias in Local Authority Decision Making." *Policy and Politics* 16:41–54.
Brady, Henry. 1999. "Political Participation." *Measures of Political Attitudes* 2:737–801.
Crozat, Matthew. 1998. "Are the Times A-Changin'? Assessing the Acceptance of Protest in Western Democracies." In *The Social Movement Society: Contentious Politics for the New Century*, edited by David S. Meyer and Sidney Tarrow, 59–82. Lanham, MD: Rowman and Littlefield.
Earl, Jennifer, Andrew Martin, John McCarthy, and Sarah A. Soule. 2004. "The Use of Newspaper Data in the Study of Collective Action." *Annual Review of Sociology* 30:65–80.
Edwards, Bob, and John McCarthy. 2004. "Resources and Social Movement Mobilization." In *The Blackwell Companion to Social Movements*, edited by David Snow, Sarah Soule, and Hanspeter Kriesi, 116–152. Cambridge, UK: Wiley.

Egelund, Niels, and Helen Laustsen. 2006. "School Closure: What Are the Consequences for the Local Society?" *Scandinavian Journal of Educational Research* 50:429–439.

Elinder, Mikael, and Henrik Jordahl. 2013. "Political Preferences and Public Sector Outsourcing." *European Journal of Political Economy* 30:43–57.

Fatke, Matthia, and Markus Freitag. 2013. "Direct Democracy: Protest Catalyst or Protest Alternative?" *Political Behavior* 35:237–260.

Gamson, Joshua. 1996. "The Organizational Shaping of Collective Identity: The Case of Lesbian and Gay Film Festivals in New York." *Sociological Forum* 11:231–261.

Gaventa, John. 1980. *Power and Powerlessness: Quiescence and Rebellion in an Appalachian Valley*. Oxford, UK: Clarendon Press.

Gordon, Cynthia, and James Jasper. 1996. "Overcoming the 'NIMBY' Label: Rhetorical and Organizational Links for Local Protestors." *Research in Social Movements, Conflicts and Change* 19:159–181.

Hirschman, Albert. 1970. *Exit, Voice and Loyalty: Responses to Decline in Firms, Organizations, and States*. Cambridge, MA: Harvard University Press.

Hutter, Swen. 2014. *Protesting Economics and Culture in Western Europe: New Cleavages in Left and Right Politics*. Minneapolis: University of Minnesota Press.

Kearns, Robin, Nicolas Lewis, Tim McCreanor, and Karen Witten. 2009. "'The Status Quo Is Not an Option': Community Impacts of School Closure in South Taranaki, New Zealand." *Journal of Rural Studies* 25:131–140.

Kilpatrick, Sue, Susan Johns, Bill Mulford, Ian Falk, and Libby Prescott. 2002. *More than an Education: Leadership for Rural School-Community Partnerships*. Kingston, Australia: Rural Industries Research and Development Corporation. Available at http://pandora.nla.gov.au/pan/36440/20030717-0000/www.rirdc.gov.au/reports/HCC/02-055.pdf.

Kitschelt, Herbert. 1986. "Political Opportunity Structures and Political Protest: Antinuclear Movements in Four Democracies." *British Journal of Political Science* 16:57–85.

Klandermans, Bert, and Jacquelien van Stekelenburg. 2014. "Why People Don't Participate in Collective Action." *Journal of Civil Society* 10:341–352.

Koopmans, Ruud. 2005. "The Missing Link between Structure and Agency: Outline of an Evolutionary Approach to Social Movements." *Mobilization* 10:19–33.

Kousis, Maria, and Charles Tilly. 2015. *Economic and Political Contention in Comparative Perspective*. New York: Routledge.

Kriesi, Hanspeter. 1995. "The Political Opportunity Structure of New Social Movements: Its Impact on Their Mobilization." In *The Politics of Social Protest: Comparative Perspectives on States and Social Movements*, edited by Craig Jenkins and Bert Klandermans, 167–198. Minneapolis: University of Minnesota Press.

Larsson-Taghizadeh, Jonas. 2016. "Informational Lobbying and Activist Resources: Comparing Mobilizations against School Closures in Sweden." Ph.D. diss., Uppsala University.

Lind, Tommy, and Olof Stjernström. 2015. "Organizational Challenges for Schools in Rural Municipalities: Cross-national Comparisons in a Nordic Context." *Journal of Research in Rural Education* 30:1–14.

McAdam, Doug, Sidney Tarrow, and Charles Tilly. 2001. *Dynamics of Contention*. New York: Cambridge University Press.

McPhail, Clark, and John D. McCarthy. 2005. "Protest Mobilization, Protest Repression and Their Interaction." In *Repression and Mobilization*, edited by Christian Davenport, Hank Johnston, and Carol Mueller, 3–32. Minneapolis: University of Minnesota Press.

Meyer, David. 2004. "Protest and Political Opportunities." *Annual Review of Sociology* 30:125–145.

Meyer, David, and Debra Minkoff. 2004. "Conceptualizing Political Opportunity." *Social Forces* 82:1457–1492.

Oliver, Pamela, and Gregory Maney. 2000. "Political Processes and Local Newspaper Coverage of Protest Events: From Selection Bias to Triadic Interactions." *American Journal of Sociology* 106:463–505.

Opp, Karl-Dieter. 2009. *Theories of Political Protest and Social Movements.* New York: Routledge.

Ortiz, David, Daniel Myers, Eugene Walls, and Maria-Elena Diaz. 2005. "Where Do We Stand with Newspaper Data?" *Mobilization* 10:397–419.

Piven, Francis, and Richard Cloward. 1979. *Poor People's Movements: Why They Succeed, How They Fail.* New York: Vintage Books.

Rucht, Dieter. 2007. "The Spread of Protest Politics." In *The Oxford Handbook of Political Behavior*, edited by Russell Dalton and Hans-Dieter Klingemann, 708–723. Oxford: Oxford University Press.

"Så röstade Strängnäsborna i folkomröstningen" [So voted the people of Strangäs in the referenda]. 2018. *SVT Nyheter* [SVT News], September 12. Available at https://www.svt.se/nyheter/lokalt/sormland/sa-rostade-strangnasborna-i-folkomrostningen.

Smith, Jackie, John McCarthy, Clark McPhail, and Boguslaw Augustyn. 2001. "From Protest to Agenda Building: Description Bias in Media Coverage of Protest Events in Washington, DC." *Social Forces* 79:1397–1423.

Snyder, David, and Charles Tilly. 1972. "Hardship and Collective Violence in France, 1830 to 1960." *American Sociological Review* 37:520–532.

Soule, Sarah, Doug McAdam, John McCarthy, and Yang Su. 1999. "Protest Events: Cause or Consequence of State Action? The US Women's Movement and Federal Congressional Activities, 1956–1979." *Mobilization* 4:239–256.

Strömblad, Per, and Gunnar Myrberg. 2013. "Urban Inequality and Political Recruitment." *Urban Studies* 50:1049–1065.

Tarrow, Sidney. 2011. *Power in Movement: Collective Action, Social Movements and Politics.* Cambridge: Cambridge University Press.

Teorell, Jan. 2006. "Political Participation and Three Theories of Democracy: A Research Inventory and Agenda." *European Journal of Political Research* 45:787–810.

Tilly, Charles. 1978. *From Mobilization to Revolution.* Reading, MA: Addison-Wesley.

Trousset, Sarah, Kuhika Gupta, Hank Jenkins-Smith, Carol Silva, and Kerry Herron. 2015. "Degrees of Engagement: Using Cultural Worldviews to Explain Variations in Public Preferences for Engagement in the Policy Process." *Policy Studies Journal* 43:44–69.

Tyler, Tom, and Heather Smith. 1998. "Social Justice and Social Movements." In *Handbook of Social Psychology*, edited by Daniel Gilbert, Susan Fiske, and Gardner Lindzey, 595–629. New York: McGraw-Hill.

Uba, Katrin. 2016a. "Deliberative Protests? Persuading Politicians Not to Close Schools in Swedish Municipalities." *Revista Internacional de Sociologia* [International Sociology Journal] 74 (4). Available at http://dx.doi.org/10.3989/ris.2016.74.4.046.

———. 2016b. "Protest against the School Closures in Sweden: Accepted by Politicians?" In *The Consequences of Social Movements*, edited by Lorenzo Bosi, Marco Giugni, and Katrin Uba, 159–184. Cambridge: Cambridge University Press.

Van Aelst, Peter, and Stefaan Walgrave. 2001. "Who Is That (Wo)Man in the Street? From the Normalisation of Protest to the Normalisation of the Protester." *European Journal of Political Research* 39:461–486.

Van Deth, Jan W., Jóse Ramón Montero, and Anders Westholm, eds. 2007. *Citizenship and Involvement in European Democracies: A Comparative Analysis.* New York: Routledge.

Van Stekelenburg, Jacquelien, and Bert Klandermans. 2013. "The Social Psychology of Protest." *Current Sociology* 61:886–905.

Van Zomeren, Martijn, Tom Postmes, and Russell Spears. 2008. "Toward an Integrative Social Identity Model of Collective Action: A Quantitative Research Synthesis of Three Socio-psychological Perspectives." *Psychological Bulletin* 134:504–535.

Verba, Sidney, Kay Schlozman, and Henry Brady. 1995. *Voice and Equality: Civic Voluntarism in American Politics.* Cambridge, MA: Harvard University Press.

Wänström, Johan, and Martin Karlsson. 2011. *Kontroverser utan avtryck* [Controversies without impact]. Gothenburg, Sweden: Nationella kommunforskningsprogrammet.

Witten, Karen, Robin Kearns, Nick Lewis, Heather Coster, and Tim McCreanor. 2003. "Educational Restructuring from a Community Viewpoint: A Case Study of School Closure from Invercargill, New Zealand." *Environment and Planning* 21:203–224.

PART II

Movement-Target Interactions

3

Protests, Precariousness, and Democracy

Cities and "Service Delivery" in the Global South

Gay Seidman

C ities have long served as the stages for the performance of popular discontent. But over the past few years, that geographic cliché has taken on new meaning: Since the 2008 financial collapse, urban protestors have snarled traffic and camped in public places around the world. As more and more people live in cities, disruptions of urban life have become ever more central to social movement strategies.

While urban protests in New York or Madrid attract global headlines, less attention has been paid to the recent explosion of uprisings in cities across the Global South. Important similarities—especially, perhaps, in the way new social media help bring young adults onto the streets—have disguised some important differences, especially in the kinds of grievances that prompt protests. In Europe and North America, protestors have used cityscapes as a broad stage to challenge austerity-driven cuts in programs that have supported middle-class lives since the mid-twentieth century (Glasius and Pleyers 2013; Standing 2014; Therborn 2014). But in cities such as Johannesburg, São Paulo, and New Delhi, protests often follow a different logic: Instead of objecting to new patterns of rising inequality, protests in the Global South tend to revolve around persistent inequalities, demanding that local authorities provide material services necessary for daily life in the twenty-first century. These urban grievances are often linked to longstanding legacies of colonial rule: Too often in postcolonial settings, basic urban infrastructure reflects long-established patterns of exclusion. Waves of protests in rapidly growing megacities such as São Paulo and Johannesburg increasingly challenge persistent inequalities in basic infrastructure and social programs, insisting that democratic citizenship involves expanded social rights as well as political participation.

In postcolonial cities around the world, inadequate public services have become a core issue, the focus of widely shared grievances against the state. In expanding megacities, protestors emphasize broad frustrations over the challenges of daily life in marginal neighborhoods and, importantly, highlight the way colonial legacies of inequality and policy biases favor wealthier urban cores, persistently neglecting rapidly growing peripheral communities. Demanding clean water, public transport services, basic foodstuffs, improved educational opportunities, or better policing, protestors have built broad movements in support of more inclusive development—especially emphasizing the need for greater investment in urban public services.

Social movement scholars sometimes view this new wave of protests through the prism of northern movements—noting, for example, how young activists with some education use social media as an organizing tool or examining transnational links between protestors in different parts of the world. But distinct differences between these patterns of protest also demand attention. In postcolonial and postauthoritarian democracies, urban protests have raised new issues, perhaps reflecting a generational shift in the character of postcolonial political movements. In country after country—from South Africa to Brazil to India—observers often describe activists demanding expanded infrastructure as reflecting a new urban middle class; raised and educated in the city, young adults may be far more insistent on the state's obligation to provide basic urban infrastructure, from electricity and public transport services to public health and schools.

Across the Global South, protestors express similar frustrations about the failure of "developmentalist" ruling parties, demanding that local governments invest in the kinds of urban services that make daily life in rapidly expanding megacities possible. Rejecting the patterns of exclusion that have long shaped postcolonial cities, disruptive protests from Johannesburg to São Paulo to Beirut have focused on inadequate public investment in urban services. Could what South Africans call "service-delivery protests" reshape the meaning of democratic rights? Could protestors' demands for expanded basic services create new momentum behind broader visions of inclusive democracy, as growing demand for public urban services reconfigures popular understandings of basic social rights and citizenship?

New Democracies, Exclusionary Legacies

As social scientists have long pointed out, city streets provide an easily accessible stage for popular demonstrations; by blocking streets, disrupting traffic, or occupying plazas, protestors demand attention to their issues. In the mid-twentieth century, Latin America's urban industrial workers used city streets to assert their demands (Conniff 1982), a pattern that continued through the twentieth century in places such as Brazil and Argentina (Holston 2009). Today public spaces continue to provide visible sites of contention, allowing protestors to draw public attention to needs that might otherwise go unnoticed; but in postcolonial societies, protestors also call attention to the stark inequalities built into basic urban infrastructure.

In colonial societies, the small urban enclaves where colonial elites once lived have often been surrounded by expanding slums, which have never been provided with basic amenities such as clean water or electricity. Those patterns have persisted into more democratic periods: Brasilia, built in the 1950s as Brazil's new capital, famously included no housing for workers in its spectacular core, leaving the workers who built it to construct their own shacks on the city's edge. Since the early 1990s, poor families everywhere have moved into expanding cities, pushed out of subsistence agriculture or drawn by new opportunities. But long-standing urban inequalities may have been even further exacerbated by that rapid growth: Global policy makers have urged local governments and city planners to attract investors rather than prioritize basic services in peripheral communities, and they have built airports, highways, and industrial parks rather than expand infrastructure in marginal areas.

Around the world, that approach continues to shape lives and opportunities: Poor households lack access to roads, water, sewers, electricity lines, or public schools. As Mike Davis memorably wrote, "Rapid urban growth in the context of structural adjustment, currency devaluation, and state retrenchment has been an inevitable recipe for the mass production of slums" (2007, 17). Beyond the areas where colonial administrators were housed in an earlier era, and outside the gated communities where better-off residents can pay for private services, poorer families often struggle, spending hours on unreliable transport to get to work or spending years in schools that are chronically crowded and understaffed.

Ironically, this restricted vision of the state's obligations—what Davis calls the "treason of the state" (2007, 50)—occurred even as democratization spread at the end of the Cold War. For some twenty-five years, international funding agencies and national policy makers have been persuaded by the ideology known as the Washington Consensus—that economic growth comes first. Pushed to balance national budgets by privatizing public services and cutting state spending, developmentalist states postponed efforts to expand public services to new urban areas. Developmentalist elites have promised that the entire nation will benefit from economic growth and industrialization; even as political participation has expanded, basic investment in urban infrastructure has been postponed. As a result, stark inequalities in the world's fastest-growing cities belie the promises of democratic developmentalism; when the state fails to provide services, citizens' access to health, education, or jobs depends on their family's wealth or status.

This pattern of inadequate public infrastructure in the context of rapid urbanization stands in sharp contrast to mid-twentieth-century urbanization in Europe and North America, where expanding electorates pushed democratically elected governments to expand public services for all city residents. As Thomas Marshall (1950) pointed out in his seminal essay on the changing meaning of citizenship in industrial democracies, in Europe and North America, political and civil rights translated into political pressure, which led in turn to expanded social rights. Unions and labor parties mobilized working-class citizens to push private employers and elected governments to improve citizens' lives, demanding not only reasonable working conditions but also transport and clean water, public health services, education programs, and other public services.

By contrast, in the twenty-first century, city planners—especially, perhaps, in poor regions of the world—have neglected service provision even as multiparty democracy spread around the world. The failure of democratic states to address the needs of cities' growing populations effectively defines life on urban margins. From Johannesburg to São Paulo, Nairobi to New Delhi, new urban patterns reveal, and exacerbate, visible tensions between the demands of development and the dynamics of postcolonial democracies.

Writing about the legacies of indirect rule in colonial Africa, Mahmood Mamdani (1996) describes sharp distinctions between people whom colonial rulers considered full "citizens"—usually European settlers and, later, educated local elites who were integrated into colonial administration—and their rural "subjects," who were ruled by local chiefs, many of whom accepted accommodation with colonial domination. This sharp line between citizens and subjects, Mamdani argues, is still reflected in deep divisions in Africa's postcolonial societies: Even after independence, a tendency to treat rural and poor communities as subjects to be ruled by unelected chiefs rather than as citizens who can articulate demands or press their claims on an elected central government still shapes Africa's postcolonial democracies.

Mamdani (1998a, 1998b) insists that this dynamic—the division between included citizens and excluded subjects—is specific to Africa's colonial regimes, but the pattern he identifies may not be unique. Similar exclusionary legacies continue to shape politics in most postcolonial societies, where sharp divisions between citizens whose voices count and poorer subjects whose voices are often marginalized in national policy debates still mark postcolonial democracies. Too frequently, educated local administrators—often descendants of settlers or of local elites—effectively dismiss the voices of poorer communities, from Latin America's marginalized indigenous communities to Asia's often-excluded "tribal" groups. Illiterate and uneducated, rural and often racially marked, these subjects are habitually treated as hapless beneficiaries of development; the voices of more educated, more cosmopolitan citizens are far more likely to shape national priorities.

In recent decades, rapid urban growth has brought this exclusionary pattern to postcolonial cities. Poor urban areas are viewed as temporary communities offering a foothold to recent migrants from rural areas—even in cities where those marginal communities have been in place for decades and even in democracies whose leaders constantly assert principles of equality and national inclusion. Politically, these assumptions further marginalize poor areas: Rather than see poor residents as citizens able to demand social rights or state services, policy makers often see those living in marginal urban communities as vulnerable to manipulation and deception, unable to make sensible political choices in their own interests. Politicians who claim to represent the urban poor may be dismissed as manipulative populists, lying to ignorant marginal communities to get their vote but rarely fulfilling their promises.

Of course, this vision of the urban poor is hardly limited to postcolonial elites. Cosmopolitan "experts" on modernization and development have often suggested that such marginal communities endanger political stability. The American political scientist Samuel Huntington (1968), for example, famously insisted that postcolonial governments would be wise to repress popular demands for inclusion rather than respond to them. Unless popular demands were tamped down by technocratic, pro-growth administrations, Huntington argued, new governments would be distracted from laying a solid basis for economic growth, delaying the long-term modernization of postcolonial societies. In fact, in the early 1980s, Huntington drew on his experiences while consulting for Brazil's military regime to suggest that South Africa's apartheid regime would be wise to pursue gradual inclusion rather than allow Black subjects to vote, arguing that "a little reform here, a little repression there" might allow South Africa's apartheid regime to maintain stability and economic growth (1981, 24). Any attempt to grant full political citizenship to South Africa's Black majority, Huntington suggested, could lead to chaos.

Scholars more sympathetic to poor communities' needs point out that in highly unequal postcolonial societies, poor communities face a dilemma: Populist manipulators may offer their only hope for access to state resources or public assistance. In his description of political dynamics in urban India, Partha Chatterjee (2004) describes a familiar pattern. As poor families move from rural villages to seek work in rapidly expanding cities, they construct crude shacks on unclaimed marginal land. Tolerated at first by elite politicians who see the slum as temporary and by businesses who need workers, poor voters become fodder for urban political machines. When competitive elections prompt local politicians to seek votes in poor areas, promises are made to improve conditions in those marginal areas; as Chatterjee points out, at least a few of those election promises may be fulfilled before the next election season rolls around, as politicians try to shore up their electoral base. Along the same lines, Liza Weinstein (2014), discussing politics in Mumbai, suggests that in the context of marginality, most slum dwellers demand simply the "right to stay put"—the right to live near jobs and the hope of new opportunities but unable to demand basic urban services, schools, or security.

This pattern is not inevitable, of course: In many developing countries, workers and poorer communities have sometimes been able to mobilize through industrial unions or political parties, asserting what James Holston (2009), calls "insurgent citizenship." Thus, for example, São Paulo's working-class communities used strikes and demonstrations, political protest and electoral mobilization, to demand both political rights and urban services, which was a central component of Brazil's pro-democracy movement, much as residents of South Africa's urban townships—an apartheid-era term for legally segregated areas such as Soweto—played a key role in bringing an end to democracy (Seidman 1994). But in the early twenty-first century, in the context of global economic pressures that undermine labor protections, most postcolonial societies lack the strong industrial trade unions and leftist political parties that Marshall saw as central in the earlier push for citizens' social rights.

Today most postcolonial democracies continue to struggle with deep divisions and the patterns of exclusion described by Mamdani. Indeed, in many rapidly expanding cities, patterns of exclusion have gotten worse since the early 1990s, not better: Globalization and deindustrialization weakened manufacturing unions and labor parties. In earlier democratic upsurges, Marshall wrote, movements for expanded social rights were generally spearheaded by trade unions and labor parties, as industrial workers and their communities used their newly granted political rights to assert new claims on the state. Today, though labor activists may sympathize with poor communities' demands for expanded public services, labor leaders in most of the world tend to focus on employers and workplace demands rather than put organizational resources into service delivery.

But around the world, inadequate public services spawn deep-seated frustration—especially in places where national governments hold out development as a promise to their supporters and where the lack of services frustrate residents' dreams. Not surprisingly, those frustrations frequently erupt into protests—often organized on social media, even in countries where only a minority of adults have access to cell phones. Much as Parisian bread riots mobilized support for the French Revolution, organizers often reach across class and ethnic lines by emphasizing shared material needs, but now, protestors' demands often reflect aspirations to modern urban realities; education, health care, water, electricity, and mass transit are increasingly seen as basic requirements for daily life.

In contrast to the labor movements Marshall described as central to democratic expansion in the mid-twentieth century, today's urban protestors focus on the state, often drawing on a cosmopolitan discourse and universal rights to describe their demands. Large cities make sharp social divisions visible: National elites live in the neighborhoods that were once reserved for colonial administrators or move into gated communities where they can count on private services for electricity, water, or security. But, importantly, while protestors draw attention to the failure of urban services in their daily lives, their demands reflect a growing insistence that states have an obligation to respond to citizens' needs—to the needs of all citizens, including those living on the edge. Often chaotic, these protests are frequently organized by relatively educated, frustrated activists who have learned that urban disruptions can provoke a more immediate response than debates in parliament.

Do these new pressures create political dynamics in today's postcolonial democracies that are significantly different from the expansion of social democracies in postwar Europe and North America? If urban activists seek to redefine states' obligations toward their citizens, demanding that all citizens be provided with the social and material conditions needed to sustain life in the postindustrial world, could these recent urban movements offer a new vision of citizenship rights? Could a shared understanding of inclusive development—building on demands for basic urban services, constructing new collective identities around community issues rather than around workplace associations—serve as the basis for a new version of Holston's "insurgent citizenship"? Will these urban protests challenge established relationships between developmentalist elites who have emphasized policies focused on economic growth and the urban populations who once supported them as new coalitions are built around the demand for a public infrastructure to support life in the city?

South Africa's Service-Delivery Protests

South Africa's recent surge of protests over inadequate urban services offers a vivid example of how demands for urban inclusion can mobilize broad support and, perhaps, shows how such protests can upend long-standing political loyalties, disrupting institutionalized political channels as well as traffic. Service-delivery protests—often small and disorganized, sometimes much larger—are sparked by daily annoyances stemming from persistent electricity outages or the lack of basic textbooks in township public schools, reflecting frustration at the failure of an elected government to provide basic services. Since the early 2000s, these protests have become a constant feature of South Africa's urban life, especially in marginal neighborhoods around major cities such as Johannesburg, Cape Town, and Durban. In 2013 and 2014, major protests were occurring every other day somewhere in the country, and by 2016, disruptive tactics had become a routine response to frustration, especially for citizens caught between the promise of postapartheid democracy and the stark inequalities of South Africa's daily life.

Since about 2013, especially as the country's mineral-based economy was hit by a global slump in commodity prices, South Africa's service-delivery protests have spread across the country, although they remain concentrated around major metropolitan areas. The specifics of protests vary from place to place, but grievances generally stem from local issues, usually centered on the perceived failure of public authorities to provide or maintain basic services or goods, from water and electricity to schools and health care. In the Johannesburg area, for example, researchers found protestors' grievances focused on "service delivery in general, housing, water and sanitation, political representation and electricity. Corruption, municipal administration, roads, unemployment, demarcation, land, health and crime also featured" in their concerns (Alexander, Runciman, and Ngwane 2013). Especially in poor neighborhoods, the term is used to describe protestors objecting to metered water provision, small groups of parents demanding improvements in their children's schools, or young adults throwing stones at police patrols.

Over the past decade, thousands, perhaps millions, of South Africans have participated in some form of these protests; many have been arrested. Relying on the disruption of life in public places—rowdy street demonstrations and traffic jams and, in some cases, arson, stone throwing, or attacks on municipal buildings such as post offices and schools—the protests rarely seem to produce new channels for discussion between residents and authorities.

Like the grievances that spark these protests, most service-delivery protests seem to be mobilized through local networks and are not coordinated with national parties or campaigns. Most of these demonstrations remain peaceful, if disruptive; but tensions can certainly escalate. In some cases, local authorities have tried to control or repress protests, sometimes using tear gas or rubber bullets or arresting demonstrators (Brown 2015). Angry protestors have often blocked roads, thrown stones, or even set buildings on fire. While it is somewhat ironic that demonstrators protesting government failure to serve poor communities have sometimes burned down post offices, school buildings, public libraries, or university auditoriums, many observers attribute these political tensions to deep frustration, especially among young adults facing high unemployment levels.

Often local political tensions also come into play. In May 2016, twenty-four schools were burned in a northern province, apparently over outrage at redrawn municipal lines; in June 2016, violent protests over city politics in Tshwane (the large municipal area surrounding Pretoria) led to burned buses, looting, and several deaths (Tandwa 2016; Masombuka, Hosken, and Quintal 2016). By mid-2016, some observers suggested that South Africa was experiencing as many as five or six violent demonstrations each day (Burke 2016)—a phenomenon that was "unlikely [to] abate in the near future as South Africans use protest activity to vent unhappiness with a range of state players, including municipalities" (Municipal IQ 2016).

It is hardly surprising that protestors would focus on South Africa's vivid urban inequalities. Today's frustrations are easily traced back to apartheid's legacies: Legally enforced segregation meant that wealth and opportunity were limited to white citizens who lived in central cities, while poor African subjects were officially designated "temporary migrants," relegated to racially defined peripheral communities, denied access to the urban infrastructure available to white neighborhoods in the city's core, and denied the vote. Especially in the informal settlements that have expanded around even midsized towns, South Africa's residential patterns continue to reflect the geography of apartheid. Stark differences between the services provided to poor Black neighborhoods set far from the city center and those available in formerly white areas continue to shape daily experiences and individuals' life chances.

Yet after twenty-some years of democratic government, the persistence of apartheid's legacies becomes a grievance in itself. In today's South Africa, wealthy households of all races enjoy relatively developed roads, water, sewage, and electricity—services originally installed for the country's white minority but now available to any South African who can afford to buy or rent in those neighborhoods (Heller and Kraker-Selzer 2010). Residents of better neighborhoods often complain that existing infrastructure is not as well maintained as they believe it was under apartheid—that is, in an era where a white-minority government concentrated government spending on white-only neighborhoods. In fact, even today, South Africa's core urban neighborhoods generally remain better off than most townships, since municipal governments generally try to keep up already-installed infrastructure; with roads already paved, electricity lines and running water pipes in place, and with long-established public schools supported by neighborhood fees on top of government funds, formerly white core areas remain far better serviced than most formerly all-Black areas.

Even so, many better-off South Africans have responded to democratization by moving into gated communities and apartment complexes, paying for private security guards, electrical generators, and private schools rather than relying on public services stretched thin precisely because democratic South Africa has tried to expand public services beyond the once white urban core (Murray 2011).

However, South Africa's poor families—almost all African or "Colored"—are generally still excluded from well-serviced areas, crowding instead into abandoned tenements in the central city, in areas still called townships, or in the informal squatter settlements that mushroomed around South Africa's cities once the government stopped enforcing apartheid's ban on African migration from impoverished rural areas. Urban services have been extended to many of these areas, but expanded demand has stretched many public services thin; in South Africa's fast-growing urban peripheries—the areas where residents are least able to afford private alternatives—water, transport, and electricity are unreliable or nonexistent. Aware that their daily lives are shaped by apartheid legacies, many township residents who might be unwilling to join in protests often refuse to pay fees for municipal services. In March 2016, the government admitted that the more than forty-two billion rands owed by residential unpaid utility fees to South Africa's local authorities were largely "unrecoverable" ("South Africans Owe" 2016).

Importantly, some of South Africa's persistent urban inequality stems from policy choices made during the negotiated transition, when the country moved to decentralize municipal budgets, a management system that often pushed city managers, even those sincerely committed to extending public services, to prioritize efforts to attract investors and sustain central business districts. As in most of the world, South African city managers face a difficult choice: They tend to maintain services that already exist rather than let them collapse entirely, a decision that only exacerbates frustration in areas where no services have been installed at all or where stalled construction projects serve as a constant reminder of unfulfilled promises. Local city managers are more likely to view poor communities as powerless supplicants than as political threats, and with little incentive to put energy or funds into expanding services to poor neighborhoods—and, ironically, often dependent on the same construction companies that built apartheid townships—many cities have failed to bring urban services for rapidly growing slums up to the levels that residents of better-off neighborhoods expect as a matter of course.

This is not, of course, to deny that postapartheid South Africa has greatly expanded citizens' rights and services for all, from public housing to social welfare benefits. Not only have public services been considerably extended, but many of South Africa's African households have become reliant on government welfare programs. But these "social grants" are small; they do not provide enough cash for poor households to ameliorate their day-to-day conditions or to address the inadequate infrastructure and services that cause daily frustration. While democratic South Africa has opened the doors to public services such as schools and clinics, too many public services are painfully overstretched—or worse, as in the case of some excellent public schools in formerly white neighborhoods, limited to the legal residents of a particular neighborhood, underscoring the persistence of unequal access to property and wealth. For South African citizens who do not own their own cars or generators, who send their children to underresourced public schools, or who wait in long lines at public clinics, life on the edge of South Africa's cities offers constant reminders that old legacies of exclusion still matter (Hart 2013).

Not coincidentally, service-delivery protests draw on a long tradition in the antiapartheid movement: Through the last decades of apartheid, as the African National Congress (ANC) and the allied labor movement tried to mobilize internal protests, many activists focused on the lack of basic services as a key grievance in the segregated townships in which Black South Africans were required to live. In part because it was illegal under apartheid to call for democratic elections, antiapartheid activists often mobilized protests over more specific issues—inadequate education or public infrastructure—rather than demand one person, one vote or directly challenge segregation. By the late 1980s, urban disruption had become a central tactic in the antiapartheid movement's repertoire of contention; activists explicitly sought to make the country ungovernable by boycotting schools for months on end, by calling on residents to stop work for weeks at a time, and by actively rejecting participation in segregated town councils or provincial governments.

Today, especially in the context of South Africa's stubbornly racialized labor markets—where Black South Africans continue to face low wages, high unemployment, and insecure labor rights—community activists find it relatively easy to mobilize broad support for local protests, demanding that the democratic state play a more active role in providing basic needs, offering services as a basic right of citizenship rather than limiting services to those who can pay for them.

Politically, today's protests remain relatively disconnected, generally mobilized by local activists with relatively little coordination across different townships. Despite efforts to form a united front of community groups, the ANC's political opponents are themselves deeply divided, and most of their efforts focus on the national state. Service-delivery protests, in contrast, tend to center almost entirely on local issues: Small groups of activists take to the streets, focused on very local complaints and lacking broader coordination, even with nearby settlements. At the national level, both ANC and opposition leaders seem unable to incorporate protestors' voices into the political debate. Moreover, because South Africa's electoral system gives party leaders a great deal of say over who can run for office on party lists, local political leaders often shy away from protests rather than provide leadership or negotiate with protestors. Unfortunately, many local municipal authorities—often lacking funds, expertise, or political will—have left protestors angry and frustrated; when protestors throw stones or burn buildings, some local authorities have arrested or even shot at them, reinforcing a sense among many protestors that local authorities refuse to attend to citizens' demands.

Perhaps the most visible example of this dynamic comes from the notorious 2012 Marikana massacre, when police killed thirty-four striking platinum miners as they left a union rally. The strikers were demanding a wage increase, but squalid living conditions and a sense of exclusion across the mining sector clearly played a central role in their discontent. Under apartheid's legally enforced migrant labor system, Black mine workers had been denied both voting rights and legal residence in white-designated areas; those who came to work in the mines were housed in single-sex hostels, leaving families behind in impoverished provincial territories. Today, although most miners—now full citizens of South Africa—move to mining areas to find work, most mining companies have stopped maintaining hostels for migrant workers. Especially in the new mines of South Africa's platinum belt, most migrant workers are offered a small "living out stipend," with which they are expected to rent their own living quarters—usually in squalid settlements near the mine shafts. Mine workers may now bring their families to live with them, but even though the government makes sure that mining companies have the water, electricity, and roads they need, mine workers' communities often lack basic infrastructure. At Marikana, this situation was worsened by disagreement between municipal, provincial, and national authorities about who bore fiscal or political responsibility for these communities, most of whom included households made up of South African citizens but whose members came from elsewhere in the country as migrants from areas such as the Eastern Cape. Even the country's shock at the massacre did not produce visible improvements; three years later, Marikana's families still lacked clean water or sewage systems, health services, and adequate elementary schools (Makgetla and Levin 2016).

For many South Africans, the Marikana massacre seems to have been a turning point, and established political loyalties began to fray as more and more South Africans turned to disruptive protests to assert their demands. Demonstrations over electricity shortages, university fees, language policies, roadway tolls, and corruption reflected growing frustration with the country's persistent inequality and increased anger at the ruling ANC. In 2016, the ANC's candidates for municipal governments faced an uphill battle as Black urban voters, in middle-class neighborhoods as well as in townships, refused to turn out in support of the party long identified with the struggle against apartheid. Especially in the country's main metropolises, the ANC's losses were widely attributed to the failure of local ANC city councilors to ensure that all households had access to urban services. In 2016, a *Reuters* headline told readers, "S. Africa's Ruling ANC Faces Rejection from Urbanites Angry over Poor Services" (Strydom 2016)—a headline that underscored a widespread recognition that South Africa's service-delivery protests could reflect an increasingly assertive understanding of democratic citizenship, creating new political dynamics in a society long shaped by exclusion.

Demanding Inclusive Growth

While South Africa's service-delivery protests—and their subsequent electoral impact—may be an especially visible example, popular demands for public services have similarly mobilized urban communities around the world, uniting residents across neighborhoods and income levels. From Turkey's protests against city plans to hand a public park to private real estate developers, to protests against Beirut's failure to remove garbage from city streets, governments' failures to provide basic services have been a central fulcrum of urban discontent.

Brazil offers perhaps the most obvious parallel to South Africa's chaotic protests. Across Brazil, massive street demonstrations in 2013 were initially sparked by anger over an announced increase in public bus fares—in the context of increased government spending on new infrastructure aimed at the upcoming world soccer games, hosted that year in Brazil. Even the activists who organized the protests were stunned by the immediate public response: Brazilians poured into the streets, demanding new attention to citizens' everyday needs.

Like South Africa's ANC, Brazil's Workers' Party was elected and reelected on a "pro-poor" platform; it expanded both public services and social programs. But as in South Africa, these programs remained woefully inadequate—especially for the aspirant middle class, who feel excluded from the opportunities promised by a government that claims to offer new opportunities to all. Brazilians who can afford to do so go to private hospitals, send their children to private schools, and live in gated communities protected by private security guards—a pattern that, as Teresa Caldeira (2000) points out, sharply curtails any egalitarian interaction between wealthy city residents and their neighbors, perhaps further exacerbating elite disregard for the needs of the poor.

Brazil's protests began with bus fares in São Paulo but quickly spread across the country and began to express a broad slate of grievances. In June 2013, a small network of activists known as the Free Access Movement (Movimento Passe Livre) began to protest a bus-fare increase; within days, the demonstrations had mushroomed, spreading to dozens of cities and involving as many as a million protestors. Activists argued that the bus-fare increase affected everyone in the country: Even middle-class Brazilians with their own cars would benefit from expanded mass transit, because easier access to bus services, by reducing the number of cars on the street at rush hour, would ameliorate traffic and improve air quality for all (Singer 2014).

Brazil's protestors seem to have been mobilized outside institutionalized party or trade union structures: A survey in mid-June 2013 found that 84 percent of demonstrators backed no political party, and 53 percent were under age twenty-five. Most had joined the protests to demand reduced bus fares and better transportation, although some also objected to corruption, police violence, and politicians in general. Within weeks, São Paulo and other major cities repealed the fare increase, but public protests continued (Leithead 2013).

Initial descriptions of the protests as middle class were quickly challenged by Brazilian observers, who argued that the protests reflected a much broader swath of frustration over the quality of the country's newly expanded public services, including education and health care as well as public transport.

> While it is true that the movement has a visible middle-class component, its dissatisfaction is not only that of aspirational young people who don't know how good they have it. The dissatisfaction is quite real: urban transportation, health care provision, and public education are in shambles. Despite the progress of recent years, there is a sense that things are not as good as they should be—that more of the population should benefit from prosperity and growth, that services should be better, and that regular citizens are left out of decisions that matter to them. (Teixeira and Baiocchi 2013)

As in South Africa's service-delivery protests, Brazil's massive street demonstrations reflected new tensions between Brazil's urban growth, rising aspirations, and new demands on both local and national governments. Noting that neither political parties nor established trade union organizations played significant roles in mobilizing Brazil's protests, Alfredo Saad-Filho and Lecio Morais argue that while rapid economic growth and a series of elected center-left governments created new opportunities and provided new services for Brazil's working poor, the Workers' Party too often failed to provide an infrastructure that would make rapidly growing cities accessible for residents:

> Economic growth, income distribution and the wider availability of credit and tax breaks to domestic industry have led to an explosion in automobile sales, while woefully insufficient investment in infrastructure and in public transport has created traffic gridlock in many large cities. Rapid urbanization has overwhelmed the electricity, water and sanitation systems, leading to power cuts and repeated disasters in the rainy season. Public health and education have expanded, but they are widely perceived to offer poor quality services. There has been virtually no progress on land reform, condemning millions to a life of marginality while agribusiness prospers. (2014, 234)

As Saad-Filho and Morais conclude, "The protests were sparked by popular demands for the improvement of services that are already available, but that have become completely unsatisfactory in the light of the growing expectations of the workers and the poor" (2014, 241). Especially as the government shifted to focus on building new stadiums and hotels in preparation for the 2013 World Cup and the 2016 Olympics, Brazilians' anger over inadequate, and much-needed, public services boiled over, and street protests became a regular feature of public life.

In contrast to South Africa, however, political parties and powerful Brazilian media conglomerates quickly began to redirect popular discontent. Especially as Brazil's economy suffered from declining commodity prices, conservative politicians were able to mobilize a wealthier (and as observers often pointed out, clearly whiter) constituency; by 2015, protestors' focus had shifted away from demands for new services to emphasize a neoliberal rejection of pro-poor social programs, blaming poor services on corruption and mismanagement. Brazil's powerful media conglomerates promoted a new framing of local grievances; right-wing political parties rather than corruption scandals eventually produced a parliamentary impasse and a successful campaign to impeach the president, Dilma Rousseff— ironically, replacing the Workers' Party with a political coalition that immediately cut back public spending, further marginalizing those living on the urban periphery.

Democratic Distemper?

In cities marked by stark inequalities, aspirant citizens turn to street protests to assert new kinds of citizenship claims. Service-delivery protests put government provision of basic services at the core of claims for new citizenship rights, focusing as much on expanded public services as on political voice. Journalists often describe today's urban protestors as members of a "new middle class." That term may say as much about the observers as it does about protest participants, but perhaps it captures a shift from the past: Whether or not they come from middle-class backgrounds, few street protestors in São Paulo or New Delhi have any intention of returning to rural communities. Most literate youth are more likely to embrace urban integration; they expect to live in the city, and they hope to earn wages rather than sell vegetables or wash car windows at intersections.

If Occupy Wall Street or Los Indignados tended to focus on rising inequality and object to cuts in existing social programs, protestors in postcolonial societies tend to focus instead on long-standing patterns of urban exclusion. Their demands revolve around aspirations that are urban, not rural; they reflect protestors' insistence on gaining access to the opportunities offered to those at the center of global cities rather than accepting relegation to the margins—an urban understanding of democratic inclusion that marks a real shift in the character of postcolonial democracies.

Through much of the late twentieth century, discussions of "poor people's movements" in the Global South have often been tinged by a romantic vision of agrarian communities and an emphasis on a vanishing world of peasant communities. For global publics, that romantic vision—often linked to agrarian movements such as Brazil's Landless People or protests by indigenous communities—can lead outside observers to assume that citizens of developing societies would prefer a sustainable peasant existence to life in the city. But those romantic visions ignore reality: Over the past five decades, rural communities everywhere have been displaced by expanding corporate agriculture, and more and more of the world's households live on urban margins. Their children may have gone to bad schools, but even poorly educated youth living in peripheral urban neighborhoods rarely hope for a return to backbreaking agricultural labor. Unlike previous generations of the urban poor, most protestors today were raised in cities, and they have grown up hoping to build lives that would be more stable and more comfortable than the households in which they were raised. Their aspirations—shaped as much by what they have learned from their parents and in school as by television shows and populists' promises—revolve around expected patterns of consumption: They need stable jobs that pay living wages, but their urban-centric aspirations also focus on state services and reasonable access to both physical public infrastructure—electricity, running water, public transport—and public social services (Braga 2012).

As they ponder their futures, most adults living in urban settings know that the quality of their lives will depend as much on improved basic public services as on their ability to earn a wage. To gain access to the city, residents need to be able to live in buildings with running water and electricity; to take buses, cars, or trains to work—and citizens are likely to demand that elected governments attend to those collective needs. Writing about Brazil, Saad-Filho and Morais point out that young urban residents expect a very different future: "The cultural identifiers and political expectations of the formal and informal working class and the middle class have been transformed, and the internet has changed radically the modalities of social interaction among the youth. . . . The demands and expectations of the formal and informal working class have shot up in the last decade. . . . Suddenly, the streets seem to explode: every social group parades its own frustrations, unprecedented rioting takes place, and the government is clearly bewildered" (2014, 240).

Nancy Birdsall, Nora Lustig, and Christian Meyer (2013) offer a term that captures that sense of frustration: "Strugglers" might best describe the activists who have taken to the streets in the cities of countries such as South Africa and Brazil, with incomes higher than the poverty line but too low, and too unstable, to be considered middle class, struggling to find an urban foothold and dependent on underfunded public services to get by. The term emphasizes economic insecurity, but it also reflects frustrations produced by unfulfilled expectations and vulnerability, the tensions between widespread aspirations to a stable urban life and the reality of urban marginalization.

The emphasis on vulnerability and precariousness also suggests an explanation for a puzzle frequently raised by policy makers: In places such as Brazil and South Africa, why have angry protestors refused to celebrate successful experiments in pro-poor policies—especially recent national programs to expand social safety nets for those living in absolute poverty through social grants or guaranteed employment schemes or through conditional cash transfers? Over the past decade, many democratic governments, including in South Africa and Brazil, have vastly expanded means-tested cash grants to the very poor—effectively promising their poorest citizens a basic income, although the amounts are painfully small. Brazil's renowned Bolsa Familia program gained more international attention, of course, but similar programs also helped poor households in South Africa, where between 50 and 75 percent of poor households received some income through means-tested social grants (Bhorat, Tseng, and Stanwix 2014).

Writing about southern Africa, James Ferguson (2015) has argued that this kind of cash-transfer program may reflect a burgeoning "politics of distribution" among policy makers, especially in emergent economies. The norms of industrial production and family structure that shaped social provision in industrial democracy, he argues, may not fit today's realities, especially as new technologies reduce demand for low-skilled labor, but most working people, especially in the postcolonial world, lack reliable access to higher education. Cash-transfer programs will hardly lift people out of poverty, but in countries that have instituted them, poor households increasingly depend on, and appreciate, these cash transfers.

Yet means-tested cash-transfer programs will never provide enough cash to cover the basic needs of poor households; the sums involved will never be adequate for citizens to pay for private services to replace inadequate public schools, clinics, or urban transport. As Jean Dreze and Amartya Sen (2013) point out, even generous cash-transfer programs cannot change the dynamics of poverty unless poor households can also rely on public schools, hospitals, and infrastructure for the kinds of services that wealthier citizens can buy for themselves. Even where social grants have provided important assistance to cash-poor households, most people living in poor communities cannot ignore persistent inequalities. While means-tested programs are certainly welcome in poor households, broad improvements in public services would help all struggling households—not only the households of the absolute poor but also of those who may be slightly above the poverty line but still struggle to get by.

In South Africa, urban politicians are increasingly taking notice of the shift: Activists outside the established parties tried to build a united front of local community groups articulating the kinds of demands often linked to service-delivery protests. Several prominent established political figures, including an ANC-affiliated mayor in Johannesburg, began to promise that they would expand and improve public services, explicitly seeking to make the city more accessible to all (Nicolson 2016).

By contrast, Brazil's early protests, which sought to promote the "decommodification of public goods and services, starting with education, health, transport, water and sanitation, and improvements in the quantity and quality of provision" were completely derailed (Saad-Filho and Morais 2014, 243). In early 2016, a political crisis led to a national crisis, as conservative politicians impeached the country's elected president and continued to restrict democratic participation. But in many other countries across the Global South, demands for expanded urban services have become increasingly visible and vocal, often serving as the basis of nascent political movements. In Lebanon, an urban coalition drew support from across sectarian lines through a focus on urban problems, especially Beirut's long-standing garbage crisis (Salloukh 2016); in Mexico, civil society groups used imaginative new tactics to demand better services and to call attention to government corruption (Tucker 2016).

Conclusion

In cities long shaped by exclusionary patterns, the urban protests that increasingly roil postcolonial democracies reflect daily frustrations. As activists from Johannesburg to São Paulo to New Delhi have discovered, spreading urban landscapes offer new opportunities to translate grievances into disruption. Increasingly, new movements of strugglers will emerge, challenging developmentalist elites to extend the public services that make urban lives sustainable. Poorer urban citizens—especially younger citizens who are more educated and more insistent on their rights than their parents might have been—have become impatient, demanding improved access to basic infrastructure and public services as a key step toward inclusion.

Instead of organizing through the workplace or working through existing political parties, urban protestors use the disruptive capacity of street protests to draw attention to their demands. As in South Africa and Brazil, these protests may operate outside institutional channels, fracturing long-established political loyalties; service-delivery protests can create chaos within long-standing political parties as well as in the streets. Even democratically elected nationalist coalitions find it difficult to channel frustration into political power: When persistent frustration leads to disruption, it often fuels further disaffection, creating new dissatisfaction. Traditional organizational forms, such as unions or ethnic associations, may well be superseded as protestors find new ways to stake claims on local government and form new coalitions to assert their demands.

In postcolonial settings, these new service-delivery protests could change established dynamics, especially where developmentalist and nationalist elites have led the state. As urban protests move outside established political channels, old political loyalties and nationalist parties may well unravel as local urban politicians explore potential new coalitions—more cosmopolitan, perhaps, and more inclusive, than the kind of bifurcated democracies built on colonial legacies.

Of course, disruptive protests may not produce expanded democracy or inclusive policies: Protestors' voices have often been lost in chaos, ignored, or repressed. In some postcolonial democracies, protests will certainly provoke authoritarian repression, a reassertion of exclusionary patterns. But as South Africa's recent experiences seem to suggest, as cities grow ever-more important, disruptive urban protests may create a new kind of pressure on local and national politicians as formerly marginalized subjects challenge postcolonial legacies, asserting new rights as citizens and using city streets to stake their claims.

REFERENCES

Alexander, Peter, Carin Runciman, and Trevor Ngwane. 2013. "Community Protests, 2004–2013: Some Research Findings." February 12. Available at https://oldsite .issafrica.org/uploads/Public-violence-13March2014-Peter-Alexander.pdf.

Bhorat, Haroon, David Tseng, and Benjamin Stanwix. 2014. "Pro-poor Growth and Social Inclusion in South Africa: Exploring the Interactions." *Development Southern Africa* 31:219–240.

Birdsall, Nancy, Nora Lustig, and Christian Meyer. 2013. "The Strugglers: New Poor in Latin America." Center for Global Development Working Paper 337. Available at https://www.cgdev.org/sites/default/files/new-poor-latin-america_1.pdf.

Braga, Ruy. 2012. *Política do precariado* [The politics of the precariat]. São Paulo: Boitempo.

Brown, Julian. 2015. *South Africa's Insurgent Citizens*. Johannesburg: Jacana Press.

Burke, Jason. 2016. "Breaking the Mould? South Africa at a Crossroads as Country Goes to Polls." *The Guardian*, August 1, 2016. Available at https://www.theguardian.com/ world/2016/aug/01/this-is-when-we-break-the-mould-south-africa-at-a-political -crossroads.

Caldeira, Teresa. 2000. *City of Walls: Crime, Segregation and Citizenship in São Paulo*. Berkeley: University of California Press.

Chatterjee, Partha. 2004. *The Politics of the Governed: Reflections on Popular Politics in Most of the World*. New York: Columbia University Press.

Conniff, Michael. 1982. "Populism in Brazil, 1925–1941." In *Latin American Populism in Comparative Perspective*, edited by Michael Conniff, 43–62. Albuquerque: University of New Mexico Press.

Davis, Michael. 2007. *Planet of Slums*. London: Verso.

Dreze, Jean, and Amartya Sen. 2013. *An Uncertain Glory: India and Its Contradictions*. Princeton, NJ: Princeton University Press.

Ferguson, James. 2015. *Give a Man a Fish: Reflections on the New Politics of Distribution*. Durham, NC: Duke University Press.

Glasius, Marlies, and Geoffrey Pleyers. 2013. "The Global Moment of 2011: Democracy, Social Justice and Dignity." *Development and Change* 44:547–567.

Hart, Gillian. 2013. *Rethinking the South African Crisis*. Durban: University of KZN Press.

Heller, Patrick, and Amy Kraker-Selzer. 2010. "The Spatial Dynamics of Middle Class Formation in Post-apartheid South Africa: Enclavization and Fragmentation in Johannesburg." *Political Power and Social Theory* 21:171–208.

Holston, James, 2009. *Insurgent Citizenship: Disjunctions of Democracy and Modernity in Brazil*. Princeton, NJ: Princeton University Press.

Huntington, Samuel. 1968. *Political Order in Changing Societies*. New Haven, CT: Yale University Press.

———. 1981. "Reform and Stability in a Modernizing, Multi-ethnic Society." *Politikon: South African Journal of Political Science* 8:8–26.

Leithead, Alistair. 2013. "Brazil Unrest: 'Million' Join Protests in 100 Cities." *BBC News*, June 21. Available at http://www.bbc.com/news/world-latin-america-22992410.

Makgetla, Neva, and Saul Levin. 2016. "A Perfect Storm: Mining and Migrancy in the North West Province." Available at http://www.tips.org.za/research-archive/in equality-and-economic-inclusion/item/3099-a-perfect-storm-migrancy-and -mining-in-the-north-west-province.

Mamdani, Mahmood. 1996. *Citizen and Subject: Contemporary Africa and the Legacy of Late Colonialism*. Princeton, NJ: Princeton University Press.

———. 1998a. "The Politics of Civil Society and Ethnicity: Reflections on an African Dilemma." In *Political Power and Social Theory*, vol. 12, edited by Diane Davis, 221–234. Bingley, UK: Emerald.

———. 1998b. "A Rejoinder." In *Political Power and Social Theory*, vol. 12, edited by Diane Davis, 259–264. Bingley, UK: Emerald.

Marshall, Thomas H. 1950. *Citizenship and Social Development and Other Essays*. Cambridge: Cambridge University Press.

Masombuka, Sipho, Graeme Hosken, and Genevieve Quintal. 2016. "'We Will Burn the Whole of Pretoria If Needs Be.'" *Sowetan Live*, June 21. Available at https://www .sowetanlive.co.za/news/2016-06-21-we-will-burn-the-whole-of-pretoria-if -needs-be.

Municipal IQ. 2016. "Press Release: Gauteng and National Service Delivery Protest Figures Fall." February 23. Available at https://cisp.cachefly.net/assets/articles/at tachments/58862_press_release_2015_service_delivery_protest_data.pdf.

Murray, Martin. 2011. *City of Extremes: The Spatial Politics of Johannesburg*. Durham, NC: Duke University Press.

Nicolson, Greg. 2016. "Interview: Parks Tau, the Mayor Who Grew into His Role." *Daily Maverick*, August 1. Available at http://www.dailymaverick.co.za/article/2016 -08-01-interview-parks-tau-the-mayor-who-grew-into-his-role.

Saad-Filho, Alfredo, and Lecio Morais. 2014. "Mass Protests: Brazilian Spring or Brazilian Malaise?" *Socialist Register* 50:227–243.

Salloukh, Bassel. 2016. "We Are All Beirut Madinati." *New Arab*, May 11. Available at https://www.alaraby.co.uk/english/Comment/2016/5/11/We-are-all-Beirut -Madinati.

Seidman, Gay. 1994. *Manufacturing Militance: Workers' Movements in Brazil and South Africa, 1970–1985*. Berkeley: University of California Press.

Singer, Andre. 2014. "Rebellion in Brazil." *New Left Review* 85. Available at https:// newleftreview.org/II/85/andre-singer-rebellion-in-brazil.

"South Africans Owe Municipalities R118 Billion." 2016. *Business Tech*, March 8. Available at http://businesstech.co.za/news/government/115844/south-africans-owe -municipalities-r118-billion.

Standing, Guy. 2014. *The Precariat: The New Dangerous Class*. London: Bloomsbury Academic Press.

Strydom, T. J. 2016. "S. Africa's Ruling ANC Faces Rejection from Urbanites Angry over Poor Services." *Reuters*, August 4. Available at https://af.reuters.com/article/ commoditiesNews/idAFL8N1AL9F6.

Tandwa, Lizeka. 2016. "Let the Schools Burn, Let Them Burn!—Vuwani Resident." *News 24*, May 7. Available at http://www.news24.com/SouthAfrica/News/let-the-schools -burn-let-them-burn-vuwani-resident-20160507.

Teixeira, Ana Claudia, and Gianpaolo Baiocchi. 2013. "Who Speaks for Brazil's Streets?" *Boston Review*, July 31. Available at http://bostonreview.net/blog/who-speaks -brazils-streets.

Therborn, Goren. 2014. "New Masses? Social Bases of Resistance." *New Left Review* 85. Available at https://newleftreview.org/II/85/goran-therborn-new-masses.

Tucker, Duncan. 2016. "Confronting Corruption: Can Guadalajara Become a Model for Transparency?" *The Guardian*, July 27. Available at https://www.theguardian.com/cities/2016/jul/27/corruption-challenge-guadalajara-mexico-model-transparent-governance.

Weinstein, Liza. 2014. *The Durable Slum: Dharavi and the Right to Stay Put*. Minneapolis: Minnesota University Press.

4

Been Down So Long, It Looks Like Up to Me

*Targets, Repertoires, and Democracy
in the U.S. Labor Movement*

Kim Voss and Pablo Gastón

How are movements governed? In the popular imagination, social movements—disruptive, antagonistic, and dependent on the courage and passions of the many who form them—defy the basic strictures of authority that apply to many formal organizations. Decades of sociological research on movements, however, have taught us that mobilizations are very rarely unbridled rebellions. More often, they are explicitly directed at powerful targets, are responsive to political contexts, and make use of tactical tools that evolve in relation to these targets and contexts. The exercise of power requires organizing, resources, and coordination. And movements usually develop some lines of authority, even when these are not necessarily desired (Freeman 1972; Polletta 2004). Movements are, in short, governed—sometimes with broad democratic participation, sometimes with clear and marked lines of authority, sometimes with obscure and unclear lines of authority. Although we have a solid handle on how targets, contexts, and arenas shape the when and the how of mobilization, there remains space to question the effect targets have on how movements are governed.

In this chapter, we interrogate the connection between a movement organization's exercise of power and its organizational governance. We build on recent work that explores the dynamics of protest against nonstate actors, including private firms (King 2008; King and Pearce 2010), asking: How do the structures and strategies of private firms shape the governance patterns of the movements that target them? If Gabriel Hetland and Jeff Goodwin are correct that social movement scholars "increasingly ignore [how] capitalism shapes social movements" (2013, 83), this new line of inquiry may well offer a critical corrective. Although this focus on private targets is relatively new to social movement studies, it is a long-standing tradition in the scholarship on labor conflict. Marxists of various stripes have long argued that patterns of worker mobilization reflect the structure of capital and the strategies of capitalists. Another example can be found in the midcentury industrial relations literature, where researchers found that through repeated interaction, employers and unions came to mirror each other in terms of aggressiveness and structure (Golden and Ruttenberg 1942), as well as in geographic scope (Ulman 1966), and they also found that strike rates reflected the social structures of work in different industries (Kerr and Siegel 1954). More recently, accounts of union revitalization argue that community-centered union tactics emerged in the 1990s in response to the changing structure of capital and the growing hostility of employers toward organized labor.

Social movement scholars can learn important lessons about the interaction between protestors and their targets from the recent history and current dilemmas of the American labor movement. In particular, the literature on union democracy draws our attention to an issue seldom addressed by social movement scholars who look at the dynamics of protest against nonstate actors: How are we to theorize the relationship between internal organizational democracy and the ways that power is exercised by protestors? We argue here that there is a strong connection between the internal distribution of power (democracy and governance patterns) and the external exercise of coercive and disruptive power. Tracing how labor's repertoire of contention (Tilly 1995) has changed as unions have confronted the neoliberal economy, we detect some surprising vulnerabilities in contemporary capitalism—vulnerabilities that have created new opportunities for the labor movement to exercise power but that have also created new dilemmas that increase the challenges of democratic governance. Through examining this recent history, we propose that where movement targets are vulnerable to forms of collective power that do not depend on direct member action and coordination, movements encounter democratic dilemmas.

Research on contemporary labor unionism suggests that the changing nature of corporate targets and the institutional environment in which labor contention takes place have altered how labor unions can successfully exercise coercive and disruptive power. As corporate structures have changed, labor's traditional tools—the strike and other forms of workplace-centered contention—have been undermined. But these same consolidations and governance changes have created new opportunities for new tactics, opportunities to which revitalized unions responded by shifting labor contention beyond the workplace and into community and market arenas. This new set of extra-workplace tactics constitute, we argue, a new repertoire of contention defined by the structures of capital and state regulation in the neoliberal order. We then analyze the effects of this changing repertoire on internal democracy. Building on the classic framework advanced by Claus Offe and Helmut Wiesenthal (1980), who argued that unions' internal governance patterns are a product of their capacities to exercise power externally, we show how unions that take advantage of this new repertoire of contention come to face new organizational dilemmas, stemming from organizational reforms pushed by union leaders to facilitate the implementation of new strategies.

We illustrate these dilemmas with an empirical case study of a union at the center of the union revitalization movement, the Service Employees International Union (SEIU). Early union activists pushing an internal revitalization program saw democracy, militancy, and growth opportunities as intimately connected. But as the union sought to counter increasingly consolidated employers in the 1990s, the repertoire they came to use challenged these assumptions and created organizational challenges, requiring extensive reforms. By the late 2000s, the union faced a series of internal political crises, as dissenters challenged as undemocratic both the organizational reforms and the repertoires they were designed to facilitate. Thus, the union most closely associated with the union revitalization movement faced intense conflicts over strategy, internal democracy, and fundamental definitions of what a union *should* do. We argue that these challenges, while certainly political in nature, arose in large part because of the strategic dilemmas that union leaders faced when confronting rapidly changing corporate targets.

Labor Movement Repertoires and the Changing Nature of Targets

The Weakening of Labor's Traditional Tools

Workplace-centered action such as the strike has traditionally been at the center of labor's repertoire of contention. Nineteenth-century workers relied primarily on strikes, which were often met by hostile courts and armed troops (Archer 2010; Hattam 1992). The denial of unions' right to strike was an important way in which the state and capital contained unions' growth potential, even if they could not stop workers themselves from striking. When legal restrictions on unions' right to organize and bargain collectively were finally surmounted in the 1930s, unions grew mainly on the basis of large and dramatic strikes against industrial employers. The right to strike was institutionalized in the National Labor Relations Act (NLRA), which not only made labor's right to strike legal but constituted it as the primary enforcement mechanism of institutionalized collective bargaining (Getman 2010; Rhomberg 2012). Strikes became the central tactic that unions used to assert workers' collective power. However, recent research reveals that the strike no longer remains as central a practice as it once was, having been steadily undermined by both political and economic developments in the neoliberal era. Strike rates have been in decline since the strike wave of the mid-1970s, from a peak of 424 major strikes involving one thousand or more workers in 1974 to 7 in 2017 (U.S. Bureau of Labor Statistics 2018).

Why has this occurred? Many scholars point toward a political attack—while the state was occasionally a milquetoast ally of organized labor in the mid-twentieth century, by the 1980s it had become openly hostile (Clawson and Clawson 1999; Fantasia and Voss 2004; McCartin 2011). Today, right-to-work laws have spread into traditional union strongholds, and public-sector unions face existential threats from state legislators and the courts. Many of these attacks have targeted labor's capacity to exercise power via the strike, amounting to what Chris Rhomberg (2012) has called the "return of judicial repression." Julius Getman (2010) argues that judicial rulings such as allowing the hiring of permanent replacements and legislation such as pro-hibiting secondary boycotts have made the strike a much riskier venture than it was when unions used strikes to grow in the 1930s. Today union strikes that do occur are rarely explicitly over workplace concerns and in-stead center on unfair labor practice (ULP) complaints about the bargaining process, because the law protects such strikers from permanent replacement (Burns 2011).

While political constraints may have increased the risk inherent in strik-ing, there are also indications that economic transformations have made strikes less effective. Jake Rosenfeld's (2006) study of strike and wage rates in the United States suggests that while strikes tended to increase wages in the postwar era, by the 1980s and 1990s, that long-standing positive associa-tion had broken down. In other words, even if unions assumed the political risks of a strike, the tactic may not have exerted the same force that it once had. Indeed, by the 1980s some employers even sought to provoke strikes to jettison union supporters or break the union itself (Getman 2010, 21, 270). While political context was important for weakening the effectiveness of the strike, this change cannot be attributed solely to a hostile state—for example, labor militancy and strike rates today are very high in China, where the state is deeply hostile to worker self-organization and independent unionism, and this labor militancy is having a positive effect on wages (Friedman 2013).

This suggests that economic changes—and in particular, changes in cor-porate targets—have played a substantial role in blunting the traditional tools of labor contention. Daniel Bell (1973) first identified the rise of the postindustrial economy as a substantial threat to unions' capacity to exercise power (see also Block 1990; Bluestone and Harrison 1982). According to this argument, manufacturing was the classic stronghold of organized labor, but service industries present distinct challenges to unions. Service workplaces tend to organize workers into smaller groups; they often center on technical knowledge and creativity, employing a greater proportion of white-collar professionals; they polarize the workforce along skill axes, separating highly skilled professionals from low-skilled service workers; and they largely exclude the semiskilled workers who wield such power in industrial settings.

But deindustrialization is not the only significant transformation in recent decades that has weakened labor's traditional tools of workplace-centered contention. Financialization has also played a key role. The increase in the share of financial activities among firms' total profit sources (Davis 2009; Krippner 2005) has shifted employers' attention toward financial markets and away from workplace dynamics. Indeed, in the shareholder value economy, workplaces themselves are seen as assets to be used or traded rather than serve as the core of a firm's activity. As workplace dynamics grow increasingly distant from powerful owners' and managers' financial calculations, the ability to induce a response from capital through strikes or other workplace-centered contention has arguably declined. Further, these trends are connected to the thorough disaggregation of many employers, as firm managers seek to concentrate on their core functions and outsource peripheral activities; for many workers in today's economy, the Taft-Hartley Act's prohibition of secondary boycotts keeps the strike weapon out of reach (Getman 2010).

In short, the causes behind the weakening of labor's traditional tools, in particular the strike, are arguably both political and economic in nature. What is unambiguous is that these tools, which had built and maintained the labor movement throughout the twentieth century, no longer carry the same weight. This is arguably one of the most important causes of unions' rapid decline in recent decades. But many unions have pushed back, developing a wide array of new tools, which move beyond the workplace as a site of contention, extending labor conflict into broader communities and political arenas.

New Repertoire of Contention: Struggle beyond the Workplace

Labor's new repertoire of contention marks a profound shift away from its traditional dependence on workplace organization and the strike. Today, the most commanding tools in labor's arsenal are tactics that extend contention beyond the workplace, using comprehensive campaign tools to exercise power in markets and local political fields and finding ways to circumvent the National Labor Relations Board (NLRB; Gastón 2018). These tools depend primarily on leverage that lies in markets and community politics rather than in the workplace; their use reflects changes in the capacities and vulnerabilities of firms.

Consider the corporate campaign: Its power rests on firms' relationships with investors, clients, shareholders, customers, and regulators. Union researchers identify a firm's flows of capital and profits; its strengths and weaknesses; and its leaders' economic, social, and political networks. Armed with this information, they unearth ways to apply economic, social, and political pressure on a firm's officials. Unions push these pressure points, using media campaigns, legal actions, consumer boycotts, political and community alliances, and other tactics (Bronfenbrenner and Hickey 2004; Manheim 2000).

Typically, corporate campaigns are combined with noninstitutionalized strategies for gaining union recognition (Martin 2008). Since 1935 the state-sanctioned procedure for union recognition in the United States has been a formal election overseen by the NLRB. But just as the bargaining-enforcement mechanisms of the NLRA, premised on the right to exercise shop-floor power, have been eroded, the current NLRB procedure allows employers to orchestrate antiunion campaigns as part of the recognition process. These campaigns have grown increasingly sophisticated since the late 1970s, allowing employers to forestall organizing in many cases (Bronfenbrenner 1994; Prosten 1979). They have grown so fierce and lopsided in the neoliberal era that unions have crafted strategies to win union recognition without an NLRB election. The most common approaches rely on card-check agreements or bargaining to organize (Fantasia and Voss 2004; Martin 2008). In the former, unions use external pressure to extract an agreement from employers that they, first, will forgo interference in the unionization process and, second, will also recognize the union without an NLRB election if more than 50 percent of workers sign authorization forms stating they want the union to represent them.[1] In the bargain-to-organize approach, unions use contract negotiations to move companies to constrain antiunion practices during organizing drives at their nonunion facilities or subsidiaries.

Corporate campaigns and non-NLRB recognition drives have moved to the center of labor's tactical repertoire largely as the result of the process of union revitalization that began in the service sector in the late 1980s and early 1990s (Voss and Sherman 2000). Virtually every high-profile union success in the private sector over the past two decades has depended on such tools. Prominent examples include Justice for Janitors campaigns in cities such as Los Angeles and Houston and at universities such as the University of Southern California and the University of Miami (Albright 2008; Chun 2009; Medina 2006), the organization of immigrant workers in Southern California (Milkman 2006), the SEIU's campaign to organize security guards and health-care workers (Bloom 2010), and UNITE HERE's Hotel Workers Rising campaign to unionize hotels in cities across the nation (Getman 2010; Gastón 2018). Although each of these campaigns has distinctive aspects, all share the same basic goals—to organize unorganized workers and to win a collective bargaining relationship without an NLRB election.

Tellingly, the effectiveness of such tools is related to the firm consolidation and financialization that lie at the heart of the contemporary economy. Union strategists have discovered that although these changes have profoundly undermined workplace-based leverage, they have also brought new sorts of vulnerabilities that can be turned into new sources of leverage. In all the prominent union victories just listed, dwindling leverage at the workplace preceded successful corporate campaigns. In the janitor and security guard campaigns, this happened when property owners contracted out the cleaning and policing of their facilities; this was followed by the rapid consolidation of the national and global companies that held the contracts. In hotels, this same trend toward consolidation and financialization happened as family-owned and locally managed hotels were replaced, either by publicly traded hospitality companies or by franchises. Today, most decision-making power in the hospitality industry lies not with hotel managers but with the real estate companies and investment banks that own hotels and for whom hotels are an asset in a larger portfolio of investments (Gastón 2018). To successfully organize workers in this changed environment, unions have developed strategies that take advantage of vulnerabilities in the realm of finance and corporate structures instead of vulnerabilities at the worksite.

This turn toward corporate campaigns and non-NLRB recognition has been accompanied by unions' growing focus on building community coalitions. Most of labor's biggest wins in recent years have involved clergy, immigrant rights activists, students, and community organizations, a reality that would have been "unthinkable 25 years ago" (Dixon and Martin 2012, 947). Many labor scholars, in fact, see this coalition work as a defining feature of social movement unionism, pointing out that it represents a fundamental shift from labor's traditional focus on the workplace (Clawson 2003; Fine 2005; Lopez 2004; Martin 2008; Voss and Sherman 2000). Some unions have committed substantial resources to building coalitions with community groups for both ideological and practical reasons. Ideologically, activists in these unions have turned away the narrow, inward form of unionism practiced by most midcentury American unions toward a more expansive understanding of unions as central to the broader struggle for social justice. Practically, coalition work is an important way to build symbolic and structural leverage in both corporate and political campaigns; such work also recognizes workers' multiple sources of identity and enables union activists to mobilize non-job-based identities in organizing campaigns (Piore and Safford 2006). Labor has also come to embrace new discursive strategies, especially as part of its focus on improving the lives of low-wage, precarious workers. Revitalized unions have learned how to produce compelling narratives that include the voices of workers, framing their claims in moral language and staging public dramas that build support and attract media attention (Chun 2005; Stuart 2010).

This shift of labor contention into community arenas reinforces the fact that local politics, while not entirely determinative of movement repertoires, are still profoundly important. *Local* governments are often the targets of unions' recent campaigns for this reason. Following years of failed efforts to change national labor laws and institutions, unions today are targeting city and county governments, especially in campaigns to establish a living wage for workers at the bottom of the labor market. Initially, living-wage campaigns focused on employees of city service contractors, such as security guards and janitors, but more recently, as in the "Fight for $15" campaign, activists have set their sights on enacting policies to cover all work performed in a local labor market, whether done by city contractors or private employers.

Altogether, these tactical changes amount to a broad shift in labor conflict from traditional, workplace-centered contention toward extra-workplace contention. We summarize these changes in Figures 4.1 and 4.2. As Figure 4.1 illustrates, traditional organizing targets—as most employers were organized when labor contention patterns were institutionalized under the NLRA—contained authority and profit flows within a specific employer. As firms deintegrated in the late twentieth century, this pushed authority away from workplaces themselves. Figure 4.2 summarizes how these changes altered the tools of labor contention, as labor's new tools push labor contention beyond the workplace and into extra-workplace fields.

This shift toward extra-workplace contention has been so pronounced that even when unions turn to the strike, a closer look reveals that such

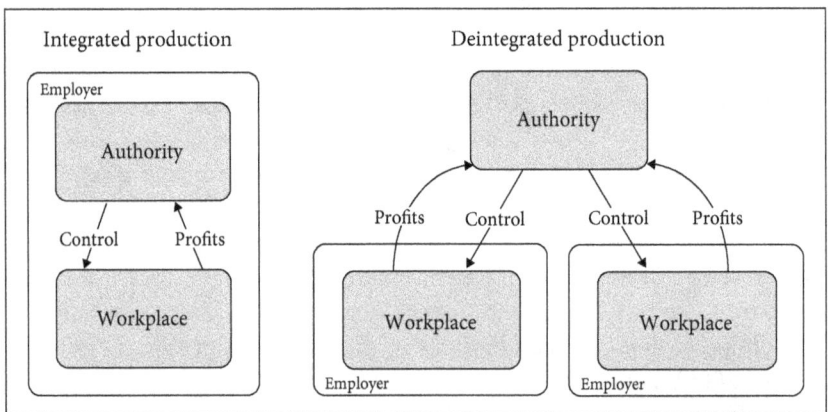

Figure 4.1. The transformation of corporate targets

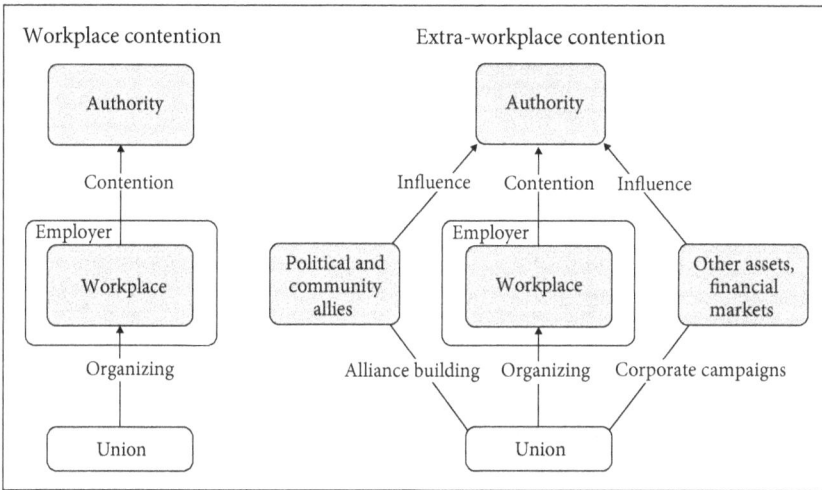

Figure 4.2. The transformation of labor contention

tactics are often repurposed. Strikes are used far less frequently today, but when they are used, they are employed as much to provide moral framing as to shut down production. Direct action on the part of workers and their supporters is now often as much about showing moral commitment and disrupting business as usual *in the community* as it is about disrupting the workplace. Another indication of repurposing the strike is the trend toward short, one-day strikes, which are often criticized as primarily symbolic (Burns 2011).

The process by which innovative unions have honed a new repertoire of contention has not been straightforward; nor has it gone unchallenged. Yet a careful look at this new repertoire suggests a surprising irony: While neoliberalism has destroyed the power of labor's traditional tools of contention, it has simultaneously enabled new forms of contention. The overall trend is clear: Successful union campaigns have shifted away from a dependence on leverage centered on the workplace and shifted toward leverage based in communities, politics, and markets.

Movement Democracy and the Exercise of Collective Power

Does how movements exercise power affect their internal governance? Social movement scholars have thus far paid relatively little attention to this relationship, more likely seeing organizational form as a product of instrumental adaptation to environments (Amenta, Halfmann, and Young 1999) or of cultural meanings and political values (Clemens 1996; Polletta 2005). Within the field of labor studies and the labor movement itself, however, the precise relationship between the external exercise of power and internal democracy is a matter of long-standing debate.

Many see internal union democracy as essential for driving member participation and deepening member commitment to struggle, make sacrifices, and assume great risks (Frost 2000; Lévesque and Murray 2005). Insofar as participation and commitment are essential for unions' exercise of power, democracy and power are positively associated. Judith Stepan-Norris and Maurice Zeitlin's (2003) study of political dynamics within Congress of Industrial Organizations (CIO) unions in the 1940s found that more democratic industrial unions were able to obtain better contracts than less democratic ones. Nelson Lichtenstein has similarly argued that even in the current era of embattled unions, internal democracy is "not a luxury, an ethical imperative divorced from the hard work necessary to rebuild the unions. . . . Instead it stands at the very center of that rebuilding process" (2013, 274). Similarly, longtime union democracy advocate and scholar Kim Moody suggests that democracy "is about more than honest elections or better democratic forms. It should begin in the workplace with strong organization and accountable shop stewards, for here is the ultimate source of working-class power" (2014, xi). Conversely, others have suggested that internal democracy and the exercise of power often exist in tension. In an often-cited statement (see Levi et al. 2009; Polletta 2004; Stepan-Norris and Zeitlin 2003; Voss 2010), A. J. Muste spoke to these inherent tensions, explaining that union leaders will often face a difficult choice between democracy and the exercise of power:

> The trade union seeks to combine within itself two extremely divergent types of social structure, that of an army and that of a democratic town meeting. . . . Imagine the conflict in the soul of a union official who must have the attitude and discharge the functions at one and the same time of both a general and a chairman of a debating society. (1948, 136)

The long persistence of this debate suggests that it is often grist for political conflict: Those claiming a negative relationship between democracy and power do so to further entrench their control, and those claiming a positive relationship do so to disperse it. Here we wish to suggest something different, that internal democracy is positively related to the exercise of certain forms of power but negatively related to the exercise of other forms of power. If, as some contend (see McAlevey 2015), union leaders have freedom of choice among these different forms of power, then democracy may well be a political choice. However, the choice of which form of power to exercise is not always an easy one. There are often substantial political or economic constraints on coercive practices, which in turn constrain movements' choices.

The character of capital shapes what unions can do. As some social movement scholars have argued, movements use tactics that match the vulnerabilities and response capacities of targets (Walker, Martin, and McCarthy 2008). Understanding the relationship between internal democracy and the exercise of power, therefore, entails ascertaining the ways in which these constraints and opportunities shape the tactical choices available to workers and their unions. We argue that it is these potential constraints and opportunities that can occasionally generate democratic dilemmas.

Democratic Dilemmas and the Exercise of Workplace Power

Most research on union democracy has centered on debates regarding Robert Michels's proposition of an "iron law of oligarchy" ([1911] 1962, 342, cited in Levi et al. 2009; Voss 2010). Scholars have sought to prove or disprove Michels's proposition by examining internal political dynamics as the primary determinants of the distribution of power. Two such theories of internal contestation have dominated the literature on union democracy. Beginning with Seymour Martin Lipset, Martin A. Trow, and James S. Coleman's examination of democratic practice in the International Typographical Union, one central theory has built on the Tocquevillian tradition, arguing that democracy is a product of "secondary organization" among members (1956, 83; see also Dimick 2009, 2010). A second approach emphasizes internal ideological contestation (Levi et al. 2009; Stepan-Norris and Zeitlin 1996, 2003). As Stepan-Norris and Zeitlin write, "Oligarchy in organized labor is no more immanent than democracy. Rather, both are the product of determinate, though contingent, political struggles among rival worker's factions and parties" (2003, 56). While these approaches differ in their relative emphasis on structural forces and agentic action, both concentrate primarily on contestation within the union organization itself.

However, democratic dilemmas—tensions and trade-offs between democracy and external power—have also been generative concepts. An influential account of such a dilemma is Offe and Wiesenthal's (1980) theory of the two logics of collective action. They juxtapose their theory with Mancur Olson's theory of a single logic of collective action, targeting the pluralist idea that all interest groups operate on the "same plane" (Offe and Wiesenthal 1980, 71). They develop their theory by specifying the "different functions that the common practice of formal association performs for labor and capital" and by looking closely at the ways "in which each of the two succeeds in gaining power through organization" (72). Much of their analysis derives from the Marxist distinction between the "dead labor" that capitalists bring to their efforts to associate and the "living labor" that workers bring (73).

From a social movement perspective, Offe and Wiesenthal call attention to the differences between the types of resources that shape the collective action logics of labor and capital. For labor, they argue that patterns of organizational governance were structured by external productive relations, in particular by unions' capacity to deploy sanctioning power. What they found was that the *distribution* of power *within* a union—including democratic practices and structures—is intrinsically related to the *exercise* of power *by* the union. Any association is able to exercise power, they argue, by mobilizing collective sanctions. For capital, this sort of collective action can be more easily achieved because there are fewer of them, they can more easily merge their (dead labor/capital goods) resources, and their interests are easily harmonized. Capital can concentrate and grow with few constraints—the coordination of action does not require extensive deliberation or the renegotiation of capitalists' identities.[2] But in an association of workers such as a labor union, mobilizing sanctions means organizing the collective withdrawal of labor—a process that involves extensive negotiation and renegotiation of individual and collective identities. This dialogic process of association in turn requires the extensive deliberation and participation of workers. This necessity for dialogic deliberation is arguably reflected in most social movements as we commonly conceive them. Like leaders of social movement organizations, union leaders' capacity for exercising power is dependent on their ability to induce a "willingness to act" (Offe and Wiesenthal 1980, 80) among their constituents.

Thus, in relatively small groups, this perspective suggests a positive association between internal democracy and the exercise of external power, an association rooted in union leaders' dependence on members themselves to exercise sanctioning power. As unions grow, however, they encounter a dilemma—greater size requires greater bureaucracy, which reduces broad participation in democratic control. Union leaders are thus compelled to seek other forms of power, becoming dependent on states rather than members themselves. It was this "optimal size dilemma" that most clearly distinguished labor from business associations, which could grow without bounds in size and in power (Offe and Wiesenthal 1980, 83). And it was this dilemma that undergirded the theoretical linkages between the distribution and exercise of labor's power.

Democracy is thus rooted in the exercise of *specific* forms of social power based on broad collective action. But the power these authors articulate is a very specific sort: workplace-centered power as exercised by workers themselves. These are the traditional tools of organized labor—the strike, the slowdown, and other collective actions organized at the point of production.

But this is not the only form of power that unions exercise. The following sections address the implications of this for our understanding of union democracy.

New Democratic Dilemmas

Unions today, particularly those most closely associated with revitalized unionism, exercise power in new and distinct ways—primarily by shifting their resources toward tactics that mobilize leverage removed from workplaces themselves. The question arises: As unions come to exercise new forms of power, is there an effect on internal democratic practices?

There is a tradition seeing the exercise of power as fundamentally related to the distribution of power within a union. Matthew Dimick builds on the Toquevillian insight that democracy flourishes where workers retain the capacity for autonomous, workplace-based secondary associations, which can range from organized caucuses to less political groups such as social clubs and other features of an "occupational community" (2009, 27; see also Lipset, Trow, and Coleman 1956, 92). These associations, he argues, need not be dedicated to democratic advocacy; rather, they are likely dedicated to more prosaic efforts such as negotiating and enforcing contracts. But they present a counterweight to centralized authority, since union leaders depend on them to exercise workplace-centered power. They are most likely to exist where there is "direct membership production of the collective good" (Dimick 2009, 38). These associations, in turn, are more likely to exist where unions make use of shop-floor tactics, particularly the strike. Dimick writes:

> Certainly, carrying out economic action or threatening to do so is one of the means by which the official union leadership produces the collective good. But . . . the union leadership and bureaucracy may sometimes have alternative, often juridified, means of producing these outputs as well—they may even accept these restrictions in exchange for these other means. Shop-floor militants aren't as fortunate. Unlike the union officialdom, their ability to achieve union goals rests on mobilizing members on the shop-floor and the consequent ability to arrest work "at the point of production." (2009, 44)

However, we have seen that many unions have adopted new repertoires of contention in response to the constraints and opportunities emergent in the neoliberal era, both economic and political. While these new repertoires are varied and adaptable, at their core they represent an increasing dependence on extra-workplace sources of leverage. Noneconomic actions, such as appeals to community and political alliances, mobilize leverage in external political and community arenas rather than within workplaces. While worker support is often necessary for building these alliances (Tattersall 2013), these efforts can be coordinated and controlled by union leadership. Corporate campaigns arguably represent "economic action" but of an entirely new form than what the term generally refers to. They exert market-based leverage through a firm's market positions rather than through the withdrawal of labor. These efforts are highly specialized, depending on substantial expertise and union research capacity. Thus, corporate campaigns also allow union leaders to exercise power in ways that are removed from the workplace and independent of the workers themselves. This allows union leaders to exercise power autonomously, undermining the possibility of secondary association and insulating union leaders from dependence on membership beyond periodic elections.

These new democratic dilemmas are further accentuated by associated organizational reforms. To pursue these new, powerful tactics, many union leaders have undertaken organizational reforms that facilitate the strategic deployment of resources to exercise extra-workplace power. Where Offe and Weisenthal saw an "optimal size dilemma" emerging from larger unions' relative inability to mobilize workers, many of today's more powerful unions have pursued membership growth as a key objective and have rebuilt themselves to maximize such growth. Andrew Martin (2008) has found that hiring professional staff, including organizers and researchers, often enhances unions' ability to grow their membership. Unions have also pursued large and dramatic mergers of unions and locals (Moody 2009), which as Jasmine Kerrissey (2012) shows, are likely to result in less democratic constitutions. Thus, while these organizational reforms facilitate the new union strategies, they may also constrain the likelihood of autonomous workplace association.

Critics of the new tactical repertoire often see union leaders' strategic choices as a product of political preference and internal political contestation (see Early 2011; Moody 2007, 2014).[3] Certainly, union leaders make strategic choices, and preferences and internal contestation will affect the choices they make (McAlevey 2015). But we must also account for how choices have become increasingly constrained in the neoliberal era, with forces largely beyond leaders' control pushing them away from workplace-centered action. Leverage based on extra-workplace sources of power are increasingly central to the repertoire. As Tom Juravich notes, "It is difficult to identify a major union victory during the past decade that did not in some significant way employ strategic research and a comprehensive campaign" (2007, 17). However, while workplace-centered organization continues to be a core value for most unionists, the centrality of workplace-centered action in campaign success is somewhat mixed; Robert Hickey, Sarosh Kuruvilla, and Tashlin

Lakhani (2010), for instance, suggest that workplace activism may no longer be as central to campaign success as it once was. The broad and rapid decline of strikes is further indicative of this shift (see Martin and Dixon 2010; Rosenfeld 2006). Today's unions thus face a new democratic dilemma, a hard choice between the adoption of new structures and practices that can undermine union democracy or efforts to resurrect tools whose utility has weakened in recent decades. It is a bind that, arguably, has been at the root of recent political conflicts within the labor movement but also one that shows few signs of abating.

Democratic Dilemmas in the SEIU

Identifying strategic dilemmas as they actually unfold has important analytic advantages (Jasper 2006). Understanding how changing structural conditions produce strategic dilemmas helps us see how environments shape movements. Focusing on dilemmas—moments when activists navigate tough choices and trade-offs under adverse conditions—also helps us see the critical role of politics and ideas, historical contingency, and human agency. In this section, we briefly explore how one large U.S. union, the SEIU, navigated the new democratic dilemmas, illustrating the connection between economic change, strategic dilemmas, and internal political turmoil.

As the union at the center of the union revitalization movement in the 1990s and 2000s, SEIU is a critical case for examining these dilemmas. In the 1980s, SEIU was losing members and faced perceived existential crises following multiple large, failed strikes. But during this period, internal activists saw opportunities to change their union, to make it more democratic, responsive, and focused on organizing and growth. In the eyes of many of these revitalizers, democracy and militancy were deeply intertwined, allowing militant workers to break free of sclerotic, if not corrupt, union leaders to turn around their unions. By the mid-1990s, reform-minded leaders took hold of the union, creating one of the most potent organizing programs in the American labor movement. While the union's reliance on such tools as card-check neutrality and extra-workplace contention was a defensive move, these tools held the promise of a new form of power for the neoliberal era.

These activists' professed and demonstrated commitment to community alliances, member militancy, and innovative confrontational tactics heavily shaped many sociologists' understanding of a changing labor movement (Clawson 2003; Lopez 2004; Milkman 2006; Voss and Sherman 2000). But a decade or so later, SEIU became the site of numerous internal crises that came to challenge some of our ideas about union revitalization. Indeed, several critical observers came to refer to these crises as labor's "civil wars" (Early 2011; Winslow 2010). Both the new tactical repertoire and the organizational changes implemented to enable it, we argue, created trade-offs between external power and internal democracy.

Democracy and Revitalization

The ideal of union democracy was a key component of SEIU's early revitalization process, insofar as progressive activists within the union saw democratic member empowerment as a means to overcome sclerotic and passive business unionism. Some key activists came out of Local 1199, a militant health-care workers' union in New York with extensive ties to both Black civil rights activists and the traditional left, parts of which had recently merged into SEIU (see Fink and Greenberg 2009). In the early 1990s, allied internal reformers began to strategize for democratic change within SEIU, attending the 1992 SEIU International Convention under the banner of "Make the Best Better" (MTBB). They saw their efforts as a call for more aggressive organizing and internal democracy. Both were seen as complementary efforts to increase worker militancy and overcome the many localized oligarchies that had formed within SEIU's relatively decentralized governance structures. A statement from the MTBB candidates read, "A strong, united, fully activated and truly participatory union can result only through full discussion and honest debate of the issues and by genuine sharing in both the decisions and the responsibilities of the international union" ("Make the Best Better" 1994).

The MTBB delegates introduced measures at that meeting calling for the direct election of SEIU officers, the election of division boards, the distribution of board agendas and decisions, and the prohibition of dual salaries. Importantly, they also called for internal reforms directed at new organizing, including the dedication of more funds to organizing and upgrading industrial division boards from advisory to policy-making bodies. From these activists' perspective, democratization and the turn toward aggressive organizing were evidently intertwined. At the convention, the MTBB-affiliated candidates were dropped from President John Sweeney's executive board slate, and the reforms they proposed were not approved at the meeting. They were, however, referred to the International's Committee on the Future, run by Andrew Stern, then the assistant to the president for organizing (Bureau of National Affairs 1992). The report of the committee called for substantially increased investment in organizing, as well as industry-based organizing and decision-making in the union, and set ambitious goals for growth. While the MTBB coalition's recommendations for further union democratization did not make the report, several key reformist activists among its ranks would soon come to occupy key positions within the union.

It was ultimately the organizing-related recommendations from the Committee on the Future that would leave a lasting mark on SEIU's transformation, playing a key role in shaping the union's revitalization. John Sweeney ascended to the presidency of the American Federation of Labor and Congress of Industrial Organizations (AFL-CIO) in 1995. Within SEIU, a contested internal election led to Stern's election as president, after he and his allies ran on implementing the platform established by the Committee on the Future. The 1996 convention marked the union's formal commitment of financial resources to organizing and growth at the local level and the development of increased strategic and coordinating capacity at the international division level. It also initiated a union-wide process to push revitalization into the union's locals, codifying a model for extending renewed militancy and tactical creativity into more reluctant parts of the union. This process began in 1996 with a requirement that 20 percent of local expenditures be dedicated to new organizing—a goal to which 80 percent of locals would come to adhere within a decade (SEIU International Executive Board Resource Committee 2004).

What followed was a period of relatively intense growth. By its own measure, the union almost doubled its membership between 1996 and 2008, though this included several large mergers. Internally, SEIU leaders and strategists attributed this success to two principal factors. First, they implemented a series of tactical changes, centered on shifting labor contention away from individual workplaces and into proximate fields. Exercising power in this new way, leaders suggested, was necessary to counter increasingly aggressive, consolidated, and powerful employers and to transcend the institutional constraints inherent in existing labor law. Second, they embarked on a series of profound organizational reforms to dedicate the union to these new tactics and to build campaigns that matched the increasing geographic scope of their targets. We address both of these transformations in turn.

Industrial Challenges and Tactical Innovation

While the union retained a diversity of approaches in the 1990s, it began to settle on a new model in which large organizing campaign victories were achieved by moving contention beyond workplaces and into political and market fields; researchers and organizers learned how to push firms to accede to extra-institutional recognition procedures, after which organizers would enter the workplace to win the formal recognition victory itself. In the private sector, SEIU achieved its nonmerger growth through transforming its tactical repertoire—a change facilitated by organizational reforms. An early tactical change was a move toward reliance on extra-institutional rec-ognition procedures, particularly card-check neutrality agreements and fast and fair election agreements. Organizers saw this tactical development as an adaptation to changing industrial contexts.

This model was arguably pioneered during the AFL-CIO's long corpo-rate campaign targeting Beverly Enterprises, a large, publicly traded nursing home management firm, during the 1980s and into the early 1990s; SEIU played a lead role in the campaign, which featured new communications practices, and ran a union-friendly candidate for the corporate board. The campaign ultimately resulted in an innovative, if not uniformly successful, agreement governing corporate conduct during organizing drives. By the late 1980s, organizers recognized in the Beverly campaign an opportunity to "pioneer [a] mass organizing approach using card check recognition agree-ments" ("Evaluation of Projects" 1988).

After this experience, SEIU developed what is one of the best-known contemporary campaign models among sociologists today, the Justice for Janitors (J4J) approach. The J4J campaign structure was invented in response to the widespread outsourcing of cleaning labor in U.S. office buildings be-ginning in the 1970s and focused on obtaining card-check neutrality agree-ments across entire urban markets so the union could quell the competitive market pressures among contractors (Milkman 2006; Savage 2006; Waldinger et al. 1998). The J4J model was a successful response to the indus-trial transformation—outsourcing—that had weakened workers' structural power. The model was also paradigmatic of the broader shift of labor conten-tion toward extra-workplace fields: Since workplace-centered action would target employers with relatively little control over the conditions of labor, the union had to devise new forms of contention that would demand the atten-tion of the property owners who held that control. By shifting attention to building owners rather than the direct employer, the new model effectively directed labor contention against those with the most control over labor conditions.

Further changes in the structure of urban commercial real estate mar-kets created new challenges and opportunities for organizers. The outsourc-ing of commercial real estate maintenance labor, in progress for decades, was initially seen as a move toward labor cost containment. But in the late 1990s, organizers discovered that labor outsourcing was part of a broader shift of commercial real estate ownership toward investment management, a trans-formation with substantial implications for the union's potential exercise of power. Organized real estate investment vehicles such as publicly traded real estate investment trusts (REITs) and private equity funds were acquiring a greater share of urban real estate to offer alternative investment vehicles to investors (Gibler and Black 2004). This produced a rapid consolidation of real estate ownership, the growth of ownership entities that spanned multiple urban markets, and an intensified functional separation between asset management and property management (McMahan 2006). It also accelerated the proliferation of firms devoted to real estate management and maintenance, which came to fill roles traditionally embraced by localized owners; some of these firms also grew, as they attempted to match the broadening geographic scope of their clients.

The resulting concentration in building ownership posed new challenges and opportunities for organizers. Workers now faced owners who were even more removed from their own day-to-day realities and who were less sensitive to traditional forms of shop-floor-centered pressure, insulated by multiple institutional layers of contracting relationships. But the opportunities were also significant. By coordinating regional and national campaigns, the union was able to leverage support from members and allies in high-density markets to organize entirely new markets from the ground up, an opportunity that was possible only because of the concentration of ownership across markets. The union was able to use its own relationships with institutional investors, primarily through the pension funds that managed investments for the union's government and hospital workers. These pension funds were sometimes able to sway real estate equity firms with which they had invested substantial capital. The union was also able to conduct national-level corporate campaigns to obtain national card-check agreements with janitorial firms.

SEIU's organizing in the private-sector health-care field faced different industrial pressures but ultimately led to a similar emphasis on extraworkplace mobilization. In the hospital sector, the union's landmark organizing campaign unionized almost fifteen thousand workers in the Catholic Healthcare West (CHW) hospital system. The CHW campaign grew out of the California Health Systems Organizing Project, an effort, beginning after the 1996 convention, to identify long-term growth opportunities in the health-care field. Here, too, the union confronted a rapidly changing industry that challenged long-standing workplace norms and had eroded many traditional bases of worker power. In the 1990s, the acute-care industry turned toward a "managed care" approach to health-care delivery, relying on capitation to control costs (see Scott et al. 2000), as increasingly powerful and consolidated health-care purchasers concerned with spiraling costs sought to pressure providers to contain them. SEIU organizers saw hospitals responding by merging into ever-larger health systems capable of controlling markets and confronting purchasers and by placing increasing pressure on labor costs (Shaffer, Worthman, and Conrad 1996). Providers integrated vertically and horizontally, seeking both economies of scale and greater negotiating leverage relative to purchasers, leading to larger, more diversified, and more geographically expansive systems, some with tens of thousands of workers. Additionally, even nominally nonprofit delivery systems began to act more like corporations, using stock and bond markets to raise capital, and they grew responsive to the exigencies of those markets (Robinson 1999). Within workplaces themselves, care workers at all levels were expected to accelerate the pace of work to reduce patients' average length of stay (Gordon, Buchanan, and Bretherton 2008). In an increasing proportion of facilities, dietary and housekeeping labor was outsourced to outside contractors (Appelbaum et al. 2003).

Confronting this situation, leaders in the International Union within the SEIU and the large California locals began to identify rapid growth opportunities, where campaigns against large and growing employers could increase density (SEIU Healthcare Division 1998). CHW, as a growing system with a high market share and a large number of nonunion facilities, was selected as a target in part on this basis ("Catholic Healthcare" 1996). The campaign unfolded along the same basic contours—a multiyear campaign to pressure CHW to agree to an expedited, extra-institutional recognition process, followed by a relatively brief and privately regulated recognition procedure. Notably, the campaign involved a substantial investment of resources, occupied many staff members for half a decade, relied primarily on comprehensive campaign tactics for leverage, and succeeded without a major long-term strike. The campaign involved symbolic actions and events across the state. These efforts focused on coalition building with community allies, patient groups, and political figures, driven primarily by appeals to the employer's professed Catholic mission. This included public agitation around CHW's legal and moral commitment to charity care, while also focusing more mundane, but potentially more costly, concerns, such as seismic retrofit requirements for hospitals ("A Time to Break Silence" 1998; "CHW" 1999; "Suits and Nuns" 1998). By 2000, the union had obtained a neutrality agreement that established restrictions on both parties and expedited the elections process—a fast and fair elections agreement.[4] Within the span of about twelve months, the union organized twenty-eight facilities.

This development of alternative tactics focused on shifting contention to non-workplace fields did not in itself require a decisive move away from workplace-centered contention. Some comprehensive campaigns involving corporate pressure tactics indeed continued involving workplace-centered contention, including strikes. But for some leaders, the promise of the comprehensive model lay in its ability to exercise power without relying on expensive and unpredictable worker-organizing efforts. As early as 1992, one high-level organizer suggested that a key goal of the International's investment in strategic organizing capacity was "to experiment with a variety of ideas to help us learn how to do large scale organizing, e.g., long-term corporate campaigning on strategic targets without conducting a worker campaign" (Lerner 1992). This goal—to identify ways to use corporate campaigns to win concessions "without conducting a worker campaign"—continued to take hold within the union. While certainly not a universal sentiment among SEIU leaders, by the 2000s many leaders were adherents to the idea that SEIU had identified campaign tools with which, as one leader more recently told Teresa Sharpe, "You can win without workers" (2010, 90).

Organizational Changes

In the eyes of SEIU leaders, the major impediments to effectively implementing the new organizing model were internal—a traditionally decentralized governance structure that, while allowing for tactical experimentation, was less well suited for the implementation of centrally coordinated strategies. Exercising new forms of power to adapt to changing employer targets necessitated internal reorganization. As Sharpe has argued, "In the eyes of SEIU leaders, union centralization follows from the centralization of capital" (2010, 89). And as a key SEIU report put it, "The decision-making structures and strategies our employers use today have changed dramatically since SEIU was founded in 1921—but ours haven't" (SEIU President's Committee 2000). One important change, the creation and empowerment of industrial divisions, had been in process for years. The divisions were originally created in 1984 as a space for local leaders to share ideas regarding organizing in their industries. Empowered divisions were "an effort," according to a 2000 report, "to respond on a sporadic basis to the initial centralization of employer decision-making" (SEIU President's Committee 2000). Over time, these divisions were vested with increasing control over targeting decisions and resources. In 2001, the industrial divisions came to control the distribution of resources from the Unity Fund, an international fund for subsidizing strategic organizing by locals and running multilocal campaigns. Whereas the 1996 convention resolutions required locals to spend a growing proportion of income on organizing, by 2008, the division structures themselves would control much of the union's organizing funds.

The union also pursued a dramatic restructuring of locals. SEIU locals had been regionally organized, with many incorporating members from multiple industrial divisions; new locals would focus on fewer industries while representing workers within a broader geographic area, which was an effort to confront employers that were no longer contained in smaller markets. Health-care locals encountered nursing home chains and hospital systems that crossed state and regional boundaries. Locals focused on commercial-property-services workers such as janitors and security guards encountered nationally organized contractors; and even when it formally bargained with locally organized contractors, the union was waging comprehensive campaigns that focused on property owners organized on a broader scale. SEIU leaders spearheaded the creation of larger locals meant to reflect the regional markets of these key employers and the creation of supralocal decision-making bodies capable of bargaining with employers that transcended the local or regional scale. Between 1995 and 2008, average local membership increased from 2,680 to 14,280 (Eaton et al. 2009). These larger locals were also more likely to follow the organizing focus of the International Union: By 2004, an internal audit found that while 80 percent of all locals had successfully implemented the International Union mandate to budget 20 percent of local expenditures on new organizing, this figure was 98 percent among locals with six thousand or more members (SEIU International Executive Board Resource Committee 2004). But more broadly, the larger locals were able to dedicate the necessary resources and staffing to expensive, targeted extra-workplace organizing campaigns. And union leaders saw them as better suited for organizing and bargaining at the scale of increasingly consolidated employers by virtue of their greater geographic scope.

Many mergers were achieved through voluntary reorganization, as local leaders adopted the organizing imperative and cooperated with the internal restructuring that many perceived as necessary. However, not all local leaders adhered to these programs, and in these cases, the international organization made use of forcible trusteeships, whereby a local's elected officers are removed and replaced with a trustee accountable directly to the International. As Adrienne Eaton and colleagues (2009) enumerate, "Whereas only two or three locals were trusteed in each four-year cycle between 1980 and 1992, that number jumped to 11 in the four years prior to Stern's election. The use of trusteeships intensified from 1996 to 2003, during which time 30 locals were trusteed."

National-level interventions in local affairs were key components of broader efforts at union reform and revitalization. As Kim Voss and Rachel Sherman (2000) show, external political intervention was an important factor in overcoming local unions' sclerotic states, paving the way for new strategies and organizational structures. Indeed, many saw the centralization of authority in SEIU as a key tool for removing largely inactive and entrenched union leaders, who often resisted change with claims to local autonomy. If, as its leaders attested, SEIU indeed needed to "change to win," they saw suspending local control as a means to that end. SEIU leader Stephen Lerner articulated precisely this tension:

> The simple fact is that the majority of local building-service unions were run by entrenched bureaucrats who didn't want to organize or

change. They were more interested in maintaining their personal power than rising to the challenges of a new workforce and a new economy. Poor workers all over the country were being held hostage in powerful local fiefdoms that, in the name of local union autonomy, claimed it was their right not to change. SEIU faced a choice and a challenge: accepting the road block these local leaders represented or remaking the union so that workers could win and take on nonunion employers. (2005, 51)

Democratic Dilemmas

Throughout the 1990s and 2000s, many mergers and trusteeships had their critics, who often contested them on the basis of claims to member sovereignty and union democracy. But by 2008, the pattern of trusteeships and supralocal decision-making structures became the grounds for a series of internal upheavals that few could dismiss as the outbursts of a reactionary old guard clinging to its position with claims to local autonomy and union democracy. And while the specific motivations and battle lines of these internal conflicts still remain substantially obscured by the passions and politics involved, the contours of the crisis nevertheless reveal important connections between internal conceptions of democracy and the union's emergent repertoire of contention.

The highest-profile conflict involved United Healthcare Workers–West (UHW), a newly merged local that organized health-care workers across California. The UHW crisis of 2008 had its origins in the emergent patterns of contention in health care, which as we argue, lodged the coercive power of the union in arenas removed from the shop floor—in politics via the mobilization of political leverage and in markets via research-intensive corporate strategies. Even during the successful CHW organizing drive in the late 1990s and early 2000s, there had been internal dissent over the wisdom of seeking card-check recognition, a basic plank of many new labor strategies. But these internal tensions came to a head surrounding what leaders came to call the "Alliance agreement," a 2004 organizing agreement with nursing homes in California. Leaders argued that in previous years, attempts to organize nursing home workers through comprehensive campaigns and NLRB elections had been relatively unsuccessful and that a new approach was needed (Hudson 2008).

At the core of the Alliance agreement was a trade of coercive power. In exchange for organizing rights in a subset of the Alliance employers' nursing homes, the union would lobby the state for a reform of Medicaid reimbursement procedures that would lead to an increase in state funds for nursing homes ("Agreement" 2004). When the agreement was introduced, Local

250's (the Northern California predecessor to UHW) newsletter heralded the agreement, calling it a "bold new course" for the union ("A Bold New Course" 2003). However, when the agreement was up for renewal in 2007, the Alliance agreement fomented substantial dissent. UHW organizers circulated a petition among their members in opposition to the agreement (Hudson 2008). Leaders later circulated a position paper that questioned the wisdom of renewing the agreement. They questioned whether the agreement achieved its potential, as it attained only $21 million in improved contract standards for nursing home workers while obtaining $119 in increased revenues for the employers, as well as its potential to meaningfully increase union density in the long term. More fundamentally, however, these leaders questioned the extent to which the agreement challenged their fundamental mission and their notions of unionism. At its core, the Alliance agreement organizing process was exercising political power but bypassing workplace contention:

> Traditionally, for workers to organize they engage in struggle to win that right. Under the Alliance agreement this is absent. The contract that newly organized Alliance workers will have is worked out in advance with the ultimate terms of that agreement discouraging— and in some cases, preventing—workers from independently engaging in struggle to improve their working conditions. (United Healthcare Workers–West 2007)

While SEIU would stall the renegotiation, the union also moved forward with a proposal to move long-term-care members out of UHW and into another local more amenable to these agreements. It was a move that, UHW leaders argued, was a retaliatory "political attack on UHW," a product of a political disagreement that "became extremely clear in negotiations for the renewal of the California Nursing Home Alliance Agreement" ("Surrebuttal" 2008). In 2009, having formally accused UHW leaders of moving union money into a fund intended to resist international trusteeship, the international trusted UHW. This reinforced critics' charge that SEIU has shifted primarily toward a model of unionism that relies almost entirely on external leverage (for more lengthy descriptions of these events, see Benson 2009; Winslow 2010).

Conclusion

Neoliberalism has produced profound challenges for unions—including political attacks on the right to strike, changes in employment structures related to sectoral shifts, and changes in the distribution of corporate power in a financialized economy—but many of these transformations have simultaneously produced opportunities for new forms of contention. Indeed, tactics like the corporate campaign, which produces leverage over an employer by extending workplace conflict into other social arenas and draws in a broad array of political actors, would arguably be less effective without the vertical deintegration that has otherwise harmed unions' ability to strike.

We argue that there is an important link between how movements exercise external power and their internal political processes. In the labor movement, the implications of this link are profound. Labor's traditional repertoire of contention was focused on the exercise of workplace-centered conflict, and this made internal democracy both more necessary and more likely. The exercise of extra-workplace forms of power associated with revitalized unionism, however, diminishes the reliance of union leaders on the deliberation and participation of workers. It insulates leaders from a dependence on members while simultaneously making them reliant on specialized staff and increased size. In short, as unions shift their tactics away from the workplace to take advantage of new opportunities for leverage inherent in neoliberalism, they are confronted with a democratic dilemma: By adopting the new structures and practices that yield greater tactical success in this political and economic context, union democracy becomes more difficult to realize and sustain.

To appreciate the profundity of this dilemma, as well as to better understand the ways that shifts in targets generate changes in repertoires of contention, it is important to underline the role of ideas and agency in our analysis. Tactical change in labor's revitalized unions was the outcome of political upheavals, with activists interacting and struggling to achieve distinct goals; it was not the result of organizational leaders quickly comprehending changing external conditions and instrumentally adjusting tactics accordingly. Instead, ongoing interaction with targets and substantial losses in the early years forced change on entrenched leaders, opening the labor movement to new approaches. Ironically, the ideal of union democracy was a crucial component of the early revitalization process in the union at the forefront of the effort to reinvent American unions in recent decades, SEIU. However, as activists experimented with new approaches to labor contention, they not only discovered the leverage that won campaigns but also found that organizational reforms enabled the successful use of that leverage. Such organizational reforms have come at a cost, as they make the practice of internal democracy more difficult, thus forcing union leaders to confront hard choices.

This democratic dilemma is at the center of labor's recent internal conflicts, yet it has thus far gone largely unrecognized. We do not contest the notion that union leaders' politics and visions matter for the choices they make. But the likelihood of internal democracy is not just a product of union leaders' oligarchic tendencies or an inevitable Michelsian law; it is also related to how collective power is exercised. Economic and political constraints often determine the forms of power that are possible and perceived as most effective, and as new practices become habitual, new organizational forms develop around them. While not all agree that extra-workplace contention is the most effective form of struggle against new corporate forms (Burns 2011; McAlevey 2015), many union leaders (and sociologists) saw the new approaches as an important corrective to earlier failures. Further interrogating the relationship between perceived tactical imperatives and internal structure is an important step toward grappling with the political tensions inherent in labor contention in the neoliberal era.

The relationship we have analyzed between social movements' repertoires of contention and their internal governance has implications for social movements more broadly. Of course, there are differences between how we conceive of democracy in unions and democracy in other social movement organizations. Unions, as Offe and Weisenthal point out, are "secondary organizers" (1980, 72), movement organizations that seek to mobilize groups that are already brought together (and thus "organized") by capital. Thus, union constituencies are usually well defined by employers. Once unions are formed, members have a structurally defined claim to representation, participation, and control, without regard to their affinity with the goals and methods of others in the organization; this is unlike many social movement organizations, where claims to self-governance and control are largely a product of participation itself.[5]

However, the broader question of the relationship between the external exercise of power and the internal distribution of power may be examined in many different settings. As social movement scholars turn their attention beyond those movements that target states and toward those that target private actors and corporations, they will uncover many similar dilemmas concerning power, practice, and governance. The different ways in which movements exercise power in these domains are likely to shape the dynamics of internal democratic practice. Although social movement scholars have made progress in theorizing how targets can shape both the tactics of movement organizations and the likelihood of success using those tactics, to date, the link between the tactics the movements choose and the internal governance of movements has gone largely undertheorized. Here, we offer one approach to this question, a set of propositions that can be explored in other settings: (1) Where targets are vulnerable to forms of collective power that depend on *direct* member action and coordination, democratic control is more likely; and (2) where targets are more vulnerable to forms of collective power that do not depend on such *direct* member action and coordination, movements encounter democratic dilemmas. These dilemmas do not imply that democracy becomes impossible. But while the precise combination of tactics is of course subject to questions of internal politics and the negotiation of member identities, the vulnerabilities and capacities of targets can shape these internal processes and should not be neglected.

Finally, the issues of democracy raised by the dilemmas facing the American labor movement extend beyond a concern with internal democracy alone. As revitalized labor unions take on an increasingly significant role in providing leadership, funding, and strategies for broader movements such as immigrant rights and the fight for a fifteen-dollar minimum wage, a case can be made that such actions contribute significantly to democratic empowerment of groups who have had little influence in the politics of their communities or nation. But the active, agentic participation of workers in struggle— the direct production of the collective good—has long been recognized as empowering workers as citizens and class actors in the workplace and beyond (Terriquez 2011). How to balance the contribution of new extraworkplace tactics against the effects that this repertoire of contention has had on internal union democracy remains an open question. It is one that we must grapple with as we think about the future of unions and other movements.

NOTES
This chapter borrows its title from Richard Fariña's novel *Been Down So Long It Looks Like Up to Me* (New York: Penguin, 1996). Both authors contributed equally to the chapter.

1. Card-check recognition is standard procedure in many countries, but in the United States, such recognition can be achieved only by circumventing the standard NLRB process (Fantasia and Voss 2004, 129; Western 1999).

2. Not all analysts agree with Offe and Weisenthal on this point. For a challenge to their conception of capitalist collective action, see Roy and Parker-Gwin 1999.

3. Just as SEIU was one of the unions most closely identified with revitalized unionism in the 1990s (Martin 2008; Voss and Sherman 2000; Waldinger et al. 1998), today it has become the target of vociferous critics from within the labor movement. Many critics point to precisely the connection between the union's democratic practices and its campaign methods (Early 2011). Moody, for instance, argues that these repertoire changes pull unions further from the "rank-and-file strategy" that focuses on union democracy and workplace empowerment (2014, 75); such a rank-and-file focus, furthermore, has been identified by labor scholars as critical to the revitalization process itself (Bronfenbrenner and Juravich 1998).

4. This process was distinct from the card-check agreements that the union was obtaining in other industries—a compromise outcome, given internal contention over card check.

5. Another way to formulate this distinction would be between constituency organizations (unions) and cadre organizations (social movement organizations such as the

Student Nonviolent Coordinating Committee or Greenpeace). Much of the literature on democracy in social movement organizations has focused on cadre organizations.

REFERENCES

"Agreement to Advance the Future of Nursing Home Care in California." 2004. Previously available at http-//img.seiu.org/pdfs/UHW-W-Exhs/Ex.214.pdf.

Albright, Jason. 2008. "Contending Rationality, Leadership, and Collective Struggle: The 2006 Justice for Janitors Campaign at the University of Miami." *Labor Studies Journal* 33 (1): 63–80.

Amenta, Edwin, Drew Halfmann, and Michael Young. 1999. "The Strategies and Contexts of Social Protest: Political Mediation and the Impact of the Townsend Movement in California." *Mobilization: An International Quarterly* 4:1–23.

Appelbaum, Eileen, Peter Berg, Ann Frost, and Gil Preuss. 2003. "The Effects of Work Restructuring on Low-Wage, Low-Skill Workers in US Hospitals." In *Low Wage America: How Employers Are Reshaping Opportunity in the Workplace*, edited by Eileen Appelbaum, Anette Bernhardt, and Richard Murnane, 77–117. New York: Russell Sage Foundation.

Archer, R. 2010. *Why Is There No Labor Party in the United States?* Princeton, NJ: Princeton University Press.

Bell, Daniel. 1973. *Coming of Post-industrial Society.* New York: Basic Books.

Benson, Herman. 2009. "Hybrid Unionism: Dead End or Fertile Future?" *Dissent* 56:79–85.

Block, Fred. 1990. *Postindustrial Possibilities: A Critique of Economic Discourse.* Berkeley: University of California Press.

Bloom, Joshua. 2010. "Ally to Win: Black Community Leaders and SEIU's L.A. Security Unionization Campaign." In *Working for Justice: The L.A. Model of Worker Organizing and Advocacy,* edited by Ruth Milkman, Joshua Bloom, and Victor Narro, 167–190. Ithaca, NY: Cornell University Press.

Bluestone, Barry, and Bennett Harrison. 1982. *The Deindustrialization of America: Plant Closings, Community Abandonment, and the Dismantling of Basic Industry.* New York: Basic Books.

"A Bold New Course." 2003. *Unity* 15 (1). Union Publications Collection, San Francisco State University Labor Archives and Resource Center.

Bronfenbrenner, Kate. 1994. "Employer Behavior in Certification Elections and First-Contract Campaigns: Implications for Labor Law Reform." In *Restoring the Promise of American Labor Law,* edited by Sheldon Friedman, Richard W. Hurd, Rudolph A. Oswald, and Ronald L. Seeber, 75–89. Ithaca, NY: Cornell ILR Press.

Bronfenbrenner, Kate, and Robert Hickey. 2004. "Changing to Organize: A National Assessment of Union Organizing Strategies." In *Rebuilding Labor: Organizing and Organizers in the New Union Movement,* edited by Ruth Milkman and Kim Voss, 17–61. Ithaca, NY: Cornell University Press.

Bronfenbrenner, Kate, and Tom Juravich. 1998. "It Takes More than House Calls: Organizing to Win with a Comprehensive Union-Building Strategy." In *Organizing to Win: New Research on Union Strategies,* edited by Kate Bronfenbrenner, Sheldon Friedman, Richard W. Hurd, Rudolph A. Oswald, and Ronald L. Seeber, 19–36. Ithaca, NY: Cornell University Press.

Bureau of National Affairs. 1992. "Convention Report: SEIU." May. Folder 12, Box 12, larc.ms.0341, San Francisco State University Labor Archives and Resource Center.

Burns, Joe. 2011. *Reviving the Strike: How Working People Can Regain Power and Transform America*. New York: Ig.

"Catholic Healthcare West Southern California." 1996. "CHW Briefing" folder, Box 111, acc#09-01, Special Collections and Archives, California State University–Northridge.

Chun, Jennifer J. 2005. "Public Dramas and the Politics of Justice: Comparison of Janitors' Union Struggles in South Korea and the United States." *Work and Occupations* 32:486–503.

———. 2009. *Organizing at the Margins: The Symbolic Politics of Labor in South Korea and the United States*. Ithaca, NY: Cornell ILR Press.

"CHW: An Open Letter to the People of Los Angeles." 1999. *Los Angeles Times*, June 13, p. A34. "CHW Memory Lane" folder, Box 75, acc#09-01, Special Collections and Archives, California State University–Northridge.

Clawson, Dan. 2003. *The Next Upsurge: Labor and the New Social Movements*. Ithaca, NY: Cornell ILR Press.

Clawson, Dan, and Mary Anne Clawson. 1999. "What Has Happened to the US Labor Movement? Union Decline and Renewal." *Annual Review of Sociology* 25 (1): 95–119.

Clemens, Elisabeth S. 1996. "Organizational Form as Frame: Collective Identity and Political Strategy in the American Labor Movement, 1880–1920." In *Comparative Perspectives on Social Movements: Political Opportunities, Mobilizing Structures, and Cultural Framings*, edited by Doug McAdam, John D. McCarthy, and Mayer N. Zald, 205–226. Cambridge: Cambridge University Press.

Davis, Gerald F. 2009. *Managed by the Markets: How Finance Re-shaped America*. New York: Oxford University Press.

Dimick, Matthew. 2009. "Labor Law and Union Democracy: A US British Comparison." Ph.D. diss., University of Wisconsin–Madison.

———. 2010. "Revitalizing Union Democracy: Labor Law, Bureaucracy, and Workplace Association." *Denver University Law Review* 88 (1): 1–60.

Dixon, Marc, and Andrew W. Martin. 2012. "We Can't Win This on Our Own: Unions, Firms, and Mobilization of External Allies in Labor Disputes." *American Sociological Review* 77:946–969.

Early, Steve. 2011. *The Civil Wars in U.S. Labor: Birth of a New Workers' Movement or Death Throes of the Old?* Boston: Haymarket Books.

Eaton, Adrienne, Allison Porter, Janice Fine, and Saul Rubinstein. 2009. "Organizational Change at SEIU: 1996–2009." Available at https://www.alvarezporter.com/wp-content/uploads/org-change-at-seiu.pdf.

"Evaluation of Projects: Beverly." 1988. Report within "Materials for Meeting," memorandum from David Snapp to Healthcare Organizers, May 20. Folder 5, Box 6, SEIU Organizing Department Collection, Walter P. Reuther Library of Labor and Urban Affairs, Wayne State University, Detroit, Michigan.

Fantasia, Rick, and Kim Voss. 2004. *Hard Work: Remaking the American Labor Movement*. Berkeley: University of California Press.

Fine, Janice. 2005. "Community Unions and the Revival of the American Labor Movement." *Politics and Society* 33:153–199.

Fink, Leon, and Brian Greenberg. 2009. *Upheaval in the Quiet Zone: 1199SEIU and the Politics of Health Care Unionism*. Carbondale: University of Illinois Press.

Freeman, Jo. 1972. "The Tyranny of Structurelessness." *Berkeley Journal of Sociology* 17:151–164.

Friedman, Eli. 2013. "Insurgency and Institutionalization: The Polanyian Countermovement and Chinese Labor Politics." *Theory and Society* 42:295–327.

Frost, Ann C. 2000. "Explaining Variation in Workplace Restructuring: The Role of Local Union Capabilities." *Industrial and Labor Relations Review* 53:559–578.

Gastón, Pablo. 2018. "Contention across Social Fields: Manipulating the Boundaries of Labor Struggle in the Workplace, Community, and Market." *Social Problems* 63:231–250.

Getman, Julius G. 2010. *Restoring the Power of Unions: It Takes a Movement.* New Haven, CT: Yale University Press.

Gibler, Karen M., and Roy T. Black. 2004. "Agency Risks in Outsourcing Corporate Real Estate Functions." *Journal of Real Estate Research* 26:137–160.

Golden, Clinton S., and Harold J. Ruttenberg. 1942. *The Dynamics of Industrial Democracy.* New York: Harper and Brothers.

Gordon, Suzanne, John Buchanan, and Tanya Bretherton. 2008. *Safety in Numbers: Nurse-to-Patient Ratios and the Future of Health Care.* Ithaca, NY: Cornell University Press.

Hattam, Victoria C. 1992. *Labor Visions and State Power: The Origins of Business Unionism in the United States.* Princeton, NJ: Princeton University Press.

Hetland, Gabriel, and Jeff Goodwin. 2013. "The Strange Disappearance of Capitalism from Social Movement Studies." In *Marxism and Social Movements*, edited by Colin Barker, Laurence Cox, John Krinsky, and Alf Gunvald Nilson, 83–102. Leiden, Netherlands: Brill.

Hickey, Robert, Sarosh Kuruvilla, and Tashlin Lakhani. 2010. "No Panacea for Success: Member Activism, Organizing and Union Renewal." *British Journal of Industrial Relations* 48:53–83.

Hudson, Gerald. 2008. "Evaluation of the Reorganization of California's Long-Term Care Locals." January 24. Previously available at img.seiu.org/pdfs/Executive-Board-Exhibits/Ex.87.pdf.

Jasper, James M. 2006. *Getting Your Way: Strategic Dilemmas in the Real World.* Chicago: University of Chicago Press.

Juravich, Tom. 2007. "Beating Global Capital: A Framework and Method for Union Strategic Corporate Research and Campaigns." In *Global Unions: Challenging Transnational Capital through Cross-border Campaigns*, edited by Kate Bronfenbrenner, 16–39. Ithaca, NY: Cornell University Press.

Kerr, Clark, and Abraham Siegel. 1954. "The Interindustry Propensity to Strike: An International Comparison." In *Industrial Conflict*, edited by Arthur Kornhauser, Robert Dubin, and Arthur M. Ross, 189–212. New York: McGraw-Hill.

Kerrissey, Jasmine. 2012. "Union Mergers in the United States, 1900–2005." Ph.D. diss., University of California, Irvine.

King, Brayden G. 2008. "A Political Mediation Model of Corporate Response to Social Movement Activism." *Administrative Science Quarterly* 53:395–421.

King, Brayden G, and Nicholas A. Pearce. 2010. "The Contentiousness of Markets: Politics, Social Movements, and Institutional Change in Markets." *Annual Review of Sociology* 36:249–267.

Krippner, Greta R. 2005. "The Financialization of the American Economy." *Socioeconomic Review* 3:173–208.

Lerner, Stephen. 1992. "Structure Recommendations." Memorandum to Andy Stern, ca. May. Folder 31, Box 2, SEIU Organizing Department Collection, Walter P. Reuther Library of Labor and Urban Affairs, Wayne State University, Detroit, Michigan.

———. 2005. "A Winning Strategy to Do Justice." *Tikkun* 20 (3): 50–51.

Lévesque, Christian, and Gregor Murray. 2005. "Union Involvement in Workplace Change: A Comparative Study of Local Unions in Canada and Mexico." *British Journal of Industrial Relations* 43:489–514.

Levi, Margaret, David Olson, Jon Agnone, and Devin Kelly. 2009. "Union Democracy Reexamined." *Politics and Society* 37 (2): 203–228.

Lichtenstein, Nelson. 2013. *State of the Union: A Century of American Labor*. Princeton, NJ: Princeton University Press.

Lipset, Seymour Martin, Martin A. Trow, and James S. Coleman. 1956. *Union Democracy: The Internal Politics of the International Typographical Union*. Glencoe, IL: Free Press.

Lopez, Steven H. 2004. *Reorganizing the Rust Belt: An Inside Study of the American Labor Movement*. Berkeley: University of California Press.

"Make the Best Better: Who We Are, What We Want." [1994]. Folder 8, Box 7, larc.ms.0341, San Francisco State University Labor Archives and Resource Center.

Manheim, Jarol B. 2000. *The Death of a Thousand Cuts: Corporate Campaigns and the Attack on the Corporation*. New York: Routledge.

Martin, Andrew W. 2008. "The Institutional Logic of Union Organizing and the Effectiveness of Social Movement Repertoires." *American Journal of Sociology* 113:1067–1103.

Martin, Andrew W., and Marc Dixon. 2010. "Changing to Win? Threat, Resistance, and the Role of Unions in Strikes, 1984–2002." *American Journal of Sociology* 116 (1): 93–129.

McAlevey, Jane. 2015. "The Crisis of New Labor and Alinsky's Legacy Revisiting the Role of the Organic Grassroots Leaders in Building Powerful Organizations and Movements." *Politics and Society* 43:415–441.

McCartin, Joseph A. 2011. *Collision Course: Ronald Reagan, the Air Traffic Controllers, and the Strike That Changed America*. New York: Oxford University Press.

McMahan, John. 2006. *The Handbook of Commercial Real Estate Investing*. New York: McGraw-Hill.

Medina, Eliseo. 2006. "Labor Will Rise Again: A Strategy for Organizing in the New South." *New Labor Forum* 15:20–31.

Michels, Robert. (1911) 1962. *Political Parties: A Sociological Study of the Oligarchical Tendencies of Modern Democracy*. Reprint, New York: Free Press.

Milkman, Ruth. 2006. *L.A. Story: Immigrant Workers and the Future of the U.S. Labor Movement*. New York: Russell Sage Foundation.

Moody, Kim. 2007. *U.S. Labor in Trouble and Transition: The Failure of Reform from Above, the Promise of Revival from Below*. London: Verso.

———. 2009. "The Direction of Union Mergers in the United States: The Rise of Conglomerate Unionism." *British Journal of Industrial Relations* 47:676–700.

———. 2014. *In Solidarity: Essays on Working-Class Organization and Strategy in the United States*. Boston: Haymarket Books.

Muste, A. J. 1948. "Army and Town Meeting." In *Unions, Management and the Public*, edited by Edward White Bakke and Clark Kerr, 187–189. New York: Harcourt, Brace.

Offe, Claus, and Helmut Wiesenthal. 1980. "Two Logics of Collective Action: Theoretical Notes on Social Class and Organizational Form." *Political Power and Social Theory* 1:67–115.

Piore, Michael J., and Sean Safford. 2006. "Changing Regimes of Workplace Governance, Shifting Axes of Social Mobilization, and the Challenge to Industrial Relations Theory." *Industrial Relations: A Journal of Economy and Society* 45:299–325.

Polletta, Francesca. 2004. *Freedom Is an Endless Meeting: Democracy in American Social Movements*. Chicago: University of Chicago Press.

———. 2005. "How Participatory Democracy Became White: Culture and Organizational Choice." *Mobilization: An International Quarterly* 10 (2): 271–288.

Prosten, Richard. 1979. "The Rise in NLRB Election Delays: Measuring Business' New Resistance." *Monthly Labor Review* 102:38–40.

Rhomberg, Chris. 2012. "The Return of Judicial Repression: What Has Happened to the Strike?" *The Forum* 10 (1): 1–18.

Robinson, James C. 1999. *The Corporate Practice of Medicine: Competition and Innovation in Health Care*. Berkeley: University of California Press.

Rosenfeld, Jake. 2006. "Desperate Measures: Strikes and Wages in Post-accord America." *Social Forces* 85:235–265.

Roy, William G., and Rachel Parker-Gwin. 1999. "How Many Logics of Collective Action?" *Theory and Society* 28:203–237.

Savage, Lydia. 2006. "Justice for Janitors: Scales of Organizing and Representing Workers." *Antipode* 38 (3): 645–666.

Scott, W. Richard, Martin Ruef, Peter Mendel, and Carol Caronna. 2000. *Institutional Change and Healthcare Organizations: From Professional Dominance to Managed Care*. Chicago: University of Chicago Press.

SEIU Healthcare Division. 1998. "Healthcare Division Organizing Plan, 1998–2000." January. Folder 3, Box 10, larc.ms.0341, San Francisco State University Labor Archives and Resource Center.

SEIU International Executive Board Resource Committee. 2004. "Resource Committee Report." May. Folder 14, Box 5, larc.ms.0341, San Francisco State University Labor Archives and Resource Center.

SEIU President's Committee. 2000. "President's Committee, 2000, Report 3: Decide." Folder 3, Box 4, larc.ms.0341, San Francisco State University Labor Archives and Resource Center.

Shaffer, Jono, Catha Worthman, and Susan Conrad. 1996. "LA Healthcare Industry: Feasibility Study." September 18. Unpublished paper in the author's possession.

Sharpe, Teresa. 2010. "Cultures of Creativity: Politics, Leadership, and Organizational Change in American Unions." Ph.D. diss., University of California, Berkeley.

Stepan-Norris, Judith, and Maurice Zeitlin. 1996. "Insurgency, Radicalism, and Democracy in America's Industrial Unions." *Social Forces* 75:1–32.

———. 2003. *Left Out: Reds and America's Industrial Unions*. Cambridge: Cambridge University Press.

Stuart, Forrest. 2010. "From the Shop to the Streets: UNITE HERE Organizing in Los Angeles Hotels." In *Working for Justice: The LA Model of Organizing and Advocacy*, edited by Ruth Milkman, Joshua Bloom, and Victor Narro, 191–210. Ithaca, NY: Cornell University Press.

"Suits and Nuns Work Plan." [1998?]. SEIU internal memorandum. "CHW Corporate Leverage" folder, Box 95, acc#09-01, Special Collections and Archives, California State University–Northridge.

"Sur-rebuttal Declaration of John Borsos." 2008. Declaration during UHW trusteeship hearing, November 21. Previously available at img.seiu.org/pdfs/Post-11-15-08 -Declarations/11-21-2008-John-Borsos-Declaration.pdf.

Tattersall, Amanda. 2013. *Power in Coalition: Strategies for Strong Unions and Social Change*. Ithaca, NY: Cornell University Press.

Terriquez, Veronica. 2011. "Schools for Democracy: Labor Union Participation and Latino Immigrant Parents' School-Based Civic Engagement." *American Sociological Review* 76:581–601.

Tilly, Charles. 1995. *Popular Contention in Great Britain, 1758–1834.* Cambridge, MA: Harvard University Press.

"A Time to Break Silence: Catholic Healthcare West; The Spiritual Cost of Corporatization." 1998. Folder 12, Box 9, larc.ms.0341, San Francisco State University Labor Archives and Resource Center.

Ulman, Lloyd. 1966. *The Rise of the National Trade Union: The Development and Significance of the Structure, Governing Institutions, and Economic Policies.* Cambridge, MA: Harvard University Press.

United Healthcare Workers–West. 2007. "The California Alliance Agreement: Lessons Learned in Moving Forward in Organizing California's Nursing Home Industry." January. Folder 18, Box 13, larc.ms.0341, San Francisco State University Labor Archives and Resource Center.

U.S. Bureau of Labor Statistics. 2018. "Major Work Stoppages in 2017." February 9. Available at https://www.bls.gov/news.release/archives/wkstp_02092018.pdf.

Voss, Kim. 2010. "Democratic Dilemmas: Union Democracy and Union Renewal." *Transfer: European Review of Labour and Research* 16:369–382.

Voss, Kim, and Rachel Sherman. 2000. "Breaking the Iron Law of Oligarchy: Union Revitalization in the American Labor Movement." *American Journal of Sociology* 106:303–349.

Waldinger, Roger D., Chris Erickson, Ruth Milkman, Daniel Mitchell, Abel Valenzuela, Kent Wong, and Maurice Zeitlin. 1998. "Helots No More: A Case Study of the Justice for Janitors Campaign in Los Angeles." In *Organizing to Win: New Research on Union Strategies,* edited by Kate Bronfenbrenner, Sheldon Friedman, Richard W. Hurd, Rudolph A. Oswald, and Ronald L. Seeber, 102–119. Ithaca, NY: Cornell University Press.

Walker, Edward T., Andrew W. Martin, and John D. McCarthy. 2008. "Confronting the State, the Corporation, and the Academy: The Influence of Institutional Targets on Social Movement Repertoires." *American Journal of Sociology* 114:35–76.

Western, Bruce. 1999. *Between Class and Market.* Princeton, NJ: Princeton University Press.

Winslow, Cal. 2010. *Labor's Civil War in California: The NUHW Healthcare Workers' Rebellion.* Oakland, CA: PM Press.

5

Protest Episodes

Shifting Actors and Targets in Local Movements

KENNETH T. ANDREWS AND SARAH GABY

I n 1957, a group of high school students led by a local minister sat down in the "whites only" section of the Royal Ice Cream Parlor in Durham, North Carolina, and in the process challenged local segregation practices. After the clerk and store owner were unable to persuade the protestors to leave, police arrested the group. Despite conflict between the National Association for the Advancement of Colored People (NAACP) youth and adult members about how to proceed, a series of pickets and a boycott of Royal Ice Cream were launched. Ultimately, this did not spark further protest or lead to desegregation. Several years later, in 1963, students organized a boycott of sixteen downtown stores. To maximize economic leverage, the boycott demanding that stores hire at least two Black employees in nonmenial jobs was scheduled around the Easter holiday. In some of the largest protest events in Durham, thousands marched and gathered outside businesses. After three days of large-scale protest and mass arrests in early May, city officials and business leaders began to respond. The mayor established the interracial Durham Interim Committee (DIC) to find a long-term resolution to the issue of segregation. By July, the committee had reached agreements with "90 percent of restaurants, all eleven motels and the one hotel in Durham" to desegregate (Greene 2005, 95).

As we detail in this chapter, the civil rights struggle in Durham was punctuated by moments of heightened protest, repression, negotiations, and concessions. These brief episodes often transformed the local arena of struggle and shaped subsequent episodes of movement activity and its consequences. This episodic quality was repeated in desegregation campaigns across the South and illustrates central characteristics of social movements:

the co-occurrence of multiple, overlapping conflicts and the uneven distribution of movement activity over time.

The civil rights movement was constituted by episodes similar to those just described, across numerous cities, as many individuals and organizations were drawn into escalating spirals of conflict. This conception differs from conventional historical accounts that characterize the civil rights movement as a singular struggle orchestrated by a small number of organizations and leaders in "chess-like fashion" (McAdam 1983, 735). In that tradition, many social scientists study how the movement as a whole contributed to federal policy changes (Burstein 1985, 1993; Jenkins, Jacobs, and Agnone 2003; Meyer and Minkoff 2004; Olzak and Ryo 2007; Santoro 2002). In contrast to this narrative, our approach understands the civil rights movement as more fragmented, comprising a "movement of movements" with competing goals, purposes, strategies, organizations, and leaders (Isaac 2008, 34; see also Luders 2010; McAdam 1982; Morris 1984).

Protest episodes merit greater theoretical and empirical attention to understand their emergence, dynamics, and consequences. But scholars routinely study events, organizations, and participants outside the context in which events occur and actors mobilize. Further, we contend that the study of movements and conflict more broadly can benefit from conceptualizing and studying protest episodes systematically. In this chapter, we demonstrate the viability of documenting protest episodes, and we show that this approach can generate new insights into basic conflict processes such as escalation, repression, and impact. As defined here, protest episodes are more delimited than what we typically mean by social movements.[1] We define an episode as a period of sustained conflict, combining the interactions with targets and other actors in the form of repression, negotiation, and/or concession. Episodes can be differentiated from discrete events as well as slower-moving processes such as building movement organizations or engaging in longer-running legal challenges.

An episode is identified primarily by its sustained nature. Episodes may be set in motion by coordinated protest campaigns, but episodes may also escalate without significant prior planning. For example, activists may initiate protest that emulates protest occurring nearby or in a response to routine politics such as a court decision or electoral outcome. As movement-related events take place, they may either be punctuated and isolated in time from prior or subsequent events or spur or interact with a series of related actions. We define the latter as episodes when they entail several weeks of collective action involving movement and nonmovement actors. Episodes may end in various ways, including through repression, the intervention of third parties, factionalism, exhaustion among movement participants, and the accomplishment of movement goals.

We argue that movements are constituted by the occurrence of many episodes spanning broad territories over longer time periods. One obstacle for incorporating an episode-centered perspective into the study of social movements is the lack of clear research strategies, a gap we attempt to address here. This approach requires a methodological shift from event-based analysis to a study focused on moments of heightened activity and contention set in social contexts. In many cases, this involves a focus on local episodes and the co-occurrence of these episodes so that they become larger waves of mobilization that may spread across regions and countries and may shift to national and transnational arenas.

The targets of protest and movement claims shape the context within which episodes occur, because they are tied to larger arenas. Here, we borrow from James Jasper's conception of arenas as "bundles of rules and resources that allow or encourage certain kinds of interactions to proceed, with something at stake" (2015, 14). In the Durham case, targets shift between the school system and courts, local merchants, and the mayor, moving across arenas that have different logics for interacting with movements.

This theoretical and methodological approach allows us to advance our understanding of the civil rights movement by contextualizing events into their broader spatial and temporal settings. In this chapter, we develop a theoretical framework for analyzing movements as sequences and clusters of episodes. Then we identify the major methodological implications flowing from this conceptualization—contrasting it to alternative approaches to studying protest and conflict. Finally, we present a case study of local activism in Durham, North Carolina, to illustrate central insights that emerge from this approach.

Protest Episodes and Impact

Using comparative analysis of protest episodes provides an important and underutilized strategy for examining social movements. As periods of sustained mobilization, episodes are the moments when social movements become most visible to both the public and their targets. Episodes may emerge from and often transform what has been referred to as "mobilizing structures," "local movement centers," or "social movement communities" (Tarrow 1998, 123; Morris 1984, 40; Staggenborg 1998). In doing so, episodes drive and may transform the trajectory of social movement activities and actors.

Social change often takes place during periods of heightened mobilization in which numerous episodes emerge in close temporal proximity (Almeida 2003; McAdam 1983; McAdam and Sewell 2001; Tarrow 1998). During episodes, movement groups are often better able to elicit responses from states and other powerful actors, who are more inclined to respond to consistent and escalating demonstrations. The volatility of these episodes shapes the dynamics of movements as activists learn from and are inspired by one another through activist networks and movement organizations or by tracking the progress of episodes elsewhere through the mass media or informal networks (Andrews and Biggs 2006).

Studying episodes has theoretical and substantive benefits that allow us to focus on important dynamics such as escalation, repression, negotiation, and bargaining (McAdam, Tarrow, and Tilly 2001). Most research focuses on the way that exogenous factors, such as the political context or prior organization, influence the onset and dynamics of protest. However, critics point to cases where protest increases dramatically without evident changes in the broader context or organizational resources (Biggs 2005; Kurzman 1996). Similarly, others have long been puzzled by the fact that repression sometimes dampens and at other times escalates mobilization (Davenport 2007; Earl 2003). Movements may be vulnerable to repression at particular moments in their development, such as the initiation of activity or after sustained mobilization has yielded few concessions (Andrews 1997; Brockett 1993). Examining repression in the context of protest episodes, rather than examining the correlation between aggregate levels of protest and repression, allows one to observe how activists respond to threats, violence, or arrests. Finally, although movement impact has often been characterized as part of a bargaining process (Burstein, Einwohner, and Hollander 1995; Wilson 1961), most studies do not examine the interaction between movements and targets. Focusing on episodes allows scholars to closely observe potential mechanisms of influence to distinguish alternative pathways of influence such as threat or persuasion (Andrews 2001).

Studying Protest Episodes

Our theoretical understanding of movements is deeply linked to the methods and analytic techniques we use in our research. Several strategies have been used to study movements systematically, the most central being the construction of event data sets or "event catalogs" based on media reporting (Tilly 2002).[2] This innovation allowed for systematic comparisons over long time periods and across multiple societies, with the capability to analyze the data using powerful statistical modeling strategies.

Despite the benefits, a focus on episodes illustrates important limitations associated with event catalogs. The central problems stem from the aggregation of event data to standardized temporal and spatial units. In most analyses, scholars group discrete events to ask questions such as "Why do some years have more protest events than others?" This approach imposes strong assumptions about the possible causal factors driving protest. Moreover, aggregation fails to address the underlying spatial and temporal dependence in event data because events are nested in many distinct (and sometimes overlapping) episodes.

Although it is possible to use event data to trace the formation and dissolution of episodes, this requires shifting the way we analyze event catalogs to the relationships that connect events as sequences of interaction. Even if we can construct the spatial and temporal clustering of events in episodes, another significant challenge concerns the strategic linkages and interactions that constitute episodes because these processes are typically beyond the attention of news media, police, or others. The type of information that is reported in news media accounts of protest is not sensitive to links between events and actors.

Our account of Durham is drawn from a larger study in which we document the origins, development, and impact of local civil rights activity in approximately fifty cities in the U.S. South. Concentrating on the movement heyday from the mid-1950s to mid-1960s, we use historical accounts to examine the characteristics and behavior of major actors, events, and the broader community. We defined episodes as sustained collective action carried out over at least one month intended to end segregation in public facilities or institutions. Our decision to set a minimum time frame of one month was informed by our assessment of this case. While some cities experience only one episode of sustained contention, others—like Durham—experienced repeated episodes over this ten-year period. We also account for actors present in and across episodes. Protest includes sit-ins as well as picket lines, boycotts, marches, petitions, and demonstrations. Key actors include movement organizations, political authorities (local elected officials, law enforcement, etc.), allies, opponents, and economic actors that the movement interacts with or targets.

Our coding and analysis are relational in that the data structure allows for information to be linked across multiple tables (e.g., actors are linked to events at which they were present). Specifically, we document characteristics in tables at the city, episode, event, and actor levels. For instance, the 1963 demonstrations in Durham contain thirty-one distinct events that are each associated with a set of actors and organizations present at those events. With this relational approach, we capture variation within (and across) cities as well as within and across episodes, while maintaining detailed analyses of the events themselves. We also examine which actors are present at which events and across which episodes or cities.

The data for this project come from secondary historical accounts for a city, and we use Cristina Greene's *Our Separate Ways* (2005) for Durham.

The descriptions of the episodes are based on Greene's book; we rely on other secondary sources as well, as indicated in the narrative that follows. The coding process was completed by a single graduate assistant to ensure consistency and then entered into a relational Filemaker database primarily by undergraduate research assistants.

Our data and analysis of each city are based on three major components of the coding scheme: episodes, event, and actors (including individuals and organizations). *Episodes* represent the macrolevel of analysis, as they encapsulate multiple events that occur in periods of contention. *Events* include protest as well as meetings, arrests, court cases, speeches, press conferences, and so forth during the period from 1954 to 1964. *Actors* include the various individuals and groups that mobilized in support of civil rights and desegregation as well as those that responded to and challenged this activity. Several characteristics of actors are captured, such as their role in the case, and connections between actors were also recorded. For instance, the Howard Johnson hotel picket was followed shortly after by a statement from Howard Johnson's managerial staff announcing that they would not cave to pressure from protest. These distinct events are linked through common actors, in this case Howard Johnson's and its manager, Clarence Daniels. Both events are included in an episode that spanned the three months surrounding the 1963 protests targeting local businesses.

Durham and the Escalation of Civil Rights Politics

The challenge to segregation in Durham occurred across five episodes that shifted and changed as participation and targets expanded. We trace the broad contours of the Durham movement in terms of civil rights activity and the major actors. Table 5.1 summarizes the pattern of protest, repression, and negotiations through the 1950s and early 1960s by year. These summary data show the aggregate pattern of movement activity. We observe an initial burst of activity related to school desegregation following the *Brown v. Board of Education* decision in the mid-1950s. Beginning in 1960, we see increasing levels of movement activity, participation, and repression culminating in a major breakthrough in 1963. The detailed analysis of the episodes that follows illustrates three fundamental points. First, civil rights activity was punctuated around distinct episodes. Second, episodes changed in terms of targets, scale, and major actors in ways that reconfigured the arena of struggle in Durham. Targets expanded from schools to single restaurants and finally more broadly to public accommodations and employment. Finally, these shifts coevolved with growing protest and increased participation, generating increases in both repression and concessions to movement demands.

TABLE 5.1 EVENTS, PARTICIPATION, AND NEGOTIATIONS IN DURHAM, NORTH CAROLINA, 1955–1963

Year	Total events	Participants	Large events (500+)	Protest events	Events with arrests	Negotiations
1955	15	6,926	2	3	0	5
1956	9	226	0	0	0	7
1957	11	910	1	3	1	3
1958	9	170	0	1	0	3
1959	8	127	0	0	0	3
1960	29	2,627	2	4	0	16
1961	12	8,778	3	3	0	3
1962	18	7,366	6	6	1	4
1963	47	19,496	9	8	5	17

From 1954 to 1957, the targets of activism were connected to education, including schools, school boards, and other local political actors. There was some limited targeting of businesses in early efforts to create equality in hiring and achieve desegregation. For instance, in 1957, public accommodations were targeted through the Royal Ice Cream Parlor protests.

Although there were several larger events, there were no large demonstrations. Instead, the large events in this early period were mass meetings. In 1954, events were relatively small, with the exception of a one thousand–person Durham Committee on Negro Affairs (DCNA) meeting. In 1955, there were a few more events with hundreds of people present, but most were small throughout the late 1950s and early 1960s. By 1962, however, several events drew thousands of people.

With the onset of the sit-ins in 1960, businesses became the primary targets of collective action events, expanding from single settings like Royal Ice Cream and the local theater to lunch counters and expanding in 1961 to the downtown business sector. Targets were pushed to both desegregate and hire Black employees in nonmenial positions. In 1962, the efforts shifted to include simultaneous targeting of businesses and political institutions and actors, a strategy that would remain and eventually lead to major gains for the movement. By 1962 and 1963, several thousand activists were part of marches, pickets, and boycotts of downtown businesses. By focusing on episodes, we show that the desegregation campaign in Durham involved a small number of relatively brief moments of heightened conflicts. In addition, we see relatively little shifting of targets within episodes but significant change across episodes as protestors became increasingly bold in challenging local businesses, elected officials, and government agencies. In addition, we argue that this episode-centered approach is crucial for observing the cumulative effect of multiple episodes that eroded elite confidence in the ability to contain protest through sanctions or minimal accommodation.

The *Brown* Decision, Local Mobilization, and Institutional Politics

We describe key features of episodes chronologically beginning with the early mobilization surrounding school desegregation. Movement activity concerning schools and desegregation followed a path of institutional politics with mass participation limited to public hearings. These efforts led to some modest reforms, but the activity was contained within the educational arena and by broader state and federal policies.

The immediate response to *Brown* in Durham included collective efforts by many Black leaders and citizens to secure implementation. In 1954, the DCNA held a meeting at St. Joseph's AME Church with more than one thousand attending to endorse candidates for an upcoming election and discuss school desegregation plans. Similarly, the Black Parent-Teacher Association pressed for desegregation in Durham. In 1955 when the *Brown II* decision was released, pressure continued to mount from parents and community leaders. A petition with more than eight hundred signatures was presented to the Durham City Board of Education, who ignored calls for school desegregation. The North Carolina legislature responded to the *Brown* decision by passing the Pupil Assignment Act in 1955 and the Pearsall Plan in 1956 in efforts to resist school desegregation. These policies created legal obstacles to desegregation by turning over control of actions such as student transfers and enrollment to local school districts and providing legal support to whites to avoid attending integrated schools. The response in Durham and at the state level involved setting up numerous institutional barriers to desegregation.

Some predominantly white organizations did press for implementing desegregation. In 1955, the Durham–Chapel Hill chapter of the Women's International League for Peace and Freedom (WILPF) came out in opposition to the Pearsall Plan. WILPF also advocated for implementation of school desegregation beginning in 1957, supported NAACP litigation, and partnered with other groups to promote integration, including the American Friends Service Committee and the Interracial Fellowship for the Schools. Other organizations such as the American Association of University Women (AAUW) were involved but played lesser roles.

Despite these organized demands for change by parents, the Durham school board obstructed these efforts by failing to approve almost all requests for pupil reassignment and deflecting related demands for school desegregation. In 1959, the school board approved reassignment plans for 9 students while denying 165 others. The procedural and minimalist response produced little institutional change despite significant legal and grassroots organizing. In this way, Durham was typical of a more moderate path than in the Deep South or some rural districts where citizens' councils emerged and white elected officials led "massive resistance" (Bartley 1969; see also Andrews 2002; Miller 1976).

Protest Politics and Business Desegregation

In contrast to school desegregation, the efforts to desegregate businesses involved direct-action protest, mass arrests, and the formation of new channels for responding to movement demands. The Royal Ice Cream protest in 1957 provided a glimpse of this new model of mobilization, but it was quickly contained. Protest politics did not emerge fully in Durham and most of the South until 1960. Four major episodes occurred in 1960, 1961, 1962, and 1963, with each typically lasting a few months. We describe these episodes with a focus on how tactics, demands, participants, and the response by targets and authorities evolved.

Beginning in 1960, tactics were similar across the episodes, combining the occupation of public settings, picket lines, and marches. The core participants were college and sometimes high school students, but this base of participation grew over each successive episode. In addition, the range of participants expanded as well with greater levels of adult support for student-initiated protest. Through a process of escalation, demands became bolder while authorities employed a dual response of greater repression and engagement through negotiation and concessions.

1960: Sit-Ins

In contrast to the Royal Ice Cream protest, the 1960 sit-ins were sustained and involved large numbers of college students throughout the spring, leading to the desegregation of lunch counters in July 1960. On February 8, a week after the Greensboro sit-ins, students from North Carolina College launched sit-ins in Durham targeting three establishments: Woolworth, Kress, and Walgreen's. Initially, managers responded by closing their lunch counters, physically blocking access for protestors, or filling the lunch counters with white customers. Although no arrests were made at the initial sit-ins, police detained two of the white participants. Local adult leaders, Reverend Douglas Moore and Floyd McKissick, went to the police station and demanded to see them. On the second day, demonstrators were arrested for trespassing, and two stores were threatened with bombing if they ended segregation (Miller 1976).

Support from established adult organizations was swift. For example, the Black Ministerial Alliance met on the evening of February 8 and pledged its "moral, spiritual, and financial support" for the sit-ins (Greene 2005, 77). On February 16, Ralph Abernathy and Martin Luther King Jr. visited Durham to offer their support, and the DCNA endorsed the sit-ins soon after. Popular support continued to grow through February, and fifteen hundred people attended a mass meeting supporting the direct-action campaign.

On February 9, Mayor Emmanuel Evans pressed the Human Relations Committee, which had been established in 1959, to negotiate a settlement (Sindler 1965). As occurred in other cities, demonstrators suspended protests during negotiations. However, on February 23, lunch counters reopened on segregated terms and protestors responded by picketing several stores. As protests resumed, local white minister and chair of the Human Relations Committee Warren Carr brought together an estimated thirty Black and white leaders in an attempt to negotiate a solution. The Human Relations Committee continued to meet throughout the spring and pursued several efforts to bring about a resolution of the conflict (Sindler 1965).

Even though the core participants in the protest from North Carolina College left for the summer, the picketing and boycotts continued with rumors of expansion to other establishments. The durability of protests combined with successful desegregation in nearby cities resulted in desegregation of lunch counters at the three targeted establishments in July 1960 (Biggs and Andrews 2015).

1961: Boycott and Pickets for Black Employment

Protest reignited in spring 1961 with activists expanding beyond desegregation to fight for better job opportunities in retail establishments. In response to the claims by employers that there were no qualified Black applicants, nineteen women completed a sales training course at Hillside High. However, none were hired at downtown businesses, spurring grievances about employment discrimination.

Durham's NAACP youth chapters made a final appeal to local businesses before launching a boycott. Not surprisingly, employers refused to hire Black employees. Having anticipated this response, students were prepared and launched a major boycott, circulating the announcement through the Black community. The *Carolina Times* provided front-page coverage. Combining mass meetings and pickets, the students maintained a disciplined focus on sustaining protest until each targeted store hired at least one Black person in a nonmenial position. In under two months, the protest helped secure employment of more than fifty Black people at twenty-three different establishments.

1962: Expansion and Escalation of Protest

In the summer of 1962, protestors focused on the desegregation of businesses beyond lunch counters to restaurants and other retail establishments. Overall there were few arrests at the protests during this episode. However, those that occurred garnered significant attention. There were only two instances of negotiations between movement leaders and city officials, which concerned the release of jailed protestors. The NAACP and Congress of Racial Equality (CORE) played central leadership roles. As in the prior two episodes, college students led the way with some additional involvement by high school students. Despite the organization of large mass meetings and protest events with thousands participating, the episode did not culminate in the establishment of new channels of negotiation or successful outcomes.

Seeing insufficient progress, activists with CORE and the NAACP launched protests at several establishments, including Howard Johnson's and the Eckerd drug store. This phase of protest was linked to CORE's "Freedom Highways" campaign that targeted segregation in establishments along interstate travel routes. During a "stand-in" at the Howard Johnson's, several youth protestors were arrested and received jail sentences following their decision not to pay fines for trespassing. As part of their thirty-day sentences, men were forced to work on road gangs, and the women were forced to work as maids. Joycelyn McKissick, daughter of Floyd McKissick and one of the first students to integrate public schools in Durham, was one of the students arrested. Dissatisfied with the response from authorities, supporters of the students' efforts gathered at the jail, singing songs.

Howard Johnson's became a primary target for mass protest that escalated because the Durham manager resisted movement demands. Responding to the arrests and growing support, Roy Wilkins, NAACP executive director, and James Farmer, national chairman for CORE, both came to Durham to speak at a mass rally. Following the rally, fifteen Blacks demonstrated at the Howard Johnson's, the site of prior arrests. Mass meetings and protests continued, including a freedom rally the following week with one thousand participants. At the close of the rally, five hundred demonstrators traveled to Howard Johnson's again to confront the store manager, Clarence Daniels.

Unlike the prior two episodes, movement activity dissipated in 1962 without any significant concessions from targets. Student leaders—Joycelyn

McKissick and Guytana Horton—were released from jail early and returned to the Howard Johnson's where they had been arrested. Clarence Daniels once again blocked the entrance and insulted the women, using racial epithets, but mass protests would not resume until the following spring.

1963 Demonstrations: April–July

Throughout the spring and summer of 1963, massive protest campaigns occurred across the South. In Durham, this episode marked the high point of local conflict and culminated in major breakthroughs for desegregation. The episode started by using the same strategy used in 1961 with a boycott in March coinciding with the Easter shopping season. The central demand was that each store hire two Black employees in sales or other nontraditional jobs, and eleven stores conceded to the movement's demand.

The major surge of protest began on Saturday, May 18, initiating three days of mass action. As part of the largest mass demonstrations in the city's history, the protests began when several hundred demonstrators marched from North Carolina College to downtown. The first day of protest ended with 130 demonstrators arrested followed by 400 more the next day (Miller 1976, 60).

The protests coincided with a significant political transition. Wense Grabarek had been recently elected but would not take office until the following Monday. However, Emmanuel Evans, the current mayor, had left town. Grabarek had benefited from the support of Black voters and the DCNA. Although Grabarek would not technically be mayor until Monday, the police chief turned to him to help resolve the conflict. Grabarek met with Hugh Thompson, the NAACP attorney who represented the Royal Ice Cream protestors in 1957.

The next day, the protest culminated in thousands gathered for a major demonstration at the Howard Johnson's. As they had the year before, CORE's James Farmer and the NAACP's Roy Wilkins spoke to a large crowd at St. Joseph's. Simultaneously, organizers were announcing the Howard Johnson's protest at churches throughout Durham. The protest at Howard Johnson's escalated with hundreds of students conducting a sit-down strike in the restaurant parking lot followed by more than seven hundred arrests. Students sang freedom songs and refused to disperse despite police threats to teargas the protestors. Later that day another confrontation developed. Quinton Baker organized North Carolina College students to march downtown in a show of support for the students who had been arrested. Meanwhile, large crowds of whites assembled, and the threat of violence loomed as fights broke out.

In an important expansion of movement targets, activists presented demands to the City Council on Monday morning, May 20, and later led a march to City Hall shortly after Grabarek had been sworn into office. Again, the threat of violence emerged as crowds of whites assembled downtown to taunt Black demonstrators. Police clashed with demonstrators at the Holiday Inn and arrested additional students, bringing the total for the three days to fourteen hundred.

On the same day that he took office, Grabarek met with student leaders. The following day he spoke at St. Joseph's AME Church, stating to the crowd of one thousand that "the demonstrations . . . have accomplished their intended purpose to the extent of alerting the entire city of seriousness and sincerity which the Negro attaches to them" (Greene 2005, 93). The next day Grabarek established the DIC and tasked it with developing a workable solution. The eleven-member committee did not include movement leaders, but it did include two Black business leaders, John Wheeler and Asa Spaulding. Wheeler coordinated closely with a leadership group of the protest movement led by Floyd McKissick and Joyce Ware. By July, the DIC had secured the desegregation of an estimated 90 percent of restaurants, all motels, and one hotel and further commitments from the city. The structure of the committee provided distance from the movements and its leaders, but the committee worked under the clear understanding that protest would resume if desegregation was not secured.

Leaders and Organizations in the Durham Movement

Here we examine the organization and leaders central to the events in Durham, building on the prior description of civil rights activity in Durham. Organizations and leaders tended to gain central roles in the movement through their ongoing involvement in the civic, political, and economic life of the Black community. However, protest episodes led to significant reorganization of this leadership structure, and established leaders and organizations were displaced because of their reluctance to embrace protest politics (Burgess 1962; Lomax 1960; Salamon 1973). At the same time, we observed substantial continuity across protest episodes in terms of the central leaders associated with protest and direct challenges to segregation. This observation opens up new questions regarding the ways that leaders gain and lose standing in the context of protest episodes (Eschen, Kirk, and Pinard 1971). Among civil rights organizations, there were several critical changes, including the increased centrality of the NAACP, the displacement of the DCNA, and the greater participation of student organizations.

The DCNA, founded in the 1930s, was the most prominent civil rights organization in the mid-1950s. Led by influential members of the Black business community, the DCNA played a central role in school desegregation and endorsed political candidates who supported desegregation. The organization was a major player in efforts to reject the school board's approach to busing and push for full desegregation. The DCNA also joined with other organizations to petition the school board. However, when the focus of desegregation in Durham shifted from schools to public accommodations, the DCNA fell out of favor, receiving criticism from the NAACP for refusing to publicly support a campaign to desegregate theaters in 1958.

Throughout this period, the NAACP supported school desegregation efforts while working toward desegregation of public accommodations. For instance, in 1957, the NAACP, especially student members, led pickets outside the Royal Ice Cream Parlor. They also pushed for equal employment as early as 1956, launching a campaign that built support and led to the creation of an employment agency. In 1958, the NAACP sued the Durham school board for discriminatory policies. However, these early efforts did not produce any substantive changes. Along with the DCNA, the NAACP rejected the school board plan for desegregation and pushed for full desegregation of schools, helping with the school board petition. The NAACP Youth Council even formed a scholarship to help low-income girls who desegregated Durham High School. Although youth in the organization wanted adults to take a more militant approach to desegregation, adults focused in 1960 on voter registration. However, by 1961, the NAACP supported youth in their efforts to implement nondiscriminatory hiring practices and supported the call for store boycotts.

Although the NAACP remained the primary organization driving desegregation activity in Durham, in 1962 a local chapter of CORE formed and worked alongside the NAACP through 1963. Together, the organizations set up pickets outside the Howard Johnson's and Eckerd drug store, pushing both to fully desegregate by hiring Black employees. The NAACP also responded quickly to emerging issues. For example, in 1963 it supported the boycott of the East End School, and NAACP members helped establish tutoring services for students who were part of the boycott. As a result of NAACP efforts in many areas and the early groundwork laid by many others, several gains were made, including a court-mandated plan for school desegregation.

Although there were thousands of participants and numerous individual leaders, many appeared at one or two events and did not occupy central leadership roles in the movement. However, there were several local actors at the time who participated in many events and became key players in the fight for desegregation. The three most prominent were Floyd McKissick and his daughter Joycelyn and Reverend Douglas Moore. During this period, established leaders associated with the DCNA such as Asa Spaulding were displaced by emerging leaders.

Floyd McKissick became a part of the movement to desegregate Durham in May 1956. By the next year, he had emerged as a central actor in the movement. He was involved in significantly more events than any other activist in Durham, including early boycotts of public accommodations, and continued through 1963. McKissick was primarily connected to other local activists, such as Nathan White Sr. and Vivian McCoy, and to activists at the national level, such as James Farmer. Affiliated with the DCNA, McKissick was a more visible leader of the NAACP and collaborated with CORE. In the 1960s, McKissick developed a cooperative relationship with the Black Muslims, which led to member protection for protestors by the Fruit of Islam in 1963. Floyd McKissick helped organize protests, guiding the progress of the movement. He was a major driver of the increased pressure put forth by the movement through direct action.

In 1960, Floyd McKissick's wife, Evelyn, brought her daughter Joycelyn into the movement when she along with another local family pursued legal action against the school board on their daughter's behalf. Joycelyn was threatened and abused as she began attending a formerly all-white school in 1960. Joycelyn joined local desegregation efforts in 1962 and helped organize a visit by Malcom X in 1963 to speak in Durham (for which she was suspended from school). She was later arrested during a stand-in at the Howard Johnson's in 1963. Joycelyn was involved in almost as many events as her father during the course of the desegregation efforts in Durham and was primarily connected to other youth activists.

Reverend Douglas Moore played a crucial link between early activism in the 1950s and the sit-in movement and led students who sat-in at the Royal Ice Cream Parlor in 1957. More important, Moore played a central in the 1960 sit-ins and also helped establish connections between local activists and Martin Luther King's Southern Leadership Conference and CORE.

For a short period during 1963, Wense Grabarek had numerous critical interactions with the movement when he was elected mayor that year. Although supportive in many ways, Grabarek desired an end to the protests and direct action, and, after he called for the cessation of protests at a mass meeting, protestors agreed to break from demonstrations to negotiate in 1963. He was supportive of the DCNA and negotiated with protestors, helping the movement gain concessions. He met with movement members, particularly youth leaders, and asked authorities to offer several concessions.

Conclusion

Protest and the responses to it coevolved over multiple episodes (Oliver and Myers 2003). Unlike what occurred in some parts of the South, white elites were prepared to negotiate with leaders in the Black community. At the same time, there was also a strong pattern of protest repression from the police and from the white community more broadly. Both forms of response were present throughout the entire period and peaked in 1963 in response to the massive level of movement support. In fact, negotiation and repression escalated in tandem with movement activity.

Over time these episodes shifted from the more institutional forms of activity directed toward schools in the 1950s to the focus on selected businesses to the broader business community and political institutions by 1963. This shift marked a further transition in the organizational composition of the movement with leaders willing to embrace a more militant style of activism and the emergence of students and a new cadre of adult leaders.

Using the case of civil rights movement in Durham, North Carolina, we highlight the episodic character of civil rights activity. The larger civil rights movement comprised multiple moments of intensive interaction between activists, opponents, targets, and bystanders followed by lengthier periods of relative quiescence. In Durham, these episodes took the form of a ratchet-like response with the scope of movement demands and participation escalating at each stage. The breakthrough in 1963 was itself the product of these prior rounds of conflict, convincing elites that a cooling-off period was unlikely to undercut support. We expect that other cities followed different trajectories. For example, early episodes were met with far-reaching repression in some cities that stymied subsequent mobilization. In some cities, episodes depended more heavily on external support. We expect the real payoff of focusing on episodes to emerge from comparative analyses showing how sequencing of episodes varies across time and location.

This case study of desegregation in Durham illustrates our larger argument about the importance of conceptualizing and studying events as connected and clustered in periods of heightened contention rather than as independent or amenable to simple aggregation. Protest event catalogs have allowed scholars to document and explain the ebb and flow of activism. Building on this tradition, we argue that tracing the sequencing and clustering of movement activity in episodes holds similar promise to deepen our understanding of the central dynamics of social movements.

NOTES

1. At a theoretical level, Doug McAdam, Sidney Tarrow, and Charles Tilly define episodes in a way similar to ours, as "continuous streams of contention including collective claims making that bears on other parties' interests" (2001, 24). In practice, though, they consider broad social movements as episodes. So the civil rights movement is an episode in their analysis; other episodes in their analysis include Spanish democratization and antiapartheid mobilization in South Africa from 1980 to 1995. Operationalized this way, the idea of episodes loses its analytic focus on interaction, sequences, and contingency.

2. Perhaps the most enduring strategy is the case study. In addition, scholars have employed in-depth interviews, individual surveys, and organizational surveys to pursue wide-ranging questions.

REFERENCES

Almeida, Paul D. 2003. "Opportunity Organizations and Threat-Induced Contention: Protest Waves in Authoritarian Settings." *American Journal of Sociology* 109 (2): 345–400.

Andrews, Kenneth T. 1997. "The Impacts of Social Movements on the Political Process: The Civil Rights Movement and Black Electoral Politics in Mississippi." *American Sociological Review* 62 (5): 800–819.

———. 2001. "Social Movements and Policy Implementation: The Mississippi Civil Rights Movement and the War on Poverty, 1965–1971." *American Sociological Review* 66 (1): 71–95.

———. 2002. "Movement-Countermovement Dynamics and the Emergence of New Institutions: The Case of 'White Flight' Schools in Mississippi." *Social Forces* 80 (3): 911–936.

Andrews, Kenneth T., and Michael Biggs. 2006. "The Dynamics of Protest Diffusion: Movement Organizations, Social Networks, and News Media in the 1960 Sit-Ins." *American Sociological Review* 71 (5): 752–777.

Bartley, Numan V. 1969. *The Rise of Massive Resistance: Race and Politics in the South during the 1950's*. Baton Rouge: Louisiana State University Press.

Biggs, Michael. 2005. "Strikes as Forest Fires: Chicago and Paris in the Late 19th Century." *American Journal of Sociology* 110 (6): 1684–1714.

Biggs, Michael, and Kenneth T. Andrews. 2015. "Protest Campaigns and Movement Success Desegregating the US South in the Early 1960s." *American Sociological Review* 80 (2): 416–443.

Brockett, Charles. 1993. "A Protest Cycle Resolution of the Repression/Popular-Protest Paradox." *Social Science History* 17 (3): 457–484.

Burgess, M. Elaine. 1962. *Negro Leadership in a Southern City*. Chapel Hill: University of North Carolina Press.

Burstein, Paul. 1985. *Discrimination, Jobs, and Politics: The Struggle for Equal Employment Opportunity in the United States since the New Deal*. Chicago: University of Chicago Press.

———. 1993. "Explaining State Action and the Expansion of Civil Rights: The Civil Rights Act of 1964." *Research in Political Sociology* 6:117–137.

Burstein, Paul, Rachel Einwohner, and Jocellyn Hollander. 1995. "The Success of Social Movements: A Bargaining Perspective." In *The Politics of Social Protest*, edited by J. Craig Jenkins and Bert Klandermans, 275–295. Minneapolis: University of Minnesota Press.

Davenport, Christian. 2007. "State Repression and Political Order." *Annual Review of Political Science* 10:1–23.

Earl, Jennifer. 2003. "Tanks, Tear Gas, and Taxes: Toward a Theory of Movement Repression." *Theory and Society* 21 (1): 44–68.

Eschen, Donald Von, Jerome Kirk, and Maurice Pinard. 1971. "The Organizational Substructure of Disorderly Politics." *Social Forces* 49 (4): 529–544.

Greene, Christina. 2005. *Our Separate Ways: Women and the Black Freedom Movement in Durham, North Carolina*. Chapel Hill: University of North Carolina Press.

Isaac, Larry. 2008. "Movement of Movements: Culture Moves in the Long Civil Rights Struggle." *Social Forces* 87 (1): 33–63.

Jasper, James M. 2015. "Introduction: Playing the Game." In *Players and Arenas: The Interactive Dynamics of Protest*, edited by James M. Jasper and Jan Willem Duyvendak, 9–32. Amsterdam: Amsterdam University Press.

Jenkins, J. Craig, David Jacobs, and Jon Agnone. 2003. "Political Opportunities and African-American Protest, 1948-1997." *American Journal of Sociology* 109 (2): 277-303.

Kurzman, Charles. 1996. "Structural Opportunity and Perceived Opportunity in Social-Movement Theory: The Iranian Revolution of 1979." *American Sociological Review* 61 (1): 153-170.

Lomax, Louis E. 1960. "The Negro Revolt against 'the Negro Leaders.'" *Harper's*, June, pp. 41-48.

Luders, Joseph E. 2010. *The Civil Rights Movement and the Logic of Social Change*. New York: Cambridge University Press.

McAdam, Doug. 1982. *Political Process and the Development of Black Insurgency*. Chicago: University of Chicago Press.

———. 1983. "Tactical Innovation and the Pace of Insurgency." *American Sociological Review* 48 (6): 735-754.

McAdam, Doug, and William H. Sewell Jr. 2001. "It's about Time: Temporality in the Study of Social Movements and Revolutions." In *Silence and Voice in the Study of Contentious Politics*, edited by Ron R. Aminzade, Jack A. Goldstone, Doug McAdam, Elizabeth J. Perry, William H. Sewell Jr., Sidney Tarrow, and Charles Tilly, 89-125. Cambridge: Cambridge University Press.

McAdam, Doug, Sidney Tarrow, and Charles Tilly. 2001. *Dynamics of Contention*. Cambridge: Cambridge University Press.

Meyer, David S., and Debra C. Minkoff. 2004. "Conceptualizing Political Opportunity." *Social Forces* 82 (4): 1457-1492.

Miller, Arthur M. 1976. "Desegregation and Negro Leadership in Durham, North Carolina, 1954-1963." Master's thesis, University of North Carolina at Chapel Hill.

Morris, Aldon. 1984. *The Origins of the Civil Rights Movement: Black Communities Organizing for Change*. New York: Free Press.

Oliver, Pamela, and Daniel Myers. 2003. "The Coevolution of Social Movements." *Mobilization: An International Quarterly* 8 (1): 1-24.

Olzak, Susan, and Emily Ryo. 2007. "Organizational Diversity, Vitality and Outcomes in the Civil Rights Movement." *Social Forces* 85 (4): 1561-1591.

Salamon, Lester M. 1973. "Leadership and Modernization: The Emerging Black Political Elite in the American South." *Journal of Politics* 35 (3): 615-646.

Santoro, Wayne A. 2002. "The Civil Rights Movement's Struggle for Fair Employment: A 'Dramatic Events-Conventional Politics' Model." *Social Forces* 81 (1): 177-206.

Sindler, Allan P. 1965. *Negro Protest and Local Politics in Durham, N.C.* New York: McGraw-Hill.

Staggenborg, Suzanne. 1998. "Social Movement Communities and Cycles of Protest: The Emergence and Maintenance of a Local Women's Movement." *Social Problems* 45 (2): 180-204.

Tarrow, Sidney. 1998. *Power in Movement: Social Movements, Collective Action and Mass Politics in the Modern State*. Cambridge: Cambridge University Press.

Tilly, Charles. 2002. "Event Catalogs as Theories." *Sociological Theory* 20 (2): 248-254.

Wilson, James Q. 1961. "The Strategy of Protest." *Journal of Conflict Resolution* 5:291-303.

PART III

Outcomes of Interactions

6

How Targets Influence the Influence of Movements

An Institutional Mediation Approach

Edwin Amenta and Nicole Shortt

Movements seek social change and target many institutions—mainly states (Amenta et al. 2010) but also the news media (Ferree et al. 2002; Sobieraj 2011), businesses (Soule 2009; King 2008), political parties (Halfmann 2011; Heaney and Rojas 2015), religious organizations (Katzenstein 1999; Kniss and Burns 2004), and universities (Arthur 2011; Rojas 2006; Moore 2008). Social movement scholars often refer to attempts to influence the various processes and outputs of these targeted institutions as potential external consequences of social movements. For these processes and results are not under the direct control of movement actors in the way that choosing appeals to supporters, strategies of influence, or press releases and websites are. But transforming movements from an object of explanation to a potential explanation for the processes and outcomes of targeted institutions changes everything about how movement scholars need to think and poses several problems for scholarship (Amenta 2014).

Probably the largest one is that movements are usually defined as representing those with little political and social power. For that reason, it seems likely that their causal influence on the processes and outcomes of institutional targets will also usually be low. Although until recently most movement scholars would have agreed with Frances Fox Piven (2006) that movements have been prominent in much political change, many scholars confronting this question, including Theda Skocpol (2003) and Marco Giugni (2007), are highly skeptical of movement influence. Scholars who follow political processes often argue that public policy, for instance, typically follows the preferences of the rich, powerful, and well organized (Hacker and Pierson 2010; Gilens and Page 2014). And sometimes movement activity backfires, leaving a movement's constituents worse off than beforehand. Doug McAdam and Karina Kloos (2014) have identified backfiring political consequences of 1960s movements, and Jennifer Earl, Sarah Soule, and John McCarthy (2003) have documented negative unintended consequences of movements on protest policing. Moreover, movements target many institutions. Yet these institutions have influences different from those of political institutions. A strategy or type of organization that proved influential for one movement regarding one institution at one moment should not be expected to be influential for a different institution or the same institution at a different time.

So studying the potential influence of movements on their targeted institutions calls for new approaches. Doug McAdam and Hilary Boudet (2012) notably called for removing social movements from the center of analyses—sound advice when social movement factors are one potential influence, among many, over institutions. Two recent scholars have already run with this recommendation. Joseph Luders (2010) places movement targets at the center of his model, applying cost-benefit analyses to those that might grant movements concessions. James Jasper's "players-and-arenas" (2015) model treats targeted institutions as important actors with their own goals and strategies. Both have advantages in taking the point of view of those actors, organizations, and institutions movement actors seek to influence.

However, we argue that scholars need to go further and adopt approaches that begin with the institutions and organizations that movements seek to influence and to theorize the potential influence of movements from there. This is the basic approach of political mediation models that theorize the influence of movements over political institutions, processes, and policy outcomes (Amenta 2006; Giugni 2007). This outside-in and target-centered approach, which might be called *institutional mediation*, requires making sense first of the standard determinants of these institutional processes and outcomes. From there scholars should theorize how movements might influence these causal processes or combine with them to yield influence. Such mediation approaches have begun to be employed regarding institutions other than political ones, including corporations, universities, and the news media (King 2008; Arthur 2011; Amenta et al. 2019). But instead of creating a new movement-related set of concepts, this mode of analysis implies immersing oneself in social science literatures outside the one surrounding social movements and then theorizing the influence of movements. Before addressing how mediation models might be applied to institutions, we discuss alternative approaches to addressing the influence of movements on targeted institutions.

Approaches to Addressing the Influence
of Movements on Institutions

The literature on the influence of movements on institutions began in a way that was deeply movement centered, focusing on the characteristics or strategies of organizations posited to advance the fortunes of movements. William Gamson's *Strategy of Social Protest* (1990) randomly sampled U.S. movement organizations over a long historical period to determine which forms of organization and strategies were most effective in winning advantages and gaining acceptance. Later research followed in Gamson's footsteps, reinforcing the movement-centered approach. This scholarship was mainly quantitative and sought to demonstrate that in some specific instance a movement, through its membership, resources, or protest, was significantly influential on a political outcome of interest in a statistical sense (Amenta et al. 2010; Uba 2009). Starting from the famous resource mobilization model of John McCarthy and Mayer Zald (1977), the best of these accounts highlighted what makes movement organizations more resourceful and better able to match strategies to political situations, often with a sophisticated view of politics (e.g., Andrews 2001, 2004).

However, problems in this line of research remained. Given the large number and wide variety of organizations in the Gamson study, there was no way to account for the influence of other organizations, including non-movement ones, or the political or other contexts of contention on movement-relevant results. And searching for successful strategies without regard to contexts seemed on its face unhelpful. Why would strategies that worked for the United Auto Workers also pay off for the American Committee for the Outlawry of War? More generally, organizations good at generating resources might not be good at strategies of influence, and framing that draws supporters might not move institutional targets. Indeed, often the opposite is true, as research has shown (see review in Amenta et al. 2010). And the sorts of political contexts that spur mobilization, such as right-wing regimes attacking labor rights or pensions, are not the most susceptible to positive change on movement-related policies.

Other approaches addressing the influence of movements on targets of interest crafted arguments that combined different aspects of movements and the political contexts they engage. Frances Fox Piven and Richard Cloward (1977) famously argued that disruptive collective action by poor people would induce concessions in public spending, but only in times of electoral instability. Skocpol (1992) argued that mass-based U.S. interest organizations had to gain a wide geographic presence to influence a district-based Congress; at the turn of the twentieth century veterans' organizations had done so, but organized labor had not. Since then, articles have made and tested claims that movement protest will work best mainly at the agenda-setting stage of the policy process (McAdam and Su 2002; Olzak and Soule 2009). And one of us (Amenta 2006) offered a political mediation model that predicted advances in movement-relevant policies that depended on the joint occurrence of movement mobilization, specific strategies, and favorable political contexts. In addition, the mediation model leaned on the policy-making literature to argue that there would be other, non-movement-related routes to change in policies that were relevant to movements' constituents.

The best of recent books on the institutional targets of movements follow these leads. They track movement-related issues over long periods of time and focus on all their determinants, not just movement-related ones. For instance, Anthony Chen (2009) addresses the causes behind U.S. equal employment opportunity policies—an issue central to African American civil rights—and Drew Halfmann (2011) addresses the determinants of abortion policy, which is a focus of abortion rights, antiabortion, feminist, and Christian right movements. Both scholars address the influence of movements on these policies but do not stop there—given that movements are only partially influential. The difference between the approach of the movement-centered articles and the policy-centered books is similar to the differences between quantitative and qualitative work identified by James Mahoney and Gary Goertz as the "effects of causes" and the "causes of effects" (2006, 230). The article writers want to identify and isolate the influence of movements, whereas the book writers, often with historical institutionalist approaches (Pierson and Skocpol 2002), want to know what accounts for important changes in movement-relevant policies, regardless of how influential movements might be.

Because movements are not always central to the relevant outcomes and processes in the institutions that they target, scholars have sought to remove movements from the center of their analyses. Doing that is a key prescription of McAdam and Boudet's *Putting Social Movements in Their Place* (2012), a study that addresses the causes and consequences of mobilizations in communities contesting fracking. They call a shift in attention away from movements to key state and economic actors a "Copernican revolution," but how exactly should this revolution be carried out?

Two Reports from the Front Lines
of the Copernican Revolution

One way is outlined by Luders (2010), who updates Michael Lipsky's (1968) classic model of protestors, protest leaders, third parties, and targets in an analysis of the influence of the civil rights movement (see also Wilson 1961). According to Lipsky, protest by disadvantaged groups typically works indirectly—and rarely. When successful, protest will draw the attention of the news media, which will accurately and sympathetically describe the protestors' demands. In turn, this attention will activate third parties with some leverage over the target, such as customers of businesses or supporters of politicians. These third parties will in turn withhold things of value to the targets, such as business or votes, and the targets will then concede to the protestors. Of course, the media might not cover the protest or publish the demands, and even if they were to do so, third parties might ignore them. And even if third parties were to act, the targets might concede something insignificant, simply to get back into the good graces of the third parties. Because so many things have to go right for the protestors to gain real concessions, Lipsky did not see protest as a highly valuable political resource.

Instead of concentrating on protest, however, Luders focuses on what movements can do to influence third parties and targets directly. Specifically, he argues that both respond to costs that can be imposed on them by movement actors and that they act according to the balance of the costs imposed on them. These include the "disruption costs"—the costs that movements would impose on them for resisting movement demands. However, there are also costs that would be incurred by giving in to movements—"concession costs" (Luders 2010, 3–4). In the civil rights movement of the 1960s, for instance, businesses that might lose boycotting African American patrons for failing to integrate might lose more racist white customers for doing so. So the target has to weigh the balance of costs. The model was built using businesses as the target, and he sees local businesses as especially susceptible to boycotts and picketing, which go beyond symbolic protest. But Luders's model also applies to other institutional targets, including political ones, with movement actors often able to impose electoral costs on political incumbents.

There are several advantages to this approach. Luders's wide focus draws important attention to a large field of contention. His focus on targets is valuable in that it can be applied to any number of institutions and actors within them. It also forces scholars to think of the constituencies of those institutional actors, the nonmovement actors that might have influence over them and processes in which they are engaged, what they care about, and how movements might influence all that. Although he refers to "disruption" costs, Luders is attentive to different lines of action that go beyond disruptive protest and that movements can employ to change the calculations of political actors. Luders shows that targets and third parties are often crucial to prospects of movement influence and that those who examine only the collective action of challengers do so at their study's peril. His model points scholars toward these important interactions.

All the same, Luders (2010) provides more of a heuristic model than a theoretical one that still looks at matters mainly from the movement's point of view and drops a lot of conceptual information in the process. The model indicates that targets will mainly concede or not, depending on the balance of their cost calculations, but does not identify what accounts for why costs are increased or lowered. For instance, targeting sitting legislators for electoral removal can increase "disruption" costs, but the account does not indicate which approaches are most effective in doing so and for which type of movements. A change in public opinion in favor of the movement's goal or a decrease in the issue's salience lowers what Luders refers to as concession costs but does not explain the conditions under which movements can change public opinion. Also, it flattens out all the various influences by movements and their various targets through the cost metric. Not every influence is a cost. It seems better to say that public opinion may influence policy makers than to say that it may turn into a cost for them.

Jasper (2015) conceptualizes movements and the institutions they seek to influence as a variety of "players and arenas," each with their own set of aspirations and idiosyncrasies, interacting complexly. This model has already been described in the Introduction to this book, but we should point out some advantages of the players-and-arenas approach. It takes movements out of the center of the discussion but does not remove them completely. It addresses interactions between movements and the various institutions and actors that they seek to influence and does not reduce these institutions and actors simply to generic "targets," taking them seriously in their own right. It provides a lively set of metaphors that can be applied to contests that might be won or lost or never happen at all. A version of the players-and-arenas model has already been used in scholarship on movements in their bids to influence news media. Notably, Myra Marx Ferree and colleagues (2002) posit a series of public discourse forums, which constitute the public sphere, with the mass news media at its center. In their heuristic model, the news media constitute a master forum and a major site of political contestation, an arena in which various players seek to make gains in public debates and discursive contests.

Yet the players-and-arenas model also has problems. One is that the language of players suggests that there is a basic equality among them, which glosses over power and access disparities. Not all actors seeking influence over the news media, for instance, are alike. The player metaphor better describes interactions between the news media and institutional political actors (Ferree et al. 2002), who receive far more courteous treatment than movement actors. By contrast, the news media mainly acts more like team owners and stadium security with regard to movement actors, making them mostly wannabe players. And journalists are more equal than others, as they are at once players and gatekeepers, purveyors of meaning and controllers of access to the forum (Amenta, Caren, and Tierney 2015). The arena metaphor is also only partially useful in depicting the interactions among journalists, institutional political actors, and movements. First, calling newspapers arenas is a stretch because only rarely do these actors physically enter newsrooms, in the way that they might walk into legislative chambers, courtrooms, or the White House. The only ones who routinely enter are the journalists, who, as noted, do not act mainly as players in the discursive outputs that are their articles and do not see themselves as players when they are acting that way. It is clear that power disparities matter when attempting to explain outcomes and processes of interest to movements, and this will be true with respect to other institutions.

Moreover, the players-and-arenas model does not address the specifics of different institutions and theorize them on their own or address previous theory and research on these various processes. This is a similar problem to the one surrounding political opportunity structure, which created a series of new and conceptually vague, political-ish concepts, all from the movement's point of view: the relative "openness or closure" of the institutionalized political system; the "stability or instability" of the broad set of "elite alignments" that typically undergird a polity; the presence or absence of "elite allies"; and the "state's capacity and propensity for repression" (McAdam 1996, 27; see also Tarrow 1996). Yet these movement-centered notions bore only distant relationships to well-established concepts in political sociology and political science and theoretical claims based on them. Afterward, critics, including some of the same scholars initially promoting these vague ideas, were bemoaning the fact that social movement scholarship failed to address standard concepts and influences in political science and sociology, including elections (McAdam and Tarrow 2010), public opinion (Burstein 2003), political parties (Goldstone 2003; Heaney and Rojas 2015), interest groups (Knoke 2001; Baumgartner and Mahoney 2005), and courts (McCammon and McGrath 2015)—all of which had causal literatures connected to the development of public policy and other political matters of interest to social movements (Amenta, Bonastia, and Caren 2001).

Similarly, there was a debate more than a generation ago in political science and sociology about referring to states as arenas. Most pluralists and many Marxists argued that states or governments were arenas in which either interest groups or classes struggled over governmental outputs (Skocpol 1985; Evans, Rueschemeyer, and Skocpol 1985). This debate ended with the rejection of the arena metaphor in favor of more sophisticated understandings of political institutions and state actors, based in part on long-standing political science and organizational theory.

Though valuable, the players-and-arenas model has problems similar to those of Luders's model: Both are mainly heuristic, too movement centered, and not closely enough engaged with relevant academic literatures regarding the institutions and actors movements seek to influence. The players-and-arenas model permits the discussion of various sorts of interactions movement actors might engage in but does not say much about how these interactions might or are likely to come out; nor does it address what the players and arenas tend to do when movement actors are not playing. It encourages a kind of flattening of all relevant institutions, organizations, and actors and a corresponding loss of ideas and information valuable to issues relevant to movements. It is not explanatory enough. There is a focus on strategic interaction, but little thought is expended on the constraints on such interactions. Anything that constrains these interactions is considered to be a structure, which is deemed to be a substandard explanation and a bad metaphor. Yet constraining social influences are not simply metaphors but are central to sociological thinking—they are why we are sociologists and not psychologists. Moreover, these constraints will vary systematically according to the various institutions and organizations movements seek to engage.

A Third Way: Institutional Mediation Models

We are proposing instead to apply the thinking behind political mediation models to institutions—an institutional mediation approach. Political mediation models take different forms (for discussions, see Amenta 2006; Amenta, Caren, and Olasky 2005; Giugni 2007; Amenta 2014). But at bottom they are theories of social movement influence through political institutions and processes and focus on public policy outcomes. Various scholars have made arguments about movement influence along political mediation lines by combining aspects of movements or their strategies and their political environment. These scholars include Piven and Cloward (1977) and Skocpol (1992), and their arguments contrast with explanations focused entirely on movements, such as Gamson's (1990). Each of these political mediation arguments theorized the influence on politics and policy of the mobilization of challengers and their strategic actions in conjunction with specific political contexts. We review one version of the political mediation model (Amenta 2006; Amenta, Caren, and Olasky 2005), which focuses on joint influences of institutional and movement causes. From there, we discuss the general form of political mediation models and indicate how the kind of thinking might be applied to scholarship regarding the influence of movements on institutions other than formally political ones.

One political mediation model (Amenta, Caren, and Olasky 2005; Amenta 2006) holds that in a democratic political system, mobilizing relatively large numbers of committed people and making plausible claims are necessary for movements to achieve political influence. Challengers' action is more likely to produce results when the institutional political actors with final say over policy decisions see benefit in aiding the group the challenger represents. To secure policy changes and concessions, challengers will typically need help or complementary action from like-minded state actors. For a movement to be influential, state actors, such as elected officials and state bureaucrats, need to see movements as potentially facilitating or disrupting their own goals—such as augmenting or cementing new electoral coalitions, gaining in public opinion, acting on stated beliefs and claims, or increasing the support for the missions of the governmental bureaus in which they work. Movement actors need to mobilize and engage in the sort of collective action that alters the calculations of institutional political actors. Generally speaking, this injunction means that movement actors should adopt organizational forms and strategic action that fit political circumstances.

The political mediation model starts with the causal literature on social policy outcomes, which focuses on determinants other than social movement actors (Hicks 1999; Amenta, Bonastia, and Caren 2001), and then theorizes about how movement actors might influence these causal processes. Policies have been studied extensively, have served as proving grounds to appraise various theories of politics, and can be analyzed according to different processes, including their introduction, enactment, and implementation. Once enacted, they can be broken into different units, including when they were adopted, how much is spent on them, and who voted for them. The political mediation model holds that there are many situations in which movements will be unlikely to have influence over policy regardless of their mobilization or collective action. For instance, underdemocratized polities are expected to deflect extensive public policy advances (Amenta, Caren, and Olasky 2005), regardless of whether other positive determinants of policies may be present. Also, policies of interest to movements may be pushed forward without the influence of movements. For instance, policy change favorable to a movement's constituency might come about through a new partisan regime coming to power in an area where domestic bureaucratic capacities are well developed. Edwin Amenta, Neal Caren, and Sheera Joy Olasky (2005) find that U.S. states with all three of these conditions—a democratized polity, a New Deal Democratic regime in power, and well-developed domestic bureaucracies—also had generous old-age pensions.

This version of the political mediation argument involves the joint appearance of causes, or what Giugni refers to as a "joint-effect" mediation model, in which movement mobilization or action combines with other conditions to produce influence (2007, 56). During such a favorable circumstance for policy advances as just described, a highly mobilized organization or movement would be expected to influence a favorable regime in power to prioritize its demands over those of less mobilized groups allied with the regime. Similarly, when a movement engages in successful assertive action, such as a sustained program of influencing elections or coming close to winning in a direct democratic process, such as an initiative, it would be expected to serve as a functional substitute for either a favorable regime in power or having such a domestic bureaucracy in place. This contention is also borne out by the evidence of generous old-age pension spending in U.S. states (Amenta, Caren, and Olasky 2005). The same study shows that these factors also influence who voted in favor of generous old-age pensions, lending further credence to the overall results.

The model also holds that it requires many simultaneous circumstances, some movement related and some not, to effect extensive change. In the U.S. setting, where controlling the government through a party is rarely an option, a national challenger with far-reaching goals is likely to need to have a favorable partisan context, its issue already on the agenda, high challenger organization and mobilization, credible claims making directed at elites and the general public, and plausible assertive action, such as electoral strategies that seek to punish policy opponents and aid friends (Amenta, Caren, and Olasky 2005; Amenta 2006). The same is likely to be true for bids to transform the structural position of groups, such as through voting or civil rights. In Giugni's (2007) own joint-effect model, tested on cross-national evidence, he argues that both a favorable regime in power and favorable public opinion—two standard determinants of public policy—as well as protest need to combine to advance spending for movement-friendly policies (see also McAdam and Su 2002 for a combinational argument regarding protest and war spending).

However, mediation models can go beyond these joint-effect models through either indirect or direct effects. Movements can engage in indirect-effect mediation (Giugni 2007, 56) by influencing known determinants of policy outcomes. For instance, movements may act to augment the potential coalitions behind policy change through directed electoral action or a highly supported but failed referendum. They might also influence public opinion, which could later have a direct influence on public policy. Indeed, Luders (2010) proposes a version of an indirect-effect political mediation model in which movements influence public opinion, which in turn influences public policy. Similarly, much movement literature indicates that protest can help place issues on the political agenda (Amenta et al. 2010), which is a necessary condition for policy change.

Finally, movements might directly influence policy, overriding the standard political institutional procedures by placing a referendum on a ballot and seeing it through to passage or forming or becoming part of governments with their own parties. Similarly, movement actors may install activists on administrative boards that implement legislation (Santoro and Mc-

Guire 1997). Of course, these direct and movement-centered routes to influence typically have joint-effect components to them at the political system level. A movement party cannot take control of governments if the political system is not democratized or if it heavily discourages movement parties; referendums are possible only when political systems allow direct democratic devices. In the United States, for instance, movement parties are highly discouraged by electoral laws, whereas many states provide for direct democratic devices. In many European countries, proportional representation encourages movement parties, whereas direct democratic devices are uncommon.

We are not advocating using the particulars of the political mediation model for those seeking to theorize about and assess the impact of movements on other institutions, but this sort of thinking and style of theorizing can also be applied widely to bids for institutional influence. As in the case of political institutions and policy, other institutions work according to their own principles and typically have well-developed literatures surrounding the determinants of their processes and outcomes. To engage in thinking similar to that behind the political mediation model and to address potential movement influence over these institutions, scholars should begin by addressing how institutions work and examining closely the causal literature surrounding them. From there, they should theorize about how movements might engage or intervene in the workings of institutions' usual determinants. Various mediation ideas have been employed in the context of business (King 2008), the university (Arthur 2011), and the news media (Amenta et al. 2012; Elliott, Amenta, and Caren 2016; Amenta et al. 2019), as each has determinants analogous to those in political settings but also determinants of their own.

The implication of this institutional mediation approach is for those seeking to understand the influence of movements on businesses start with businesses and the mainly organizational theory that focuses on them, those seeking to understand the influence of movements on policing practices start with these organizations, those seeking to understand movement influence on legal decisions begin with courts, and so on. More generally, this approach means thinking not in terms of movement outcomes but of institutional outcomes that may sometimes be influenced directly, indirectly, or in joint ways by movements. The approach is institution centered in that it relies on the specific determinants of the institutional processes in question. Needless to say, this institution-based approach promises little consistency in the literatures on the external consequences of movements, but it does not mean that they have to be completely unlinked.

Those studying the impacts of movements on institutions may gain some guidance by thinking through how closely these processes resemble or do not resemble political processes—the institutional ones that have been most closely examined. Scholars have claimed that institutions and organizations such as universities and the news media are importantly political institutions. Some of the same concepts employed in political analyses, including partisanship, professionalization, and bureaucratization, can be used to explain processes and outputs in these organizations. We have engaged in some work along these lines regarding how and why movement actors sometimes receive extensive news media coverage and are sometimes covered substantively in news articles (Amenta et al. 2012; Elliott, Amenta, and Caren 2016; Amenta et al. 2019). These projects start with the ways news media institutions are organized and the determinants of influence over these institutional processes and outcomes, focusing on news organizations, news values, and journalistic practices (Schudson 2011). Their forms of organization, including degrees of professionalism and partisanship, and news rules are central in determining if and how events and groups, including movements, are covered. All of these originate from the literature on the news media and the influences on its processes and outcomes. From there we theorize about how movement actions and organizational identities and capacities may influence media processes that typically determine whether certain events and organizations will be covered and how. This goes along with an understanding that movements may not influence most movement-relevant coverage, given that there are more powerful influences on the news media and its coverage than movements.

Scholarship on policing as an institution has begun with organization characteristic of the police force that makes them more likely to monitor protest (Earl, Soule, and McCarthy 2003) and the way that the institution of policing has changed since the beginning of the War on Terror, which in turn influences interaction with movements (Earl 2009). Work on corporations as targets of movements holds that corporations are more likely to make concessions when they have recently experienced declining sales or when the media draws attention to boycotts (King 2008). Discussion of universities has found that those that have larger budgets and are more inclusive of student participation in curriculum planning are more likely to adopt new academic programs (Arthur 2011). In each instance, scholars begin with the character and determinants of the institutional target, which is treated as important in its own right, to discover the extent to which the movement is likely to gain influence or benefits.

Conclusion

Scholarship regarding the influence of movements over institutions has many obstacles not present in treating movements as the thing to be explained. Movements do not control these outcomes and processes, and movements typically represent groups with little power or are concerned with issues that are not routinely considered by targeted institutions. For those reasons, movement influence over these targeted institutions is not likely to be the main driver of change in them. Scholars have begun to remove movements from the center of their analyses of institutions that movements target, including Luders's cost-benefit model and Jasper's players-and-arenas model. Although these models have shed valuable light on processes and outcomes shielded by movement-centered analyses, they replicate some problems in that scholarship and limit the possibilities of understanding the consequences of movements and their influence on institutional targets. Creating a new set of concepts meant to be applicable to all institutional targets does not take these institutions seriously enough and will limit the possibilities of theorizing about the influence of movements.

We argue that instead of creating new movement-related models, scholarship on the potential institutional influence of movements needs to employ institutional mediation models based on a more complete understanding of the institutions that movements seek to change. This approach implies a mastery of the literature on these institutions, ascertaining what others have found to influence them, and then piggybacking on it. They should focus on how movements might intervene in the causal processes surrounding these institutions in the manner of political mediation models. Following this suggestion would also mean becoming expert in the literature on the institution in question and employing concepts and theories in this literature while avoiding concepts created to explain movements. Adopting this approach also means that scholars should avoid proliferating new opportunity structures of different sorts. These concepts are invariably movement centered and discount the institutions that movements seek to influence, as well as the literatures surrounding them. Instead, we should bear in mind that probably most institutional processes and outcomes of interest to movements have determinants with little to do with movements. More generally, this approach means thinking not in terms of movement outcomes but in terms of institutional outcomes that may sometimes be influenced by movements.

In rethinking how we study the influence of social movements on their targets, we can both improve movement scholarship and contribute to the various literatures that focus on different institutions. The literature on political institutions has greatly benefited from work of social movement scholars seeking to understand the political influence of movements. Social movement scholars should also lend their energy and expertise to other institutions of interest while expanding their knowledge of how these institutional processes work and how their outcomes are typically generated. The back and forth between movement theorizing and institutional theorizing will sharpen both lines of inquiry.

REFERENCES

Amenta, Edwin. 2006. *When Movements Matter: The Townsend Plan and the Rise of Social Security*. Princeton, NJ: Princeton University Press.

———. 2014. "How to Study the Influence of Movements." *Contemporary Sociology* 43 (1): 16–29.

Amenta, Edwin, Chris Bonastia, and Neal Caren. 2001. "U.S. Social Policy in Comparative and Historical Perspective: Concepts, Images, Arguments, and Research Strategies." *Annual Review of Sociology* 27:213–234.

Amenta, Edwin, Neal Caren, Elizabeth Chiarello, and Yang Su. 2010. "The Political Consequences of Social Movements." *Annual Review of Sociology* 36:14.1–14.21.

Amenta, Edwin, Neal Caren, and Sheera Joy Olasky. 2005. "Age for Leisure? Political Mediation and the Impact of the Pension Movement on U.S. Old-Age Policy." *American Sociological Review* 70:516–538.

Amenta, Edwin, Neal Caren, and Amber C. Tierney. 2015. "Put Me In, Coach? Ump? Owner? Security? Why the News Media Rarely Cover Movements as Political Players." In *Players and Arenas: The Interactive Dynamics of Protest*, edited by James M. Jasper and Jan Willem Duyvendak, 229–250. Amsterdam: Amsterdam University Press.

Amenta, Edwin, Thomas Alan Elliott, Nicole Shortt, Amber C. Tierney, Didem Türkoğlu, and Burrel Vann Jr. 2019. "Making Good News: What Explains the Quality of Coverage of the Civil Rights Movement." *Mobilization* 24 (1): 19–37.

Amenta, Edwin, Beth Gharrity Gardner, Amber Celina Tierney, Anaid Yerena, and Thomas Alan Elliott. 2012. "A Story-Centered Approach to the Newspaper Coverage of High-Profile SMOs." *Research in Social Movements, Conflict, and Change* 33:83–107.

Andrews, Kenneth T. 2001. "Social Movements and Policy Implementation: The Mississippi Civil Rights Movement and the War on Poverty, 1965–1971." *American Sociological Review* 66:71–95.

———. 2004. *Freedom Is a Constant Struggle: The Mississippi Civil Rights Movement and Its Legacy*. Chicago: University of Chicago Press.

Arthur, Mikaila Mariel Lemonik. 2011. *Student Activism and Curricular Change in Higher Education*. Burlington, VT: Ashgate.

Baumgartner, Frank R., and Christine Mahoney. 2005. "Social Movements, the Rise of New Issues, and the Public Agenda." In *Routing the Opposition: Social Movements, Public Policy, and Democracy*, edited by David S. Meyer, Valerie Jenness, and Helen M. Ingram, 65–86. Minneapolis: University of Minnesota Press.

Burstein, Paul. 2003. "The Impact of Public Opinion on Public Policy: A Review and an Agenda." *Political Research Quarterly* 56:29–40.

Chen, Anthony. 2009. *The Fifth Freedom: Jobs, Politics, and Civil Rights in the United States, 1941–1972*. Princeton, NJ: Princeton University Press.

Earl, Jennifer. 2009. "Information Access and Protest Policing Post-9/11: Studying the Policing of the 2004 Republican National Convention." *American Behavioral Scientist* 53:44–60.

Earl, Jennifer, Sarah A. Soule, and John D. McCarthy. 2003. "Protest under Fire? Explaining the Policing of Protest." *American Sociological Review* 68:581–606.

Elliott, Thomas Alan, Edwin Amenta, and Neal Caren. 2016. "Policy Influence on Social Movements: The LGBT Movement and Five National Newspapers, 1969–2000." *Sociological Forum* 31:926–947.

Evans, Peter B., Dietrich Rueschemeyer, and Theda Skocpol. 1985. *Bringing the State Back In*. Cambridge: Cambridge University Press.

Ferree, Myra Marx, William Anthony Gamson, Jürgen Gerhards, and Dieter Rucht. 2002. *Shaping Abortion Discourse: Democracy and the Public Sphere in Germany and the United States.* Cambridge: Cambridge University Press.

Gamson, William A. 1990. *The Strategy of Social Protest.* 2nd ed. Belmont, CA: Wadsworth.

Gilens, Martin, and Benjamin I. Page. 2014. "Testing Theories of American Politics: Elites, Interest Groups, and Average Citizens." *Perspectives on Politics* 12:564–581.

Giugni, Marco. 2007. "Useless Protest? A Time-Series Analysis of the Policy Outcomes of Ecology, Antinuclear, and Peace Movements in the United States, 1977–1995." *Mobilization* 12:53–77.

Goldstone, Jack A., ed. 2003. *States, Parties, and Social Movements.* Cambridge: Cambridge University Press.

Hacker, Jacob, and Paul Pierson. 2010. "Winner-Take-All Politics: Public Policy, Political Organization, and the Precipitous Rise of Top Incomes in the United States." *Politics and Society* 38 (2): 152–204.

Halfmann, Drew. 2011. *Doctors and Demonstrators: How Political Institutions Shape Abortion Law in the United States, Britain, and Canada.* Chicago: University of Chicago Press.

Heaney, Michael T., and Fabio Rojas. 2015. *Party in the Street: The Antiwar Movement and the Democratic Party after 9/11.* Cambridge: Cambridge University Press.

Hicks, Alexander M. 1999. *Social Democracy and Welfare Capitalism: A Century of Income Security Politics.* Ithaca, NY: Cornell University Press.

Jasper, James M. 2015. "Playing the Game." In *Players and Arenas: The Interactive Dynamics of Protest*, edited by James M. Jasper and Jan Willem Duyvendak, 9–33. Amsterdam: University of Amsterdam Press.

Katzenstein, Mary. 1999. *Faithful and Fearless: Moving Feminist Protest inside the Church and Military.* Princeton, NJ: Princeton University Press.

King, Brayden G. 2008. "A Political Mediation Model of Corporate Response to Social Movement Activism." *Administrative Science Quarterly* 53:395–421.

Kniss, Fred, and Gene Burns. 2004. "Religious Movements." In *Blackwell Companion to Social Movements*, edited by David A. Snow, Sarah Soule, and Hanspeter Kriesi, 694–715. Oxford, UK: Blackwell.

Knoke, David. 2001. *Changing Organizations: Business Networks in the New Political Economy.* Boulder, CO: Westview Press.

Lipsky, Michael. 1968. "Protest as a Political Resource." *American Political Science Review* 62:1144–1158.

Luders, Joseph E. 2010. *The Civil Rights Movement and the Logic of Social Change.* New York: Cambridge University Press.

Mahoney, James, and Gary Goertz. 2006. "A Tale of Two Cultures: Contrasting Quantitative and Qualitative Research." *Political Analysis* 14:227–249.

McAdam, Doug. 1996. "Conceptual Origins, Current Problems, Future Directions." In *Comparative Perspectives on Social Movements: Political Opportunities, Mobilizing Structures, and Cultural Framings*, edited by Doug McAdam, John D. McCarthy, and Mayer N. Zald, 23–40. Cambridge: Cambridge University Press.

McAdam, Doug, and Hilary Boudet. 2012. *Putting Social Movements in Their Place: Explaining Opposition to Energy Projects in the United States, 2000–2005.* New York: Cambridge University Press.

McAdam, Doug, and Karina Kloos. 2014. *Democracy Imperiled: Race, Class and the Emerging Politics of Inequality, 1960–2012.* New York: Oxford University Press.

McAdam, Doug, and Yang Su. 2002. "The War at Home: Antiwar Protests and Congressional Voting, 1965 to 1973." *American Sociological Review* 67:696–721.

McAdam, Doug, and Sidney Tarrow. 2010. "Ballots and Barricades: On the Reciprocal Relationship between Elections and Social Movements." *Perspectives on Politics* 8:529–542.

McCammon, Holly J., and Allison R. McGrath. 2015. "Litigating Change? Social Movements and Court." *Sociology Compass* 9:128–139.

McCarthy, John D., and Mayer N. Zald. 1977. "Resource Mobilization and Social Movements: A Partial Theory." *American Journal of Sociology* 82:1212–1241.

Moore, Kelly. 2008. *Disrupting Science: Social Movements, American Scientists, and the Politics of the Military, 1945–1975*. Princeton, NJ: Princeton University Press.

Olzak, Susan, and Sarah A. Soule. 2009. "Cross-cutting Influences of Environmental Protest and Legislation." *Social Forces* 88:201–225.

Pierson, Paul, and Theda Skocpol. 2002. "Historical Institutionalism in Contemporary Political Science." In *Political Science: The State of the Discipline*, edited by Ira Katznelson and Helen V. Milner, 693–721. New York: W. W. Norton.

Piven, Frances Fox. 2006. *Challenging Authority: How Ordinary People Change America*. Lanham, MD: Rowman and Littlefield.

Piven, Frances Fox, and Richard A. Cloward. 1977. *Poor People's Movements: Why They Succeed, How They Fail*. New York: Pantheon Press.

Rojas, Fabio. 2006. "Social Movement Tactics, Organizational Change and the Spread of African-American Studies." *Social Forces* 84:2147–2166.

Santoro, Wayne A., and Gail M. McGuire. 1997. "Social Movement Insiders: The Impact of Institutional Activists on Affirmative Action and Comparative Worth Policies." *Social Problems* 44:503–519.

Schudson, Michael. 2011. *The Sociology of the News*. New York: Norton.

Skocpol, Theda. 1985. "Bringing the State Back In: Strategies of Analysis in Current Research." In *Bringing the State Back In*, edited by Peter Evans, Dietrich Rueschemeyer, and Theda Skocpol, 3–37. Cambridge: Cambridge University Press.

———. 1992. *Protecting Soldiers and Mothers: The Political Origins of Social Policy in the United States*. Cambridge, MA: Harvard University Press

———. 2003. *Diminished Democracy: From Membership to Management in American Civic Life*. Norman: University of Oklahoma Press.

Sobieraj, Sarah. 2011. *Soundbitten: The Perils of Media-Centered Political Activism*. New York: New York University Press.

Soule, Sarah A. 2009. *Contention and Corporate Social Responsibility*. New York: Cambridge University Press.

Tarrow, Sidney. 1996. "States and Opportunities: The Political Structuring of Social Movements." In *Comparative Perspectives on Social Movements: Political Opportunities, Mobilizing Structures, and Cultural Framings*, edited by Doug McAdam, John D. McCarthy, and Mayer N. Zald, 41–61. Cambridge: Cambridge University Press.

Uba, Katrin. 2009. "The Contextual Dependence of Movement Outcomes: A Simplified Meta-analysis." *Mobilization* 14:433–448.

Wilson, James Q. 1961. "The Strategy of Protest: Problems of Negro Civic Action." *Journal of Conflict Resolution* 5:291–303.

7

Bolivian Water, Mexican Corn

State Response to Subsistence Protests

Erica S. Simmons

Why do the targets of social movement activities respond to social mobilization in the ways they do? Why do they choose to ignore social movements in some moments, co-opt them in others, and repress them in still others? Exploring these questions not only uncovers dynamics of a given target's structures and decision-making practices (for example, states or corporations) but also sheds light on why and how social movements develop in the ways they do. Social movements do not operate in isolation from their targets; interactions between the two shape both the target and the social movement itself. This chapter approaches these questions by focusing on how well the targets of a social movement's claims understand those very claims. Most basically: What do the actors charged with responding to the movement think that the movement is really about? How might those perceptions be different from or similar to the perceptions of the participants in the movement itself? A target's understanding of a social movement's claims will help determine whether the target perceives the movement to be particularly threatening and what kind of threat it might pose. These perceptions shape a target's response, which, in turn, shapes the evolution of the social movement. If we want to understand social movement trajectories, we must pay attention to both the actions and the perceptions of a social movement's target.

Two cases of social mobilization, one in response to water privatization in Bolivia and the other in response to rising corn prices in Mexico, serve as a lens through which to explore these issues. This chapter shows how differences in the ways in which public authorities understood the movements' core claims helps explain why the two governments reacted in starkly different ways to the emerging movements. Where government officials appreciated the symbolic value of the goods at stake, they acted quickly to curtail resistance. Where officials failed to grasp the meanings with which the good was imbued for movement participants, they dismissed the potential for widespread mobilization, not only allowing the movement to grow but also intervening in ways that directly encouraged movement acceleration.

The Cases

In January 2000, the Bolivian city of Cochabamba erupted in protest. Thousands of Cochabambans took to the streets to protest the privatization of their water supply. While the privatization had been in process for more than three years, the Bolivian government had found a buyer and reached an agreement for the concession only the previous June. The buyer, a consortium called Aguas del Tunari, gained rights not only to Cochabamba's municipal water system but also to water collected through private and communal wells. In January when bills came due for water that had, in some cases, doubled in price, the water wars began, shutting down the city for days at a time. A cross-class, cross-ethnic, cross-urban-rural movement took hold in the region. Protests then spread throughout the country, and the government was forced to renationalize Cochabamban water by April.

Seven years later and thousands of miles away, in January 2007, Mexicans filled the Zócalo in Mexico City to express opposition to rising corn prices and corn imports. The price of tortillas had risen dramatically across the country—in some regions prices had quadrupled since the summer. Marching under the banner "Sin Maíz No Hay País" (without corn there is no country), consumers and producers, middle class and campesinos united to demand access to affordable, explicitly *Mexican* corn. Recently inaugurated President Felipe Calderón moved quickly to cap prices, and large-scale mobilization subsided.

As they began, the Bolivian water wars and the Mexican *tortillazo* protests looked strikingly similar. In both cases, broad-based resistance movements formed to protest a perceived threat to a subsistence good. Attention to the grievance at stake—understood as materially *and* ideationally constituted—helps shed light on the movements' similar origins and composition (Simmons 2014, 2016c). In spite of their initial similarities, the movements' trajectories quickly diverged. In Bolivia, protests escalated, shutting down the Cochabamba region and, later, the country for days at a time. In Mexico, the movement quickly collapsed. This chapter begins with the premise that in each case the state's response to the protests played a critical role in shaping the trajectory of mobilization. The chapter then focuses on this response, asking: How do we understand why state actors in Bolivia and Mexico make such different choices when faced with similar possibilities for broad-based, widespread social mobilization?[1]

The Questions

The questions posed here build on recent efforts to put contention in context (Goodwin and Jasper 2012), acknowledge that social movements develop in fields with multiple players and arenas (Jasper and Duyvendak 2015), and understand social mobilization as part of a dynamic relationship between movements and their targets (e.g., McAdam 1983; Lichbach 1995; Skrentny 2006; McDonnell, King, and Soule 2015; also see the Introduction). Social movement scholars have made important contributions to our understandings of how targets influence social movement trajectories (e.g., Bishara 2015; King 2011; Soule 2009; Amenta et al. 2002; McAdam 1983). We know that a target's response can dramatically shape how an episode of contention unfolds.

Yet even as there is a growing literature on the dynamics of corporate response to social mobilization (e.g., King 2008), scholars pay relatively little attention to why targets in general, and state actors in particular, respond to social mobilization in the ways they do.[2] Discussions of response based on perceived threat, cost, or risk (e.g., King 2008; Boudreau 2004; Cunningham 2004; Kriesi 1995), the meanings that policy elites attribute to groups (Skrentny 2006), and the reasons that states engage in repression (e.g., Davenport, Mueller, and Johnston 2005; Davenport 2007) offer important exceptions. However, even as these works draw attention to the importance of threat perception and offer insights into repressive responses, our general explanations for state response to social mobilizations remain limited. We have few tools with which to systematically understand why states perceive particular movements at particular moments as threatening.

Furthermore, the importance of culture in why state actors choose to respond as they do has gone undertheorized. Culture plays a central role in our understandings of why social movement actors do what they do (e.g., Jasper 1997). Yet there is little attention to how culture might shape state responses to those same movements.[3] We know a target's perceptions of threat matter, yet we know little about how culture shapes the target's understandings of what might be threatening or costly. For example, in Christian Davenport, Carol Mueller, and Hank Johnston's (2005) analysis of repression and mobilization, culture is incorporated into analysis of the movement, but how culture shapes state choices is less clear. As a result, we have only a partial understanding of why targets make the choices they do. Some scholarship has focused on how the meaning-making practices of targets shape social movement trajectories. In particular, John Skrentny (2006) shows how the meanings that policy makers attach to different groups fundamentally shapes response to movement demands. This chapter builds on Skrentny's insight that perceptions matter but focuses our analytic lens not on the type of challenger but rather on the claims those challengers are making. As Jasper and King argue in the Introduction, "The target remains a hollow creature in the social movement literature—largely lacking in strategy, motivation, and cultural tools." This chapter aims to help fill the void by offering one set of tools with which to explore this question: Why do targets respond the ways they do?[4]

The question is critical because a target's response can dramatically shape how an episode of contention unfolds. Indeed, the responses of actors within the Bolivian and Mexican states mattered enormously for how and why the trajectories of the two mobilizations differed. In Bolivia, even in the face of early resistance and projected rate hikes, authorities forged ahead with privatization plans. As demonstrations grew, public officials showed little willingness to compromise and chose instead to send troops into the streets to thwart the protests. The central government's unwillingness to compromise, combined with conflicts between protestors and troops on the streets, served to strengthen the resolve of the movement leaders and encourage rapid movement growth.[5] In Mexico, at the first signs of tortilla price increases public officials worked to placate potential resistance. In just over two weeks, high-level government officials successfully implemented a voluntary pact that effectively served to stabilize tortilla prices. The social movement quickly lost momentum.

The Argument

The argument developed here is built on an approach that focuses the lens of social movement theory on the meaning work done by grievances (Simmons 2014, 2016c). By paying attention to the ways in which different grievances are imbued with similar or different meanings in different contexts, we can come to think of grievances differently than as the relative gain or loss of a material "thing" or a set of political privileges. The approach builds on literatures that treat grievances as endogenous to mobilization identities and mobilization efforts (e.g., Johnston, Laraña, and Gusfield 1994; Opp 1988) but focuses on the meaning work done by grievances in the mobilization process. The basic argument is that while grievances maintain material power, their ideational aspects, as well as the reciprocal relationship between the two, play a critical role in developing understandings of what the grievance is. By understanding grievances as embedded in cultural context, we can productively engage with the ways in which the claims themselves, not sim-

ply how those claims are articulated by movement entrepreneurs, shape social movement outcomes.

Understandings of water and corn help explain policy makers' responses
to social mobilizations in Bolivia and Mexico. In Mexico, government officials charged with responding to the movement appear to have understood
the symbolic value of corn for social movement participants. As a result they
perceived the movement to be a serious political threat and acted quickly to
curtail resistance. In Bolivia key government officials appear to have failed
to grasp the meanings with which water was imbued. As a result, they dismissed the potential for widespread mobilization, making critical choices
that not only gave the movement the space to grow but also directly encouraged movement radicalization and acceleration. By paying attention to the
meanings that each movement's claims took on for the policy makers
charged with responding to them, we shed light not only on how and why
they responded in the ways they did but also on what the trajectories were of
each movement.

Theorizing Coherence

To understand social movement trajectories, we need to understand the
meanings at work not only among social movement organizers and participants but also among a social movement's targets. We need to look at how
culture works both among social movement participants to help produce a
movement and among state actors charged with responding to the same
movement. Yet I do not intend to suggest that cultures at work in each of
these spaces are bounded, separate, or contained.[6] I draw on William Sewell's
conceptualization of cultural structures to understand them as both multiple and overlapping. Cultural structures, Sewell argues, should be seen as
"corresponding to spheres or arenas of social practice of varying scope that
intertwine, overlap, and interpenetrate in space and time" (2005, 206). Semiotic networks may not be easily pried apart, but we can still recognize that
"structures need to be seen as multiple in the . . . sense that difference institutional realms, operating at varying social and geographical scales, [may]
operate according to different symbolic or cultural logics" (208).

We may understand particular signifiers in different ways depending on
the institutional context or geographic location, but those signifiers do work
in different semiotic networks and may be in tension with each other in ways
that participants fail to grasp. Cultural meanings derived from one structure
may be transposed to others, but they also may not. The boundaries of semiotic communities are difficult to determine, if for no other reason than because the concept of a boundary is conceptually inappropriate for describing
semiotic relationships. Yet people are not always able to comprehend the

symbolic actions of others; all conceptual systems are not always or equally shared.

An example from the cases discussed here helps illuminate the point. Multiple, overlapping cultural structures exist within (but are not necessarily confined by) the Bolivian nation-state. Some symbolic actions across the institutional realms of, for example, agricultural production, mining, or state policy making or across the geographic spaces of La Paz, Santa Cruz, or Cochabamba may be mutually comprehensible, while others are not. For example, references to Bolivia's loss of access to the sea at the end of the nineteenth century may work to produce patriotism across institutional realms or geographic spaces. The privatization of water, however, worked symbolically in Cochabamba in ways that do not appear to have been widely intelligible to high-level government policy makers, most of whom were from and resided in different geographic areas of the country. Many also expressed logics of development based on individual, market-based conceptions of the good life.[7] While policy makers largely understood water privatization as a step in the path toward modernization, international integration, efficiency, and progress, for many Cochabambans water took on community-related meanings that were directly threatened by the privatization process.

This is not to say that there was an internal, logical consistency to the meanings that water took on in the Cochabamban context—these meanings were, indeed, multiple and often contradictory. Nor is it to say that a similar logical consistency existed for the meanings that water took on for the policy makers responsible for approving the privatization contract and responding to the protests. What this chapter brings to the fore are the ways in which the tensions produced by the variety of meanings that water took on informed the responses of both the Cochabambans who took to the streets and the policy makers charged with responding to the mobilization.

Target Response

There are two levels on which policy makers' understandings of the grievance operated. First, the subsistence resource was sometimes imbued with community-related meanings for the government officials themselves. Relevant decision makers understood corn or water to index, for example, national identity or local community relations. Second, even if decision makers did not themselves understand the good to be imbued with community-related meanings, they understood that these meanings were produced and reproduced by *others* in ways that might be conducive to collective action. While corn or water may have meant little to the government officials themselves, those same officials understood that the goods were imbued with meanings for the communities affected by the threat. While the first-level understandings can help explain the reactions of public officials, they do not appear to be necessary. The cases suggest that, while government decision makers' own understandings of water or corn informed their decisions, intervention to avoid protest required only that they perceive the potential meaning of the good for others.

Evidence from interviews after the fact and newspaper coverage at the time, both of which appear in the following discussion, suggests that Bolivian officials saw little potential for mobilization around a threat to water in Cochabamba. Water had little symbolic meaning to the relevant government officials; few were from Cochabamba. Furthermore, those same officials failed to understand the meanings with which water was imbued in the Cochabamba Valley. As a result, relevant public officials did not anticipate the scope or scale of the potential resistance movement and did little to try to contain the movement in its early stages. Officials remained tied to the ideological importance of privatization, and they understood implementation of the Cochabamba concession as a critical step in the path to a modern Bolivian economy. Government officials failed to anticipate the potential for a broad-based movement and, as a result, failed to act to effectively demobilize resistance.

When faced with a similar challenge, Mexican officials' actions stand in stark opposition to those of their Bolivian counterparts. In Mexico, high-level government actors quickly appreciated the potential for mass mobilization around a threat to tortillas. Some members of the Calderón administration understood that their constituents perceived corn to have meanings deeply rooted in a sense of self and community. Others not only understood the meanings with which corn was imbued for constituents but also themselves understood corn to be highly symbolic. Whether or not corn was symbolic to the officials themselves, the perception that it was to constituents was enough to orchestrate an immediate government response to rising tortilla prices; public officials anticipated the potential for widespread mobilization and acted to avert major social unrest.

The chapter cannot offer a full accounting of all the causal mechanisms at work in shaping state response. I do not argue that the meanings water and corn took on for government officials are the only relevant factors in explaining either government decisions to respond or the effectiveness of those responses. There are a host of relevant differences, both structural and specific to the contested policies, between the two cases. Both Bolivia and Mexico experienced extended periods of market-based economic reforms—including severe austerity measures, extensive privatizations, and widespread elimination of subsidies and price supports—yet the countries share few social, economic, or political structures. The movements took place in different arenas that undoubtedly informed the strategic actions of players in different ways (Jasper and Duyvendak 2015). Even as state resources and policy independence were severely constrained by national and international contexts, divergent responses to social mobilization are overdetermined; differences in economic, social, and political structures, as well as those specific to the contested policies, shaped why and how state actors responded as they did.[8]

Addressing all of the political, social, and economic factors at work is beyond the scope of the chapter. I can, however, make a more modest claim. Through thick description and attention to discourse and symbols I can demonstrate connections between understandings and actions without having to rule out alternatives. The comparison of the Bolivian and Mexican cases shows how state actors' understandings of the meanings with which a social movement's grievances are imbued influence their response to the movement; grievance interpretation is a consequential part of the picture. Through attention to the meanings with which grievances were imbued I can shed light on the seriousness with which state actors took the potential threat generated by the movement, a factor that, no doubt, informed the particular responses that policy makers adopted. Furthermore, grievance interpretation is a particularly important mechanism on which to focus, as it sheds light on the ways in which multiple structures help facilitate shared understandings; diverse political contexts, conditions, and constraints can foster similar (mis)understandings of grievances. My claim is not that the mechanism I describe is the only one that matters but rather that it can explain an important part of the empirical puzzle.[9]

Bolivia

Either they pay the bills or there isn't water.

—OFFICIAL FROM THE BOLIVIAN CENTRAL GOVERNMENT, quoted in Alberto García, Fernando García, and Luz Quintón, La "Guerra del Agua"

The water war brought two perceptions of water face to face in confrontation—one economic and the other social and cultural.

—CARLOS CRESPO FLORES, "Water Privatisation Policies and Conflicts in Bolivia"

Bolivia was arguably the poster child for market economic reforms; water privatization in Cochabamba was not an isolated policy program. Faced with economic crisis, Bolivia's first democratically elected president in almost two decades, Victor Paz Estenssoro, spearheaded a sweeping marketization program. Implemented in 1985, the New Economic Policy included cuts in social subsidies, liberalization of capital and trade accounts, and privatization of public enterprises. Water privatization in Cochabamba began in the early 1990s as part of a renewed commitment to privatization under then-president Gonzalo Sanchez de Lozada. When the presidency changed hands (and parties) in 1997, the political commitment to markets did not waver. Former dictator Hugo Banzer took the reins, this time as the democratically elected leader of the Acción Democrática Nacionalista (ADN; Nationalist Democratic Action), and forged ahead with the privatization plans.

From the first moments of the Bolivian initiative to privatize water in Cochabamba, the actions of government officials suggest that they either assumed to understand already or perhaps did not care to understand what the reaction in Cochabamba would be. Cochabambans were not consulted during the initial bidding process in 1997 or during the revision of the bidding requirements in 1999 (Crespo Flores 2003), both of which were managed in La Paz, Bolivia's functional capital. Both local governmental officials and the public were ignored as potential stakeholders or potentially productive contributors to the process. Civic organizations were similarly sidelined, as were officials from the municipal water company, Servicio Municipal de Agua Potable y Alcantarillado de Cochabamba (Semapa; Cochabamba Municipal Drinking Water and Sewage Service), and the national government negotiated the concession (Maldonado Rojas 2004). Engineer and local politician Gonzalo Maldonado remarked that "the government consulted with political parties and forgot to consult with the people" (quoted in Crespo Flores 2003, 237). Herbert Müller, who was minister of the treasury at the time, recalls that the government failed to "socialize the process. . . . We believed," he recalled, "that economic rationality would be enough to convince the people."[10]

Cultural Structures of Water

Müller's comments offer a clear reflection of the logics that drove both the process of contract development and the perceptions of what was at stake. The understandings of development and progress generally, and water specifically, that dominated the policy-making process drew on cultural logics grounded in conceptions of individual ownership and the benefits of private markets. For policy makers, water appears to have been understood as an "abstract" industrial product to which the logics of markets could easily be applied (see Bakker 2003, 42). Most were from La Paz or Santa Cruz, regions where access to water could be taken for granted by many residents. Questions of water access were not a daily source of worry or concern for those in charge of negotiating the Aguas del Tunari contract or those responsible for responding to the unrest in Cochabamba after its implementation. Furthermore, their narrative was one in which privatization would bring much-needed investment to Cochabamba's municipal water system. Markets would bring new resources and introduce efficiencies. It might not expand networks to Cochabamba's unconnected neighborhoods, but a municipal-run water system had also been unable to meet this need. Government had been managing the resource poorly, and it was time for the private sector to step in. Müller recalls his perspective at the time: The contract would "solve the water problem in Cochabamba, so why would Cochabambans be opposed?"[11]

Many Cochabambans, however, had understandings of water very different from those that were informing the policy-making and implementation process. Cochabamba's history of, and contemporary experiences with, scarcity combined with both irrigation practices and understandings of an agricultural past to imbue water with meanings tied to local and regional identities. Access to water was a personal, daily struggle for many (see Simmons 2016c), as well as a regional struggle that framed broader community needs and discourses. As Marion Fourcade (2011) has shown, when goods like water become parts of our daily life and practice, they become part of our cultural narratives, shaping their possibilities for valuation. For many Cochabambans, regardless of their occupation or place of residence within the valley, water helped produce and reproduce conceptions of regional rights and communal identity. Water was not only a critical component in their continued livelihood but also a good that took on national, regional, and ethnic significance. The Aguas del Tunari contract threatened not only relationships with a critical material good but also imagined communities of nation, region, and ethnicity as well as quotidian communities—communities constituted by face-to-face interactions where the members know each other directly—created by everyday social interactions and relationships (Simmons 2016b, 2016c).

Not surprisingly, the meanings that water took on in the Cochabamban context are multiple, varied, and sometimes apparently contradictory. Yet for many Cochabambans water worked to symbolize something more than its biophysical characteristics. In sidelining local voices, the officials in charge of policy development (and later response to the social mobilization that emerged) left little space to develop an appreciation for the meanings with which water was imbued in the Cochabamban context. These community-related understandings emerged as incommensurable with conceptions of water as a good that could be exchanged for profit. However, during the crucial moments when Cochabambans could have made clear the ways in which the concession and the new law threatened their perceptions of community, there were few Cochabamban voices involved in the process.[12]

Without an understanding of how Cochabambans might perceive the contract, state officials proceeded according to their own understandings of what water privatization meant. Vice Minister of Governing José Orías (who was also a Cochabamban) observed that the government "treated it like buying or selling a house, not like they should have treated water."[13] While a house certainly has symbolic value for its owners, some houses have symbolic value for entire communities, and certainly homeownership itself is symbolic in many places, Orías's comparison implies that government officials treated water as a purely material good, something that could be individually owned and managed with few—beyond a concerned neighbor or two—caring how the house might be transformed by new occupants. For the government officials involved, Cochabamba's concession contract was a transaction—a complicated one, but a transaction nonetheless—between the government and a private firm. They seemed to fail to see how this particular transaction was not simply an exchange of property but rather a violation of community. By the time protestors effectively conveyed this message and government officials appear to have understood that compromise would be necessary, movement leaders were unwilling to negotiate.

Early Mobilizations

Apparently certain that opposition would be minimal, officials claim to have been confident that they could ignore the early attempts to organize a resistance movement. When asked about potential civil unrest during a visit to Cochabamba in September, the president of Bolivia, Hugo Banzer stated, "I'm used to that kind of background music" (*Los tiempos*, September 3, 1999). Banzer dismissed the possibility of large-scale mobilizing, suggesting that it would remain only in the background and would be unlikely to affect the contract's implementation.

Even as irrigators and urban organizations mobilized in large numbers on the eve of the passage of critical reforms that would allow for the privatization process to move forward, most government officials remained unconvinced of the potential for large-scale resistance. Civil society leaders organized a roadblock of the Cochabamba-Oruru highway—a major national artery—on October 27, but reaction from government authorities was minimal. Carlos Saavedra, the minister of trade, and Luis Uzín, the superintendent of basic sanitation, remarked that they understood these early protests to simply be a manifestation of divisions in the municipal electoral process (*Opinión*, December 10, 1999; *Los tiempos*, December 12, 1999).[14] The government representatives who arrived from La Paz to negotiate an end to the blockade made few concessions. The movement was not yet well organized and ultimately called an end to the protest without extracting significant concessions (Peredo, Crespo Flores, and Fernández 2004).[15]

Even as the potential for dramatic rate hikes became clear, government officials did little to dampen local fears or express empathy for the challenges that the Aguas del Tunari contract might pose to local relationships with water. Officials consistently stated, "O pagan las tarifas o no hay agua" (Either they pay the bills or there isn't water) (García, García, and Quintón 2003, 47). Cochabamban scholar and activist Carlos Crespo Flores argues that "neither the government nor the superintendency understood the collective perception of water as a social and cultural good and the implications for any attempt to introduce market disciplines" (2003, 244).

By the beginning of January it was becoming increasingly apparent that any government response would continue to come from La Paz and be shaped by Paceños's and Cruzeño's understandings of water. On January 3, seven hundred police officers and a "special security group" arrived from La Paz to control the bridges and points of access to the city (García, García, and Quintón 2003, 49). In an attempt to avert the work stoppages and mobilizations called for January 11, representatives of the central government—all of them from La Paz or Santa Cruz save for Orías—tried their hand at a second round of negotiations. Public officials with seemingly little understanding of what was at stake for movement leaders and participants continued to serve as the key decision makers.

But once again, there appeared to be little willingness on the government's side to reach a compromise. On January 10, Minister of Trade Carlos Saavedra arrived in Cochabamba to convince the leaders of the central organizational vehicle for the movement, the Coordinadora para la Defensa del Agua y de la Vida (the Coordinadora) and the Cochabamban Civic Committee to call off the strike.[16] A Coordinadora member recalled that "the government was deaf to the people's complaints [reclamos]. At the beginning, if they had changed just four or five clauses, most of the movement would have compromised and the rest wouldn't have had enough of a following to continue."[17] His comments were not unique.[18] Mauricio Barrientos, president of the Civic Committee, concurred that, at this stage, compromise had been possible. But he thought that "the government didn't want to solve the problem because they thought it would go away."[19]

The protests took place as scheduled, and the water movement brought Cochabamba to a halt on January 11. Protestors remained in the streets for three days when government actors finally agreed to negotiate. But after three weeks of meetings, the government's final proposal seemed to reflect a failure to understand Cochabamban concerns. Saavedra offered a reduction of the rate hike from 35 to 20 percent. The reduction was neither sufficient nor credible; with many Cochabambans experiencing rate hikes of more than 100 percent, the government's promise to reduce rates from the 35 percent that Aguas del Tunari maintained was the extent of the hike to 20 percent seemed out of touch and nonsensical.[20] Furthermore, in spite of a signaled willingness to negotiate on these points, the proposal did not address concerns with Law 2029 or the elements of the Aguas del Tunari contract that Cochabambans feared would affect communal or private wells or halt further investments in long-term access to a sustainable water supply. The proposal reflected a fundamental misunderstanding of what many Cochabambans understood to be at stake; the protests were not simply about the material impact of a price increase (see Simmons 2016b, 2016c).

Having failed to achieve what they claimed to have considered central objectives, movement members rallied once again to stage large-scale public protests in early February. At the same time, Walter Guiteras, the minister of governing, arrived from La Paz to order the Coordinadora to suspend the march or face the consequences, mobilizing the army and the La Paz police force to make good on the threat (García, García, and Quintón 2003). Guiteras revealed a fundamental misunderstanding of the dynamics in Cochabamba when he interpreted the protests as driven by economic interests, stating that "strong economic interests are distorting the true interests of the people of Cochabamba to have water in the short and middle term" (quoted in Crespo Flores 2003, 241).

The reactions of the public officials charged with thwarting the protests suggest they thought the movement could be contained through a display of physical force. The march quickly turned into a violent confrontation as the La Paz police force (known as the *dálmatas* [dalmations] for their spotted uniforms) tried to keep protestors from occupying the Plaza 14 de Septiembre, Cochabamba's symbolic center. Neighborhood organizations set up barricades throughout the city; local shopkeepers closed their stores, partially, of course, for protection but also, at least according to reports in *Presencia*, to "attach" themselves to the protestors ("Bloqueo de protesta" 2000). The police used tear gas and lead bullets to keep the march from entering the plaza. The numbers of those reported wounded varied, but there were no fatal injuries.

The damage, however, was more than physical. The presence of the *dálmatas* conjured images of a repressive regime and heightened local solidarity. Crespo Flores remarks that "the spectacle of more than 70 motorbikes with heavily armed police in strange uniforms produced an environment of fear and indignation among the population" (2003, 240). On February 5, the headline for *Los tiempos*, a Cochabamba daily, read "Como en la dictadura" (Like in the dictatorship). The headline not only referenced the repressive government response but also alluded to the president, Hugo Banzer, who was democratically elected in 1997 but had governed Bolivia from 1971 to

1978 as the leader of a military junta. The period is known as the most repressive in recent memory. Once shots were fired and protestors beaten, support for the movement manifested itself with increasing numbers on the
streets.

Consequences of Target Response

Water remained the movement's central commitment; many Cochabambans
who participated only after the government repression began claimed that
water was a central concern.[21] Yet the show of force from the central government appears to have helped trigger increased participation, tapping into
feelings of Cochabamban solidarity. One university student told me, "We
were protecting Cochabamba, Cochabambans. The government wanted to
take away our right to water, so it was us against them."[22] Divisions between
the central government and Cochabamba now manifested themselves in a
physical battle; the necessity of a fight to retain Cochabamban control over
Cochabamban water was clear.

   Government rhetoric both performed the divide between La Paz and
Cochabamba and brought it into being. Movement leader Gonzalo Maldonado recalls that one of the representatives of the central government repeat-
edly claimed that the objective was to keep the *poblada* (a demeaning term
for "the masses") from entering the main plaza.[23] Government officials were
clearly setting themselves apart from the Cochabambans who took to the
streets. Many Cochabambans who had supported the protestors silently were
now willing to take action. One participant recalled, "Water was important
to our lives, but only when people started falling in the streets did I leave my
house. . . . Our way of life was at risk. It was the government against Cochabamba, and we had to fight for what was ours."[24] What was "ours" was most
immediately water—they were fighting to continue to access water through
established routines and practices. But it was also the quotidian communities that water encouraged and sustained, as well as the imagined community of region, nation, and ethnic group. As Rogers Brubaker suggests, the
kinds of events that took place on the streets of Cochabamba could "galva-
nize group feeling and ratchet up pre-existing levels of groupness" (2004, 14).

   With the central government literally waging a physical battle to fight
Cochabamba for its water, Cochabamban regional and Bolivian national
identifications became increasingly powerful, as did the sense that water was
ours. It was perceived as something that belonged to Cochabamba and to
Bolivia—not to a central governmental authority that could sell the water
and undermine its communal role.[25] With the willingness to use violence,
the central government further divorced itself from Bolivia, becoming an
"other" that could be an enemy to both region and nation. It did not repre-

sent Bolivia and was no longer a part of the conception of "ours" or "us." At the same time, the violence heightened the regional and national sense of "groupness" of the Cochabamban community, which in turn increased both support for and participation in the rallies on the streets. Yet the government continued to fail to appreciate the dynamics at work. Vice President Jorge Quiroga offered his own interpretation, arguing that "the Cochabamban movement is against Cochabamba and against satisfying Cochabamba's need for drinking water" (quoted in Crespo Flores 2003, 242).

The perspective of the director of the Cochabamban division of the national military (the seventh military division), José Antonio Gil, offers insight into the divide between the central government, the region, and the nation, as well as the ratcheting up of a feeling of "Cochabambanness." Like Orías, Gil was a Cochabamban and an employee of the central government—he could potentially both share the same understandings of water as his fellow Cochabambans and offer insight into why and how the government was responding in the ways it did. Gil recalls, "The government thought that by showing a lot of force, they would stop the taking of the plaza. But they just didn't understand the local dynamics, what role water played for all of us . . . and once the people were repressed in the way they were, it created solidarity in the region."[26]

Gil called the perspective of the officials who came in from La Paz both to direct the army and to negotiate with the movement "the CNN perspective, not the perspective from knowing Cochabamba."[27] By comparing them with CNN, the government negotiators, most of whom were from the "media luna"—Bolivia's Amazonian region—became not only decidedly un-Cochabamban but also un-Bolivian. They were foreigners, descending briefly to analyze a situation without any understanding of local history or practices. They could render a verdict about what was right or wrong with the information at hand, but they could never base that verdict on anything more than calculations rooted in understandings of the practices and values of their own communities. Ultimately, Gil explicitly stated, it was this "*terquedad* [stubbornness, or thick-headedness]" of the government that was responsible for things "arriving where they arrived" in Cochabamba.[28]

The Catholic Church stepped in to mediate an end to the February demonstrations; the government again agreed to revisions in the Aguas del Tunari contract. The resulting *convenio por Cochabamba* (agreement for Cochabamba) was intended to freeze prices at January 1998 levels until the conclusion of the negotiations ("Retornó la calma a Cochabamba" 2000) and set the terms for negotiations to, among other things, establish a new tariff structure (García, García, and Quintón 2003). But by many accounts the Coordinadora had also become unwilling to compromise. Many movement leaders now seemingly understood the extent of their mobilizing capacity and believed that they could demand the annulment of the contract.[29] Oscar Olivera recalls, "Yes, we radicalized after what happened in February. The people were behind us. Ending the *tarifazo* was no longer enough."[30] Movement leader Victor Gutierrez reflected that "nothing would have happened if the government had accepted our early demands. But they didn't, so we went all the way."[31]

By the end of March it was clear that the negotiations had once again reached an impasse. On April 4 the "final battle" began. The Coordinadora occupied the Aguas de Tunari headquarters, rallied thousands of people to march in the local plaza, and instigated blockades throughout the urban and periurban areas (Albro 2005, 252). As Crespo Flores argues, the "government failed to comprehend the diversity of the composition of the movement brought together under the banner of the Coordinadora" (2003, 242) and as a result continued to act in ways that served only to further escalate the movement. The April 6 arrest of the Coordinadora delegates, including Coordinadora leader Oscar Olivera, appears to have been a fundamental miscalculation. News of the arrests drew crowds of more than ten thousand into Cochabamba's central plaza that evening (Shultz 2003). On April 8 President Banzer issued a declaration of martial law. Protestors formed new roadblocks that afternoon, and bands of "water warriors" defended the plazas. On Monday, April 10, the Bolivian government announced that Aguas del Tunari would leave the country. The contract would be revoked, and Semapa would regain total control over the water system.

The blunders of Bolivian officials—from the failure to conduct public consultations during the initial contract negotiations to the unwillingness to negotiate in January 2000, to calling in the *dálmatas* and authorizing the use of force in February, play an important role in the trajectory of the Cochabamban water movement. Attention to the meanings that water had for Cochabambans and the failure of the government officials both making and implementing policy to understand those meanings shed light on why those blunders occurred.

Mexico

These kinds of things can bring down governments.

—Official from the Mexican Department of the Economy,
interview by the author, 2009

From the first moments of the *tortillazo*, government officials in Mexico City were intent on devising a solution that would quell and contain any social unrest. This section argues that we can explain Mexican policy choices during this period, at least in part, as a reflection of officials' understandings of the meanings of tortillas, and corn more broadly, to many Mexicans. Corn signifies different things to different people in Mexico, yet there is the sensibility that, across the country, it is imbued with special meaning. For many Mexicans, corn has come to mean "Mexico"; it is deeply imbricated in understandings of Mexican family life and serves as a foundation for perceptions of communal belonging, indexing both imagined identifications at the national level and quotidian communities within neighborhoods or families (see Simmons 2016a, 2016c). Mexican officials understood that tortillas indexed far more than their simple material value. This appreciation allowed them to anticipate the potential for widespread mobilization and develop policy responses that effectively contained the mobilization.

In December 2006 Felipe Calderón of the Partido Acción Nacional (PAN; National Action Party) took office as the new president of Mexico. Tortilla prices rose precipitously only a month later, and social actors began to organize their constituencies in protest. Almost immediately Calderón's advisers met in Los Pinos (the Mexican president's home and offices) to determine a course of action. High-level officials from Secretaría de Hacienda y Crédito Publico (Ministry of Finance), Secretaría de Economía (Ministry of the Economy), Secretaría de Desarrollo Social (Sedesol; the Ministry of Social Development), and Los Pinos were among those in attendance. An official from the Ministry of the Economy who was present for these early meetings recalls, "We all felt like we had to act immediately." Unrest, he claims to have believed, was inevitable.[32] Another attendee of early sessions at Los Pinos argued that there would have been a *desmadre* (loosely translated as "disaster") without quick, early action.[33]

But solutions were difficult to devise. For a government committed to free-market principles, a fixed price was an unattractive solution. While the exact origins of the concept of a "price pact"—a commitment from major corn-flour and tortilla producers to maintain the price of corn flour and tortillas at or below mutually agreed-on levels—are unclear, it is evident that the idea gained quick approval among the inner circle at Los Pinos. Even most of the "technocrats"—policy makers heavily identified with free-market policies and ideologies—in attendance were on board. Felix Vélez, undersecretary of social development at the time, recalls that he was the only one voicing opposition to the plan. "The Los Pinos meeting," he recalled, "worked how I would imagine the central planning office for a communist regime would work—and this was the PAN!"[34] While other attendees paint a picture of a slightly more contentious meeting, most recall that even those for whom the pact was a betrayal of their fundamental principles of "good" policy were on board. That so many professed hard-line free-market politicians were on board is just one indicator of how large they perceived the potential crisis to be.

On January 18 the Agreement to Stabilize the Price of the Tortilla took effect. Signed by cabinet officials, representatives of the *maíz*-tortilla manufacturing industry, *maíz* and tortilla distributors, and the president of the Confederación Nacional Campesina (CNC; National Peasant Confederation), the "voluntary" agreement committed the signatories to sell tortillas at prices no higher than $8.5 pesos/kilo, corn flour at no more than $5 pesos/ kilo and *maíz blanco* (white corn) for no more than $3 pesos/kilo (Rubio 2007).[35] Felipe Calderón spoke at the signing in Los Pinos. The agreement carried all of the weight of the presidency.

Of the more than forty-five thousand *tortillerías* in Mexico, only five thousand were directly affected by the agreement.[36] Yet Mexicans were now guaranteed an option for a stable price. Whether through rural Diconsa stores or Walmart, many Mexicans would be able to take direct advantage of the agreement. The president claimed that at more than 320,000 locations, Mexicans would find tortillas sold at the "just" price established by the pact (Calderón 2012, 39). He went on, "We will not tolerate speculators or hoarders; we will apply the law firmly and punish those who seek to take advantage of the needs of the people" (quoted in Javier Jiménez 2007). Even many who did not have access to a participating supermarket or store claim that the pact assuaged fears of continued rapid growth in tortilla prices.[37] With the large-scale producers and distributors on board, many smaller *tortillerías* would have to step in line as well—if not at 8.5 pesos per kilo, then at something relatively close to it—if they wanted to compete.[38]

Almost two weeks to the day after tortilla prices started to make headlines, the Calderón administration had produced what appeared to be an effective response. Why had officials acted so quickly and with the full force of the highest levels of the Mexican government? Mirroring the language used by protestors in both Mexico and Bolivia, government official after government official offered the same response: "Teníamos que . . ." (We had to . . .). While there were variations in how each official finished the sentence, the sentiment was usually the same. "We had to act." "We had to resolve the crisis." "We had to deal with it." "We had to find a solution." The urgency of the language betrays a sense that there was no choice; if prices were going to continue to rise, the only option was to intervene in the markets in some way. What was a political contingency seemed like a moral imperative or inevitability. Because an increase in corn prices meant a threat not just to Mexican pocketbooks but also to the very notion of what it meant to be Mexican, officials "had to" act.

The speed with which the pact was orchestrated, the high-level positions of both the designers and the signatories, and the decision that the president himself would speak at the signing ceremony offer ample evidence of how critical the Calderón administration understood the challenge to be. The agreement was not issued through the Department of Agriculture or Economy, but rather the discussions for it and the signing itself took place at Los

Pinos. Advisers reported that the president had taken a direct interest in making sure his administration developed a plan that would serve to calm the growing unrest.

In spite of the similar sense that something had to be done, officials offered a variety of explanations for why. A few cited the importance of the first one hundred days of Calderón's presidency, arguing that continued price increases would undermine public support and derail the president's agenda. Others discussed the "legitimacy" crisis created by the controversy over Calderón's election and the continued claim by his opponent, Andrés Manuel Lopez Obrador, that there was extensive electoral fraud, arguing that there was a need to demonstrate a commitment to the whole population. As conversations continued, every interviewee expressed a fear of a large-scale, widespread protest movement; even those who would not feel the financial pinch themselves might take to the streets to defend access to tortillas as a fundamental component of what it means to be Mexican.

Some officials did not hesitate to identify potential protest as a motivating factor. Two attendees of early Los Pinos meetings recalled a long discussion of the French Revolution. "That was not going to be us," one said. "Are you kidding? These kinds of things can bring down governments. No way we were going to let that happen. We could not have another French Revolution on our hands," he concluded. The French Revolution can signal a variety of different images, events, or emotions. For these government officials in Mexico City in early January 2007, it appears to have conjured images of people in the streets, of the toppling of a government, of the politicization of people and groups that had been previously unorganized. And they drew a clear connection between tortillas and bread. "For Mexicans, corn is our bread. They worry about bread in Europe; we worry about corn here," one official remarked.[39] Another offered a stronger statement: "You think bread was important in France? You haven't seen anything like what could happen with tortillas here."[40] While it may no longer be popular in scholarly circles to explain the French Revolution with reference to rising bread prices, that connection is exactly what Mexican officials had in mind. Just as bread had brought down the ancien régime, so, too, could tortillas upend the current Mexican government.[41]

They understood this kind of organized unrest as possible and the potential for widespread unrest as high because of the special place that tortillas have in Mexico. Some insisted that the importance was purely economic, but the language they used betrayed their understandings of the deeper role the good played for many Mexicans, and sometimes themselves. One of Calderón's advisers stated clearly that "it was not about the symbolic power of corn." But he immediately followed up: "It was about defending the rights of the people." Why and how are tortillas or corn a "right"? If "rights" are based on the pure economic need of feeding a family, then it is difficult to understand how tortillas are part of the equation. In almost every Mexican town, tortillas can be easily substituted for bread or other grain products. If it is a Mexican's right to have access not just to affordable food but to affordable tortillas, as this official's statement suggests, then the symbolic power of the good was, indeed, at work in the administration's decision-making process, in spite of the protests of this particular official.[42]

Other officials had equally skeptical reactions when questioned directly about the symbolic power of corn as a potential motivator for social protest. But their answers to other questions suggested again that there was, indeed, something more than a simple economic calculus at work. Graciela Aguilar, director of Agencia de Servicios a la Comercialización y Desarrollo de Mercados Agropecuarios (Aserca; Agency of Services for the Commercialization and Development of Agricultural Markets—the agricultural trade arm of Secretaría de Agricultura y Desarrollo Rural [Sagarpa; Ministry of Agriculture and Rural Development]), both at the time of the *tortillazo* and at the time of her interview for this research, questioned the mobilizing power of corn's meanings in Mexico. But when I asked why the administration had chosen not only to act quickly but also to do so in a way that betrayed its most fundamental ideological principles, Aguilar looked at me as though I were in kindergarten. "Where are you from?" she asked, her tone implying that my own question bordered on idiotic. "Of course the government acted quickly. You must not understand what corn means in Mexico." She continued: "It is part of our ancestry. . . . It is the culture. We did not have time to think; we had to act."[43] According to her, there was something that I, as a foreigner, would clearly never understand about corn and its intersection with everyday life and identity in Mexico. Had I understood, I never would have asked the question. For Aguilar, corn indexed Mexico in the same ways it did for the thousands who took to the streets demanding access to cheaper tortillas. As a result, government response seemed inevitable for Aguilar.

Other officials discussed the mobilizing potential of the tortilla's place in the national imaginary more directly. Many remarked that tortillas were fundamental to "being Mexican," so of course a threat to it would bring people to the streets. They appear to have understood a sense of self—both collective and communal—and nation to be at stake. Tortillas were, by their accounts, part of what it was to be Mexican. Officials claimed that even for those who could afford to pay the high prices, the idea that others could not violated a sense of country. They also contended that this feeling of violation could motivate widespread unrest. Corn is "like the flag," remarked one official.[44] The simile suggests that corn indexes national identity in a way that not only symbolizes country but also implies that its desecration would be understood as an affront to nation, a potentially treasonous act.[45] Even Felix Vélez, the adviser who took a clear stand on the side of markets, remarked that "alongside the Virgin de Guadalupe and soccer, corn is part of national identity. . . . [There is an understanding that] if the government is committed to the people, it will guarantee this basic staple."[46] While he disagreed with the policy choice, Vélez claims to have understood what was behind the decision.

But it was not just the idea that eating tortillas every day helped produce a sense of nation. Calderón's advisers also talked about the sense that the "myth of Mexico" was at stake. Corn evokes an image of a Mexican countryside, of legends of the Popul Vuh, of a faraway past and an imagined present. Tortillas reflect what many *want* Mexico to be—a vision steeped in history, community, and a distinct culinary tradition that sets the nation apart. The "myth of Mexico," as one put it, was also wrapped up in the accessibility of the tortilla and corn. With the price increases, he argued, "the myth was at stake."[47] The possibility that high prices would diminish the centrality of the tortilla in the Mexican diet threatened an understanding of what set Mexico apart from the rest of the world, of what makes Mexico and Mexicans distinct. By evoking this myth, government officials revealed one more layer of their own understandings of the meanings with which corn is imbued.

Some of Calderón's advisers made explicit reference to the mobilizing power of the threat to tortillas, as well as to the kind of broad-based coalition that such a threat could create. They did not simply picture unorganized riots. Instead, many described the potential for a well-organized opposition coalition leading the protest. "This kind of thing could bring the unions . . . together with the more radicalized sectors like the miners. And Lopez Obrador's followers along with the [previously] demobilized middle classes," one official hypothesized. "But they didn't have the time to organize this kind of resistance," he went on. "We moved in to address everything too quickly."[48] Officials expressed an understanding of the potential for a threat to tortillas to bridge divides and bring together disparate organized groups and the unorganized. An Economía official stated that "of course there would have been a revolt. . . . Tortillas are an emblematic product that can bring everyone together. Milk, bread, all of the prices could rise, but it was the tortilla that the government feared." He went on to say that "tortillas and corn are unique; there is nothing like corn."[49] Officials appear to have understood exactly why a threat to tortillas could cross salient divides—between city and country, across ethnic backgrounds, between squabbling unions or social organizations. The threat would appeal to something "more profound," as one official put it, than the divisions that kept them from working together.[50]

Officials also capitalized on the connection between tortillas and "being Mexican" to bring the crucial players for a successful price pact on board. As the agreement was voluntary, with no compensation for the companies that participated at the outset, Calderón's advisers needed to convince at least a few major participants in the *maíz*-tortilla chain that it was in their interest to participate. There appear to have been a number of reasons these players came on board so quickly. Interest in seeing the Calderón government remain stable and the potential to gain a larger market share of the tortilla business certainly played a role. But the minister of the economy two years later, Gerardo Ruíz Mateos, echoed the sentiments of others who had put the pact together when he recalled that the pact also "appealed to their [the business participants'] consciousness as Mexicans."[51] Even if the companies did not agree to the pact out of their own commitment to nation, they understood that they could be painted as traitors for continuing to raise tortilla prices.

With the price pact in place, the movement seemed to lose momentum. The major social groups that had been organizing for the January 31 march continued, and the march took place. But the movement ground to a halt shortly thereafter. As one public official put it, the government had "already killed the dog" by the time January 31 arrived. Another simply said that after the January 18 pact, the issue "fizzled." Nevertheless, the coalition that had already begun to organize the January 31 march forged ahead. In spite of the plural participation in the events, interviews and newspaper coverage suggest that the demands no longer had the same mobilizing power that had driven early participation. The issues at stake had become more abstract—the neoliberal economic model and free trade specifically, neglect of the countryside, and a lack of transparency more broadly. While these kinds of concerns could unite the leadership of a variety of sectors, the rank and file did not come out in numbers that might make the Calderón administration worry.

Furthermore, many of the unorganized members of the middle class who had participated in earlier *reclamos* (complaints/demands) throughout the city stayed home. One woman from the Tlalpan neighborhood reflected the sentiment of many others when she said, "Sure, there were still problems, but I knew I could buy tortillas."[52] One of her neighbors commented that "they [the government] are not ignoring us, the importance that tortillas have. There is no need to make *reclamos* anymore."[53] Many who had been willing to participate in earlier mobilizations were now confident that tortillas and corn would be protected. The administration had effectively communicated that tortillas and corn were special and would receive the protection they were due. In doing so, the administration severed the connection between movement leaders and the general population. The people did not need to mobilize to put corn and tortillas at the center of the state's agenda.

The administration had effectively convinced many Mexicans that access to corn and tortillas would not be subject to the vicissitudes of markets.

The Calderón administration, however, did not want to take any chances. While many public officials contended that they no longer feared widespread unrest, they were quick to respond publicly and sympathetically to the simultaneous marches.[54] La jornada reported that Calderón "'shared' the concerns of the diverse organizational participants that marched" through the center of the city (Roman 2007). Government officials were also quick to reach out to movement organizers, establishing "tables of dialogue" that began to meet the first week of February. All of the major organizations that had called the march were invited to participate in these "regular" sessions with officials from Los Pinos, Sagarpa, Sedesol, and Economía.[55] Representatives from the Ministries of the Economy, Agriculture, and Labor sat down with representatives from farmers' organizations, workers' organizations, and a broad citizens' coalition. In spite of a shared "Declaration" there was little agreement between the groups once they sat down together to negotiate. Historical divisions between the organizations that split after mobilizations in the early 2000s, as well as new splits resulting from the 2006 election outcome (some groups continued to actively support López Obrador, while others, still Partido de la Revolución Democrática [PRD; Party of the Democratic Revolution] sympathizers, chose to respect Calderón's right to be in office), plagued the negotiations. One participant remarked that the plurality of the groups represented made it easy for government to take advantage of disagreements. The groups met a few times between February and the end of April, and the government offered concessions to various participants. Gradually, participants dropped out, but the conversations continued and the meetings functioned as a link, albeit tenuous, between the administration and organized civil society. By bringing the opposition to the table quickly, the government effectively undermined any momentum that might have been produced by the January 31 march. Furthermore, government policy makers effectively capitalized on divisions within such a plural group, offering enough favors to some to take them out of the movement and highlighting differences among those that remained.

Conclusion

The comparison of the Bolivian and Mexican cases reveals the critical role that government officials' perceptions can play in a social movement's trajectory. But why and how are such different perceptions possible? Why would government officials in one case understand the symbolic nature of the good at stake, while in the other officials appeared to have understood little beyond the good's material role? Why and how did the "cultural structures"

(Sewell 2005, 205) in Bolivia develop so that Paceños, Cruceños, or Cochabambans might understand water differently? Or in Mexico in ways that
made understandings of corn broadly shared at the national level?

Any answer to these questions requires a close treatment of how relevant
semiotic networks are produced and reproduced in Bolivia and Mexico. The
evidence presented thus far offers some clues as to where we might begin to
develop an answer; attention to geography and long-term governance structures offer potentially fruitful avenues for future inquiry. Regional splits and
governance structures that isolated policy makers from their constituents
may have combined to help produce an environment in which relevant Bolivian officials had little understanding of the meanings that water took on
in the Cochabamban context. Conversely, the national implications of a
threat to corn, combined with institutionalized structures of communica-
tion that persisted in spite of the transition away from official corporatist
rule under the Partido Revolucionario Institucional (PRI; Institutional Revolutionary Party), may have helped Mexican policy makers anticipate and
work to quickly diffuse potential unrest. These two factors might have helped
create the conditions of possibility for different cultural structures to be produced and reproduced.

People experience social and political order in heterogeneous ways. Yet
something helps facilitate moments of shared intelligibility. How that shared
intelligibility is produced and reproduced, as well as why some things may
be more intelligible to some groups than others, is a question that emerges
from the evidence presented here; shared political and geographic structures
may shed light on how some semiotic networks are produced and reproduced. Attention to these structures might also help us better understand the
ways in which processes and practices of valuation shape perceptions of
commodification (see Fourcade 2011; Zelizer 2011). For many Cochabambans, intimate, daily connections with water helped produce understandings
of the resource as something that should not be sold for profit. For the officials from La Paz and Santa Cruz charged with responding to the mobilization, the logic of the market was the only way to both preserve and develop
Cochabamba's water resources. Different logics of valuation and understandings of development helped produce different relationships with the
good. This, in turn, helped produce different understandings of what was at
stake in Cochabamba in the fall of 1999 and winter of 2000.

Of course, there is much that is contingent during periods of political
contention; these structures are not the beginning of a unilinear causal
chain that makes the (mis)understandings highlighted here somehow inevitable. But the Bolivian and Mexican cases suggest that patterns of meaning
making surrounding the perceived grievances at the core of social mobilizations can help shape what state actors perceive as threatening, how they

evaluate potential responses, and, as a result, how a social mobilization develops.

NOTES

A modified version of this chapter was previously published as Erica S. Simmons, "Targets, Grievances, and Social Movement Trajectories," *Comparative Political Studies*, October 29, 2018, available at https://doi.org/10.1177/0010414018806532.

1. The divergent outcomes in these cases come as no surprise to social movement scholars or experts in the politics of Latin America. There is increasing recognition of the importance of contingency in explaining the trajectories of contentious episodes (e.g., McAdam, Tarrow, and Tilly 2001), and Mexico and Bolivia share few social, economic, or political structures. Yet there is much we can learn from comparing divergent outcomes in the Bolivian and Mexican cases.

2. This chapter draws on insights from the literature on corporate response but agrees with the implications of Brayden King (2011) that many of the dynamics shaping state responses are likely to be different. I hypothesize that one place of overlap is in precisely the dynamic outlined here: Corporate actors' understandings of grievances likely play a role in shaping response.

3. The literature on corporations appears to pay more attention to questions of cultural processes as they shape target responses. See de Bakker et al. 2013 for an interesting discussion. They call for understanding "strategic interactions as cultural practices that are situated in pluralistic institutional fields" (580).

4. Implicit in this approach is, of course, an understanding of states as made up of multiple arenas themselves. Responses to social movements are developed within particular branches of the government and by particular people; the state cannot be treated as a unitary actor.

5. In his analysis of the events, Carlos Crespo Flores argues that the state was simply incapable of handling the opposition that arose in early 2000. However, his argument focuses on establishing the role of the government's "authoritarian, clientelistic, and manipulative measures" (2003, 5). He argues that these "measures and attitudes adopted by the Bolivian government throughout the conflict failed to facilitate a democratic and consensual conflict resolution" (5). He does not, however, explore the roots of the impasse.

6. As Sewell notes, a singular notion of structure is conceptually problematic, not the least because "boundaries are notoriously difficult to delineate" (2005, 205).

7. For a relevant discussion of economic valuation of symbolically important goods, see Fourcade 2011.

8. There is also increasing recognition of the importance of contingency in explaining the trajectories of contentious episodes (see McAdam, Tarrow, and Tilly 2001).

9. See Fearon and Laitin 1996 for a similar methodological approach. They use comparative case analysis to uncover relevant causal mechanisms without claiming an exhaustive account of all of the causal processes at work.

10. Herbert Müller, interview by the author, February 2010, La Paz.

11. Müller, interview by the author.

12. Ultimately, Cochabamba's mayor, Manfred Reyes Villa, and the governor of the prefect (state) of Cochabamba, Guido Camacho Rodríguez, worked alongside the general director of Semapa, Arturo Coca Seleme, as the Cochabamban voices during the final negotiations. Other negotiators included Vice Minister of Investment and

Privatization Miguel López Bakovic, Superintendent of Basic Sanitation Luis Guillermo Uzín, and Superintendent of Electricity Alejandro Nowotay Vera. See García, García, and Quintón 2003.

13. José Orías, interview by the author, February 2010, Cochabamba.

14. Municipal elections were scheduled for December.

15. This was confirmed by additional author interviews, including a conversation with Marcelo Delgadillo in January 2010 in Cochabamba.

16. Civic Committees emerged throughout Bolivia in the 1970s in an effort to combat centralist governmental tendencies. They included a "range of organizations [and] were largely controlled by the local business sector." Assies 2003, 34n1. The water wars were plagued by a split between the Coordinadora and the Civic Committee. See Simmons 2016c, chap. 3, for a discussion of this split. The Civic Committee was active throughout, but the Coordinadora was largely responsible for the later push to annul the Aguas del Tunari contract.

17. Coordinadora member, interview by the author, January 2010, Cochabamba. Some of the names of interviewees are withheld by mutual agreement.

18. Coordinadora leaders, interviews by the author, August–September 2008 and January–February 2010, Cochabamba and La Paz.

19. Mauricio Barrientos, interview by the author, January 2010, Cochabamba; Marcelo Delgadillo, Oscar Olivera, and Víctor Gutiérrez, interviews by the author, September 2008 and January 2010, Cochabamba. Six separate interviews, including three with government officials who preferred to remain anonymous, confirmed this impression of these early negotiations. It is, of course, possible that Saavedra is being painted as a scapegoat by the other interviewees, particularly since the government officials present at these talks requested that I not attribute any comments about Saavedra to them. The three interviews cited here are with movement leaders. Saavedra would not agree to an interview for this research; for his account of these events I must, therefore, rely solely on the statements published in newspaper coverage.

20. Víctor Gutiérrez and Marcelo Degadillo, interviews by the author, February 2010, Cochabamba.

21. Water wars participants, interviews by the author, August–September 2008 and January–February 2010, Cochabamba and La Paz.

22. Water wars participant, interview by the author, February 2010, Cochabamba.

23. Gonzalo Maldonado, interview by the author, January 2010, Cochabamba.

24. Water wars participant, interview by the author, August 2008, Cochabamba.

25. It was not until March that the foreign connections of the Aguas del Tunari conglomerate were revealed; the selling of the water to a foreign company was not yet a rallying cry of the movement.

26. José Antonio Gil, interview by the author, 2010, Cochabamba.

27. Gil, interview by the author.

28. Gil, interview by the author.

29. Gonzalo Maldonado, Walter Antezana, Oscar Olivera, Omar Fernandez, and Gabriel Herbas Camacho, interviews by the author, 2008, La Paz and Cochabamba.

30. Oscar Olivera, interview by the author, 2008, Cochabamba.

31. Victor Gutierrez, interview by the author, 2008, Cochabamba.

32. Ministry of the Economy official, interview by the author, 2009, Mexico City. Most members of the Mexican government at the time of the *tortillazo* would not allow me to attach their names to any quotations. Interviewees are named only in cases in

which the speaker gave explicit permission before, during, or after the interview for the use of his name. In all other cases, they are anonymous.

33. Los Pinos attendee, interview by the author, 2009, Mexico City.

34. Felix Vélez, interview by the author, 2009, Mexico City.

35. Signatories included the minister of the economy, the minister of agriculture, the president of the National Association of Industrial Corn, the vice president of corporate events for Walmart, the general director of Bimbo, and the presidents of Grupo Maseca and Grupo Minsa. Only *maíz blanco* intended for sale to *nixtamaleros* (those who nixtamalize corn) was included in the $3 pesos/kilo price.

36. Participating *tortillerías* were those with representation at the price pact negotiations. The relatively low percentage of *tortillerías* affected does not mean that the agreement affected a similarly low percentage of the quantity of tortillas sold. Participants tended to be larger *tortillerías* with wider distribution.

37. Interviews by the author, January–July 2009, Mexico City.

38. Tortilla prices did, indeed, continue to rise. But there appeared to be a sense among many Mexicans that Calderón had dealt with the issue. This suggests that concerns are not with prices per se but with how those prices are perceived. In particular, the idea that corn and tortilla prices should not be subject to the vicissitudes of markets appears to have been a critical component in explaining the timing of the protests and the lack of protest around price increases in subsequent months. Calderón had established that corn and tortillas would not be subject to the ups and downs (or at least just the ups) of markets. Future increases, while none included as dramatic a rise, did not spark social movement mobilization. Calderón staged a performance in Mexico—the price pact was part of a political dance to which many Mexican citizens responded. The intervention on January 18 was a public show of commitment to Mexico's poorest people. Regardless of how much material relief the price pact brought (arguably little), it served to demonstrate that the government was committed to protecting tortillas from market fluctuations.

39. Government official, interview by the author, 2009, Mexico City.

40. Government official, interview by the author, 2009, Mexico City.

41. When pressed, most officials conceded that they did not think "real" revolution was likely. Yet a widespread movement that brought the end to Calderón's administration entered the realm of the imaginable. This is particularly surprising in a state where political stability had been a hallmark of governance for more than seventy-five years. While Mexico has experienced its share of unrest, most notably in the late 1960s with the student movement, in the mid-1990s with the emergence of the Ejército Zapatista de Liberación Nacional (EZLN; Zapatista National Liberation Army), and more recently with the contestation over the 2006 presidential election, the president's ability to fulfill his electoral mandate has rarely come into question. In contrast to the political turmoil that remained in recent political memory in Bolivia (the 1978–1985 period in particular), every Mexican president since 1934 has completed his full term. To imagine a serious threat to a president's term was to imagine something that few living Mexicans could recall.

42. I anticipate that this misrecognition is possible because the symbolic and the material are so intimately intertwined where corn is concerned in Mexico. It is easy to see how individuals might think they are only evaluating corn's "material" role in Mexico when, in fact, their conceptions of what the material "is" are rooted in semiotic practices. While some of the statements and slogans during the *tortillazo* are easily read

as symbolic references (e.g., without corn there is no country), other elements of the actions may be less transparently symbolic and therefore harder for someone approaching the event with a positivist analytic lens to interpret as rooted in meaning-making practices.

43. Government official, interview by the author, 2009, Mexico City.

44. Government official, interview by the author, 2009, Mexico City.

45. In some contexts, flag destruction may very well be imbued with patriotic meanings, but the destruction of a symbol of the nation can be read most straightforwardly as an unpatriotic act.

46. Government official, interview by the author, 2009, Mexico City.

47. Government official, interview by the author, 2009, Mexico City.

48. Government official, interview by the author, 2009, Mexico City.

49. Government official, interview by the author, 2009, Mexico City.

50. Government official, interview by the author, 2009, Mexico City.

51. Gerardo Ruíz Mateos, minister of the economy, interview with the author, 2009, Mexico City.

52. Government official, interview by the author, 2009, Mexico City.

53. Government official, interview by the author, 2009, Mexico City.

54. Government officials, interviews by the author, January–June 2009, Mexico City.

55. Not one interviewee reported the same frequency for the meetings.

REFERENCES

Albro, Robert. 2005. "'The Water Is Ours, Carajo!' Deep Citizenship in Bolivia's Water War." In *Social Movements: An Anthropological Reader*, edited by June Nash, 249–271. Malden, MA: Blackwell.

Amenta, Edwin, Neal Caren, Tina Fetner, and Michael P. Young. 2002. "Challengers and States: Toward a Political Sociology of Social Movements." *Research in Political Sociology* 10:47–83.

Assies, Willem. 2003. "David versus Goliath in Cochabamba: Water Rights, Neoliberalism and the Revival of Social Protest in Bolivia." *Latin American Perspectives* 30 (3): 14–36.

Bakker, Karen J. 2003. *An Uncooperative Commodity: Privatizing Water in England and Wales*. New York: Oxford University Press.

Bishara, Dina. 2015. "The Politics of Ignoring: Protest Dynamics in Late Mubarak Egypt." *Perspectives on Politics* 13 (4): 958–975.

"Bloqueo de protesta contra el gobierno paralizó Cochabamba" [Antigovernment protest blockades paralyzed Cochabamba]. 2000. *Presencia*, February 5.

Boudreau, Vincent. 2004. *Resisting Dictatorship: Repression and Protest in Southeast Asia*. Cambridge: Cambridge University Press.

Brubaker, Rogers. 2004. *Ethnicity without Groups*. Cambridge, MA: Harvard University Press.

Calderón, Felipe. 2012. "Firma del acuerdo para estabilizar el precio de la tortilla" [Signing of the agreement to stabilize the tortilla price] (January 18, 2007). In *La voz de los hechos: Discursos del Presidente Felipe Calderón Hinojosa* [The voice of the facts: Speeches of President Felipe Calderón Hinojosa], 39–40. Mexico City: Fondo de Cultura Económica. Available at https://felipecalderon.org.mx/wp-content/up loads/2017/12/La-voz-de-los-hechos-PARTE-1.pdf.

Crespo Flores, Carlos. 2003. "Water Privatisation Policies and Conflicts in Bolivia: The Water War in Cochabamba (1999–2000)." Ph.D. diss., Oxford Brookes University.

Cunningham, David. 2004. *There's Something Happening Here: The New Left, the Klan, and FBI Counterintelligence*. Berkeley: University of California Press.

Davenport, Christian. "State Repression and Political Order." 2007. *Annual Review of Political Science* 10 (1): 1–23.

Davenport, Christian, Carol Mueller, and Hank Johnston. 2005. *Repression and Mobilization*. Minneapolis: University of Minnesota Press.

de Bakker, Frank G. A., Frank den Hond, Brayden King, and Klaus Weber. 2013. "Social Movements, Civil Society and Corporations: Taking Stock and Looking Ahead." *Organization Studies* 34 (5–6): 573–593.

Fearon, James D., and David D. Laitin. 1996. "Explaining Interethnic Cooperation." *American Political Science Review* 90 (4): 715–735.

Fourcade, Marion. 2011. "Cents and Sensibility: Economic Valuation and the Nature of 'Nature.'" *American Journal of Sociology* 116:1721–1711.

García, Alberto, Fernando García, and Luz Quintón. 2003. *La "Guerra del Agua": Abril de 2000, la crisis de la política en Bolivia* [The "Water War": April 2000, political crisis in Bolivia]. La Paz: Fundación PEIB.

Goodwin, Jeff, and James M. Jasper. 2012. *Contention in Context: Political Opportunities and the Emergence of Protest*. Stanford, CA: Stanford University Press.

Jasper, James M. 1997. *The Art of Moral Protest*. Chicago: University of Chicago Press.

Jasper, James M., and Jan Willem Duyvendak. 2015. *Players and Arenas: The Interactive Dimensions of Protest*. Amsterdam: Amsterdam University Press.

Javier Jiménez, Sergio. 2007. "Gobierno e IP logran el 'Pacto de la Tortilla'" [Government and IP archive the "Tortilla Pact"]. *El universal*, January 19.

Johnston, Hank, Enrique Laraña, and Joseph R. Gusfield. 1994. "Identities, Grievances, and New Social Movements." In *New Social Movements: From Ideology to Identity*, edited by Enrique Laraña, Hank Johnston, and Joseph R. Gusfield, 3–35. Philadelphia: Temple University Press.

King, Brayden G. 2008. "A Political Mediation Model of Corporate Response to Social Movement Activism." *Administrative Science Quarterly* 53 (3): 395–421.

———. 2011. "The Tactical Disruptiveness of Social Movements: Sources of Market and Mediated Disruption in Corporate Boycotts." *Social Problems* 58 (4): 395–421.

Kriesi, Hanspeter. 1995. *New Social Movements in Western Europe: A Comparative Analysis*. Minneapolis: University of Minnesota Press.

Lichbach, Mark Irving. 1995. *The Rebel's Dilemma*. Ann Arbor: University of Michigan Press.

Maldonado Rojas, Gonzalo. 2004. *H2O: La guerra del agua* [H2O: The water war]. La Paz: Fondo Editorial de los Diputados.

McAdam, Doug. 1983. "Tactical Innovation and the Pace of Insurgency." *American Sociological Review* 48:735–754.

McAdam, Doug, Sidney G. Tarrow, and Charles Tilly. 2001. *Dynamics of Contention*. Cambridge: Cambridge University Press.

McDonnell, Mary-Hunter, Brayden G King, and Sarah A. Soule. 2015. "A Dynamic Process Model of Private Politics: Activist Targeting and Corporate Receptivity to Social Challenges." *American Sociological Review* 80 (3): 654–678.

Opp, Karl-Dieter. 1988. "Grievances and Participation in Social Movements." *American Sociological Review* 53:853–864.

Peredo, Carmen, Carlos Crespo Flores, and Omar Fernández. 2004. *Los regantes de Cochabamba en la guerra del agua* [Cochabamban irrigators in the water war]. Cochabamba: CESU-UMSS.

"Retornó la calma a Cochabamba" [Calm returned to Cochabamba]. 2000. *Presencia*, February 6.

Roman, Jose Antonio. 2007. "Atender el llamado al diálogo, orden Calderón" [Comply with the call for dialogue, Calderón order]. *La jornada*, February 1.

Rubio, Blanca. 2007. "El campo no aguanta más: Claroscuros de un movimiento campesino" [The field cannot stand it anymore: Chiaroscuros of a peasant movement]. In *El campo no aguanta más*, edited by Armando S. Albarrán, 15–38. Mexico City: Universidad Autónoma Metropolitana Miguel Angel Porrúa.

Sewell, William H., Jr. 2005. *Logics of History: Social Theory and Social Transformation*. Chicago: University of Chicago Press.

Shultz, Jim. 2003. "Bolivia: The Water War Widens." *NACLA Report on the Americas* 36:34–37.

Simmons, Erica. 2014. "Grievances Do Matter in Mobilization." *Theory and Society* 43:513–536.

———. 2016a. "Corn, Markets, and Mobilization in Mexico." *Comparative Politics* 48:413–431.

———. 2016b. "Market Reforms and Water Wars." *World Politics* 61:37–73.

———. 2016c. *Meaningful Resistance: Market Reforms and the Roots of Social Protest in Latin America*. New York: Cambridge University Press.

Skrentny, John D. 2006. "Policy-Elite Perceptions and Social Movement Success: Understanding Variations in Group Inclusion in Affirmative Action." *American Journal of Sociology* 111 (6): 1762–1815.

Soule, Sarah A. 2009. *Contention and Corporate Social Responsibility*. New York: Cambridge University Press.

Zelizer, Viviana A. 2011. *Economic Lives: How Culture Shapes the Economy*. Princeton, NJ: Princeton University Press.

8

Missing Targets

Contemporary Slaveholder Responses to Human Rights Advocacy

A<small>USTIN</small> C<small>HOI</small>-F<small>ITZPATRICK</small>

The individuals and institutions that social movements target are a black box. There is a reason for this. From the 1960s onward, social movement scholarship has illuminated a range of collective endeavors. This has included name-brand movements (civil rights, women's, LGBT, peace) and a host of causal factors, including emotion (Goodwin, Jasper, and Polletta 2009), resources (McCarthy and Zald 1977), cultural dynamics (Snow et al. 1986), and structural factors (McAdam 1999; Tarrow 2011).

Only recently are we starting to see studies on right-wing movements (Blee 2002; McVeigh 2009; McVeigh and Estep 2019), elite mobilization (Martin 2013), and the impact of countermobilization on movement outcomes (Andrews 2004). This previously sparse list has exploded, fueled by the persistence of conservative religious mobilization in the United States, increased mobilization in the Muslim world from the Arab Uprising onward, and, of course, the 2016 election of Donald Trump.

However, studies of awkward movements and the one percent continue to be exceptions to trend lines sketched by scholars who occupied the barricades in the 1960s. Our best case studies are of progressive movements. Movement scholars' more nuanced assessments are reserved for that which we understand the best and perhaps sympathize with the most. While our assessments of activists are rich, our understanding of their adversaries—those in power—are less sophisticated. Often, movement targets are reductions: "The Establishment." "The Man." Faceless, nameless, and legion.

This is probably due to a selection effect. It is very unlikely that anyone from the Occupy movement is going to join a Wall Street firm and generate participant observation data on Goldman Sachs's decision-making processes.

It is hard to get a job at Goldman Sachs, for example, in the first place. And with more than thirty-six thousand employees, there's simply no way to guarantee one will be at the right place at the right time when the firm decides how to respond to any particular collective action effort (Statista 2019).

Movements, in contrast, are where the action is—or at least where it is most visible. It may also be that movement scholars are reluctant to legitimate the actions of those who may enjoy general support. People engage in collective action to shed new light on old behavior and to thereby gain support for new ideas, individuals, or institutions. Perhaps appreciative inquiry among targets runs the risk of humanizing movement opponents and undermining the efficacy of injustice frames.

As a consequence, movement scholars have a general practice of deploying our methodological arsenal to tell half of the story. We apply the vivid colors in our palette to the movement and our droll and reductionist gray hues to the monolith of empire, capital, and systemic injustice that "The People" struggle against. This may provide a calming sense of solidarity, but it does not illuminate the full range of complexity at play in most collective action efforts. Half the story does an injustice to scholarship. Partial understandings also sell our movement allies short, as we regularly overestimate the simplicity and strength of a movement's impact. It is harder, but more honest, to take targets seriously. This chapter is a commitment to the "healthy conversation about movements and targets" that will "shift our analytic focus to the strategic interactions between various players" (see the Introduction).

Incumbents

Across our definitions, movements mobilize resources; rally people; frame issues; identify or create opportunities; create collective identities; and generate new political, cultural, and economic realities. Adversaries are targeted by the movement. Despite being significant actors in the real world, movement adversaries are *targeted by* movements—that is, they are the direct object of another's action. They are acted on. Rarely do they earn their own verbs. Yet they are clearly sophisticated actors. An abusive police force may be a movement's adversary while simultaneously engaged in fractious collective bargaining negotiations with the local government, all the while collaborating in an interagency coalition on crime prevention. What should we call such social actors? I prefer "incumbent" and "social movement target." Other terms work as well: Dieter Rucht (2004) uses "adversaries," which includes other movements, institutions, parties, administrative units, and public officials. "Adversary" emphasizes the conflict that often accompanies collective action yet overlooks a host of other configurations. Sidney Tarrow's definition of social movements specifies that they interact with "elites, opponents, and authorities" (2011, 9). This approach is simultaneously broad and exclusive because target composition, for Tarrow, appears to be part of the political opportunity context. Indeed, elites, opponents, and authorities are evidenced by "shifting political alignments" (165), "influential allies" (166), and "divided elites" (166). Rather than have three different types of actor, we have one group that is best understood as part of a political opportunity structure. Both approaches are also fundamentally movement-centric. Recent scholarship, as this book readily attests, suggests that movements target complex social and economic actors rather than static and fixed targets. The result is a series of strategic engagements between complex social actors.

For James Jasper and his fellow travelers (Jasper and Duyvendak 2015; Duyvendak and Jasper 2015), movements engage in a number of arenas and in the process engage with a host of strategic players. For scholars such as Neil Fligstein and Doug McAdam, incumbents exist in broader "socially constructed arenas within which actors with varying resource endowments vie for the advantage" (2012, 10). Both approaches provide more sophisticated ways of conceptualizing movement targets as actors simultaneously working or playing (choose your metaphor) at one or more levels. Movements target incumbents—those already in positions of power and authority. Most social movements, whether violent or nonviolent, aim to secure new rights or recognition from those in power. Thinking in terms of incumbents takes us closer to a value-neutral and less movement-centric analysis of this set of actors. Slaveholding was an incumbent practice worldwide two hundred years ago. It was supported by an incumbent notion of inequality and paternalism. Incumbent legal, financial, and religious institutions reinforced these practices and ideas.

What good does it do to know that a board of directors is simultaneously operating at three different levels? Or in the case I indicated earlier, what good does it do to know that the police are simultaneously the targets of mobilization and mobilizing themselves through collective bargaining? This is not a rhetorical question but an open one that has yet to be addressed by social movement scholarship. The current approach has been to explore whether an embattled board of directors or well-connected police force represents a political opportunity or threat to movements.

In the end, I propose that social movement incumbents are individual, collective, or conceptual subjects of collective challenges for resources, recognition, or change (Choi-Fitzpatrick 2017). This definition has the benefit of emphasizing a wide range of target types, including private and institutional individual actors, collective groups or institutions, and cultural factors such as norms and ideas. Incumbent actors—indeed the emphasis in this chapter is on incumbent social actors, leaving incumbent *ideas* for another day—may be engaged in collective action efforts of their own at the very moment they are also targeted by social movements. Incumbency is an emergent property of dense concentrations of intellectual, cultural, and structural power and authority. It arises when incumbent justifications predominate in sociocultural spaces.

Complex institutions are inhabited by competing networks of groups and individuals intent on changing particular policies, negotiating certain settlements, extracting certain concessions, obtaining new identities, and generally securing for themselves the sorts of gains associated with progressive collective action efforts. Actors within complex institutions, such as churches, universities, and governmental departments, are regularly acting according to the principles identified by social movement theory. A new body of work (King 2008; Walker, Martin, and McCarthy 2008; Martin, McPhail, and McCarthy 2009) suggests that social movement theories can be applied in many contexts. Stripping away the normative objectives that make movements so intriguing to scholars allows for a new and unblinkered view of social movement activity itself. There is no "view from nowhere," but perhaps we would be aided by a "few from someplace new."

In what follows I advance six general observations about social, political, or economic actors who have been targeted by social movements. Incumbents play a critical role in collective action insofar as they:

1. Shape movement tactics
2. Rely on resources
3. Rely on culture
4. Respond to opportunities and threats
5. Affect outcomes
6. Vary in willingness and ability to respond to movements

I discuss each observation in turn, referring to relevant literature as appropriate and referring to my own work in a handful of cases (Choi-Fitzpatrick 2015, 2016, 2017). Along the way I illustrate these possibilities by drawing on interviews with contemporary human rights violators. Interviews with perpetrators of bonded labor (a form of modern slavery) in India shed light on the extent to which their unique attributes shape movement efforts, the extent to which they rely on critical political and economic resources and cultural norms, the way they perceive broader changes as either opportunities or threats, and the way they choose to respond to collective action. Bonded labor is a labor relationship in which an individual exchanges his or her total economic capacity for an initially fixed amount of money. Subsequent debts often compound the years spent in the charge of a more powerful and often upper-caste employer. Fieldwork in communities targeted by social movement organizations led to surprisingly frank interviews with landlords, factory owners, managers, and recruiters. Interviewees across fifteen intervention sites spoke about each of the factors listed, and these findings are cursorily introduced in the pages that follow (and discussed in greater length in my previous publications).

I conclude each section with a hypothesis for future research. While I conclude this essay with a brief exploration of how these approaches may explain incumbent behavior, robust quantitative analysis must be brought to bear on some of these questions. As we see in the chapter's concluding observations, other puzzles elude empirical assessment, including the question of whether movements modulate or transform oppressor consciousness, as measured by changes in attitude. I am skeptical about our ability to measure such phenomena accurately but look forward to any attempts to do so. In what follows I am arguing that if social movement scholarship has helped us understand "The Masses," perhaps these same movement tools may help shed some light on "The Man."

Possibilities

Incumbency Shapes Movement Tactics

Social movement targets are not passive recipients of movement efforts. Recent work by Tim Bartley and Curtis Child (2014) has demonstrated the "social production of targets." This process relies on activities at two levels. The first is relative to the business itself (Bartley and Child's unit of analysis). Social movements do not simply target offending corporations. Bartley and Child demonstrate this with a comparative approach that points to a host of targetable corporations that have simply escaped movement attention (e.g., American Eagle, Columbia Sportswear, Converse, Timberland, Vans), while others have been the result of sustained campaigns (e.g., Nike, Walmart, the Gap, Guess, Levi Strauss). Large firms with recognizable brand names are more likely to be targeted in Bartley and Child's study than are smaller or less visible companies (2014, 15). Here targeting is the product of firm behavior (e.g., violating labor or environmental standards) together with firm legibility as a target.

Visibility matters. This structural component of targeting is complemented by a second, more cultural, process. Some corporations are more targetable than others because of a combination of prior corporate social responsibility commitments and a particular crisis. A crisis within a company wanting to be seen "doing something" in response to growing criticism may thus result in scrutiny and the emergence of a campaign. Once this has happened, reputational stickiness comes into play (Fischer and Reuber 2007), with public/stakeholder knowledge about past infractions shading perceptions of current behavior. A firm's reputation may be critical to unions and other movement actors, but it is also of interest to the general public, policy makers, stockholders, and competitors. Bartley and Child convincingly argue that "certain firms (firms that were large, leading advertisers/branders, and with good reputations and recognition for social responsibility) were almost guaranteed to be targets of anti-sweatshop activism, while firms lacking structural power and cultural vulnerability were almost guaranteed not to become targets, even though some of them could credibly be charged with profiting from sweatshops" (2014, 21). Targets shape movement decisions, however passively and unintentionally (see also Walker, Martin, and McCarthy 2008). Movements also target institutions that have the kind of profile that will have a demonstration effect. Targetability, from the movement's perspective, is the result of both what a target does and who the target is.

Incumbent behavior, in turn, has an effect on the ultimate movement outcome. The reason for this is fairly straightforward: Targets are complicated social actors. This is particularly true if the target is an individual making decisions at the fraught intersection of values and interests. It is also true if the target is a publicly held corporation whose decision-making is complicated by pressure from managers, stockholders, customers, and regulators. Ion Bogdan Vasi and Brayden King (2012) have recently used social movement theory to illustrate the impact that stakeholder activism has on a firm's assessment of environmental risk. This negative assessment, in turn, negatively affects financial performance. How targets—individual antagonists or decision-making individuals within institutions—emote and assess shapes whether and how they respond. This is clearly demonstrated in earlier work by James Jasper and Jane Poulsen (1993) that emphasizes the ways targets respond tactically and iteratively to collective challenges. Some creativity and trial and error are required for institutions to get their approach right. An initial response might be based on a misunderstanding of the public's support for the incumbent's behavior. Likewise, a heavy-handed response from an incumbent may confirm the challenger's narrative, further undermining incumbent claims to legitimacy.

In my own work on the contemporary antislavery movement I found that targeting decisions among groups working to end bonded labor in India cluster around three interconnected considerations: (1) the organization's theory of change, (2) factors specific to the incumbent, and (3) probability of success. I have not found these features to be discrete. A legal aid organization focused on deterrence may choose only cases of trafficking and slavery that have a high likelihood of gaining public attention and setting important precedents (the American advocacy group International Justice Mission matches this description). A community organizing effort, however, may train organizers in communities ripe for collective action challenges for clearly defined rights or recognition (the global advocacy group Global Alliance against Trafficking in Women [GAATW] matches this description). In each case challengers assess the extent to which the incumbent matches the movement's ideal-type target. It is not necessarily the worst or most visible offenders who get targeted. It might be the low-hanging fruit in one situation and the toughest nut in another. Work alongside advocacy groups has led me to conclude that there is a clear interaction effect between these three factors. The probability of success increases when a powerful tactic thwarts a weak rights violator—but this is unsatisfactory for an organization like the International Justice Mission, whose theory of change requires it to pursue precedent-setting cases. Challenger tactics emerge from a decision-making process that varies in complexity based on actor type.

Targets respond in turn. The nature and extent of incumbents' response have a lot to do with their ability to respond. When a legal aid organization drags a powerful trafficker to court, it can expect a prolonged fight that is often punctuated by corruption, threats, and violence. When a community organizing group mobilizes a women's savings collective to thwart avaricious moneylenders, the incumbent's response has a lot to do with its reliance on this market, access to other markets, ability to deploy coercive force, and so forth. Conversations with rights violators in a rapidly changing India suggests perpetrators' ability to respond to collective action has a lot to do with the extent to which they are connected to fast-growing segments of the Indian economy or are trapped in its economic backwaters.

Perpetrators may preemptively trade in old forms of power for new ones, as when my fieldwork identified a small-time operator who voluntarily emancipated his two bonded laborers to align himself with an internationally recognized effort to create new markets for employers who denounced exploitation. The operator in question simultaneously rejected feudal exploitation and embraced a leadership role in a new-economy operation.

Rather than be passive recipients of collective action, targets are active and engaged social actors embedded in complex fields and arenas of action. Individuals, and individuals working within institutions, exercise judgment and take action in response to movements. Relatively unexplored, however, is the general question of why targets respond the way that they do. Movement scholars are rarely in the position to engage movement opponents in frank interviews or to "'man' the battle stations" as participant observers when the movement's salvos begin.

HYPOTHESES
- Incumbent features and behavior shape movement tactics.
- Incumbent features and behavior shape target response.

Incumbents Rely on Resources

This observation is obvious, but its implications are significant. The point of resource mobilization theory was that opponents have more resources. So this fact was controlled for, as *movement* resources became the focus. The selective incentive of solidarity combines with the tangible resources provided by institutional support (buildings, staff, publicity materials) to mobilize the marginalized. As a result, incumbent resources are widely recognized yet poorly understood. Social movement targets are not evenly and equally able to respond to cost-raising behavior from movements. Boycotts, work slowdowns, and declining stock valuations are believable pressures for target leadership to grapple with, just as these same factors were previously considered their resources—for example, large workforce, low wages, and high-profile stock.

As the previous section suggests, social movements take key resources into consideration when they decide whom to target. It stands to reason that these factors also affect how this targeting takes place. Sociologist Kevin Bales has suggested that boycotts are not the best sanction for multinationals that rely on exploited labor to drive costs down. The reason is that the blunt pressure of a boycott will force a multinational to respond with an equally blunt action: eliminating forced labor from its supply chain by firing subcontractors and forced laborers. The offending multinational overcomes a public relations threat and perhaps raises its prices to cover higher wages (Luders 2010). The victim of forced labor, Bales argues, then becomes a victim of a hasty housecleaning.

Incumbent resources also shape their ability to respond. There is good reason to expect that institutions targeted because they have strong reputations are best positioned to initiate a countermobilization but may be the least likely to do so out of fear of a backlash. Incumbent resources are both a blessing and a curse, allowing for a range of responses in theory while limiting them in practice. This limitation is linked to the source of the incumbent's resources.

Most complex organizations rely on an admixture of resources, from cash to critical approval, and must engage in sophisticated decision-making when responding to collective action demands. Political patronage might allow for a certain amount of repression at the same time as challenges to a monopoly threaten the cash flow that makes this patronage possible. Social movement scholars have long debated whether resources lead to mobilization (McCarthy and Zald 1977) or to capitulation (Piven and Cloward 1977). This tension is easily traced through our assessment of incumbent behavior.

Cash and caste are king in rural India. The former is rapidly supplanting the latter in areas that are also experiencing changes in physical infrastructure—that is, when people have a chance to leave. Fieldwork in the midst of economic transformation highlights the changing role of key resources. Caste and land were once the only currency for powerful landlords, who set themselves up as lenders of last resort and subsequently benefited from systems of bonded labor. Over time, however, caste is being replaced by cash and connectivity. A static notion of incumbent resources would suggest that incumbent power is stable—yet in India, as in every place besieged by the market economy—power is in flux. When the devalued resource is status or identity—for example, caste—it is harder to convert into the new coin of the realm. Of course it is not impossible, something Charles Tilly clearly demonstrated in *Durable Inequality* (1998). The point here is that resources are not static.

HYPOTHESES

- Tactics targeting incumbent resources are more successful.
- Stability of resources depends on their location in social, political, and economic systems and on the relative stability of those systems.
- Increased resources allow for a greater range of responses.
- Resources weaken incumbents when those resources rely on the opinion of external stakeholders.

Incumbents Rely on Culture (Opinions and Assumptions)

Social movements are congregations of people working together for some change-oriented goals. The status quo they wish to change includes key stakeholders who have grown comfortable with, and benefited from, the way things are. This state of affairs manifests itself in culture and resources—as we see in the prior two sections—that combine into a general sense of *incumbency*. Incumbency is an emergent property of intellectual, cultural, and structural power and authority. It generates a sense of natural everydayness and normality.

Thus, for those employing bonded laborers, "the enslavement of a worker is simply a small variable among many in a much larger economic equation" (Bales 2004, 27). While this variable may be one of many, it is not inconsequential, since it has an impact on an ordered cultural system shared by victim and perpetrator alike. For many rights violators who find themselves targeted by social movements, this ordered cultural system is shaped by social, political, legal, and economic advantages that are reproduced through social action (Sewell 1992) and give rise to an oppressor consciousness that Paolo Freire aptly described as transforming "everything surrounding it into an object of its domination. The earth, property, production, the creations of people, people themselves, time—everything is reduced to the status of objects at its disposal" (2018, 58; see also Buber [1923] 1970).

Yet while Freire argues that this reduction is rooted in sadism (2018, 59, 89), Mary Jackman (1994) has more plausibly argued that the oppressor's worldview is punctuated by a toxic paternalism that masks the expropriative relationship from both the subordinate and dominant. "That ideology," Jackman argues, "is a collective property" that "permeates the main institutions and communications networks of organized social life and is propagated with an easy vehemence that can come only from uncontrived sincerity" (1994, 8). In this way the unequal relationship is "swathed in a morality" that links the worth of the oppressed to a relationship defined by the oppressor (8). Perhaps increased oppositional consciousness and resistance lead to an increase in concerns about insubordination—what E. P. Thompson has called "the diminution of deference" (1993, 36) and what Thavolia Glymph may as well have called a "diminution of difference" (2008, 223).

Incumbency matters because it shapes these expectations about social relations. It also shapes expectations about what sorts of responses are appropriate: Is it a countermovement or repression that will do the trick? Power begets power. Power also begets expectation. Simply put, incumbents almost always have more power than movements. The appearance of that power—the projection of a closed opportunity context—is critical to thwarting mobilization. It may also invite that very mobilization if it is combined with self-proclaimed moral authority and significant market share (Bartley and Child 2014).

Being an incumbent involves occupying a relatively stable position in relation to a challenger. This flexibility is one of the reasons I prefer the term "incumbent." Further, it does not imply any normative bias. Incumbents may be powerful in absolute terms but are just as likely to be powerful only relative to challengers. In other words, incumbents possess power and authority relative to a particular challenger. This approach borrows heavily from newer theoretical approaches that emphasize the extent to which movements occur within or are nested in overlapping fields or arenas (Fligstein and McAdam 2012; Jasper and Duyvendak 2015).

Dominant conceptualizations of gender and sexuality, and the real institutional and individual behavior that reinforced it, faced significant challenges from the women's movement starting in the 1960s. Likewise, the

second-wave feminists who led this challenge themselves held dispropor-
tionate power and authority in the movement and soon faced challenges
from a more diverse array of movement actors—leading to what we now call
third-wave feminism.

The analytic flexibility provided by the term "incumbent" should not
mask the fact that the structural reality of incumbency is manifest in a paradigmatic worldview. Incumbents often possess greater resources than do
movements. They are also better positioned to guide popular interpretations
of movement efforts. Incumbency, I argue, emerges at the intersection of
these two factors. In my own work a shared notion of *caste*—and the atten-
dant duty to a moral order—has long served as a restraint to challengers,
effectively offering to incumbents a coercion discount. Less force is exerted
when it is not needed. Obvious, but true. Powerful landlords in rural India
did not invent the caste system, but they used it deftly to their advantage. As
the caste system is undermined by the market, new cultural norms and
forms are emerging to accommodate new forms of exploitation. As seen
from earlier vignettes, some incumbents are better positioned than others to
take advantage of these times of change.

HYPOTHESES
- Incumbent interpretations of reality predominate in popular
  culture.
- Incumbent interpretations of reality may also be present among
  challengers.

Incumbents Respond to Opportunities and Threats

Social movements are thought to respond to opportunities and threats. This
same logic can be applied to the incumbents they challenge. Incumbents
lacking internal consensus on how to respond to challengers or lacking the
resources necessary to counter movement gains may find themselves put off
balance. This state of affairs is typically thought of as an opportunity for the
movement. It is just as accurate to think of this as a threat to the incumbent.
Threats can be thought of as cost-raising conditions. Violent repression
raises the costs of mobilization, and in the absence of deep philosophical
commitments and strong social bonds this is likely to result in movement
failure (a point made by Jeremy Weinstein [2005] in his work on armed
rebels).

The same is true for incumbents—credible threats emerge only when
movements are able to begin exacting true costs. As preceding sections demonstrate, incumbency comes in many forms and some targets are more

vulnerable than others to variation in public opinion. Publicly traded corporations, for example, may be threatened by rumors, since negative publicity can instantly wipe important value off the books, regardless of the merit of a particular story. Likewise, privately held companies may be impervious to even damning findings as long as they have the cash reserves to offset state-initiated fines and sanctions, should the movement ever secure such an outcome.

Jack Goldstone and Charles Tilly have modeled much the same thing regarding the state: Protests emerge when gains are expected to outweigh costs (including threats, like repression) (2001, 184–185). But the state's ability to respond is conditioned on its own weakness (or strength), popular support, and the strength of the movement's allies and opponents. Movement targets must also make such cost-benefit calculations. While incumbency may provide some cultural capital for antimovement issue framing, there is no guarantee that it will succeed, especially in times of broader social and economic transformation.

As mentioned earlier, in some cases movement challenges create opportunities for incumbents, as occurs when a small-time operator effectively traded in his bonded laborers for a position at the head of a network. Any observer of market economies can see the wisdom in this move, independent of ethics, as he moved from the caste economy to the cash economy. For others the loss of a laborer is treated as a profound threat—whether economic, psychological, or both. In another instance a former slaveholder searched high and low for a runaway, expressing to me great frustration that the worker would be so ungrateful. Such impudence, like insurgencies more broadly, are seen by perpetrators as economic threats (compliant workers are seen as an economic necessity) and an insult to one's honor. Even more challenging is the possibility that one person's threat is another's opportunity.

HYPOTHESES
- Threats and opportunities are subject to incumbent perception.
- Incumbent institutions' perceptions may be multiple and heterogeneous (i.e., directors, managers, and stockholders may not agree).

Incumbents Affect Outcomes

Incumbents shape outcomes. The most obvious way in which they do this is tied to the very position, capacity, resources, and structural affordances that incumbency provides. These attributes shape not only short-term but also medium- and long-term outcomes. Institutional actors, states especially, are often limited to the acceptance and advantages first identified by William Gamson's (1990) breakthrough work on movement outcomes. Early scholarship, including Gamson's, focused on movement "success" and "failure" (see, e.g., Gamson 1990, 195), while later work broadened to include an expanded range of outcomes. Here, too, the implicit category is the movement—the success or failure of a movement has given rise to a broader assessment of movement outcomes.

Dynamic interactions between incumbents and challengers generate new social realities: new actors, new resources, new tactics, new ideas and ideals, new opportunities and threats, and new incumbents. Some of these realities are immediately obvious; others take much longer to manifest, perhaps themselves grist for subsequent mobilization. Popular pressure to reduce crime in the 1990s led to the harsh sentencing policies that two decades later produced popular pressure to rein in the harsh policing tactics that flourished within an anticrime environment (Alexander 2012). Kenneth Andrews's (2004) work on the establishment of alternative educational institutions in response to gains by the civil rights movement demonstrates the way local attitudes and resources shape movement outcomes. This is complicated comparative-historical work of the most demanding sort.

Shorter-range studies may also shed light on nearer-term outcomes. A focus on incumbent outcomes prompts us to recognize that while movements may win or lose, they may also engage in countermobilization or repression. In fact, incumbents have a wider-than-recognized range of responses available to them. They may certainly support or create a countermovement in the hope of undermining the challenger. This can happen through the funding of a radical-flank effort or supporting grassroots efforts to counter the movement's claim in public discourse. Incumbents, states especially, are in a position to initiate soft and hard repression. Such repression may trigger a new wave of mobilization, but it is more likely to drive away the sort of general-affinity supporters that social movements rely on to demonstrate worthiness, unity, numbers, and commitment (WUNC, in Tilly's [1999] formulation). These two short-term responses have been the focus of excellent scholarship (Davenport 2007, 2015; Earl 2003). Yet not every incumbent has the willingness or ability to engage in these tactics.

Three additional tactics have attracted less attention, perhaps as a result of their pedestrian quality: persistence, adaptation, and quitting (Choi-Fitzpatrick 2017). Simply put, some incumbents possess the right combination of hubris and resources to continue on with the behavior that originally drew movement attention in the first place. Other incumbents may, for whatever reason, elect to instead adapt to the new state of affairs by retaining as many of the key features of the old practice as possible. This response is known as greenwashing in the environmental justice movement. Finally, incumbents who are unwilling or unable to persist or adapt may elect to simply succumb to movement claims. How exactly this occurs is the topic of the next final observation. In the preceding pages I describe characters who fit into each of these categories.

HYPOTHESES
- Incumbents select tactics that they feel are appropriate considering their capacity and the broader context.
- Incumbents may use preemptive tactics to prevent consolidation of grievances.
- Most incumbents respond to movements in one of five ways: cooptation, countermobilizing, repressing, persisting, or quitting.

Incumbents Vary in Willingness and Ability to Respond to Movements

At the individual level, incumbents' response to challengers is shaped by their ability and willingness to meet the movement's demands. By ability I mean the actual capacity to pursue a desired plan of action, whether repression or resignation. It is clear that the ability to respond is unevenly distributed, whether the unit of analysis is the sole individual or established institution. The ability to respond is empirically measurable, at least in general terms. The state's monopoly on coercive violence, the corporation's tight relationship with advertiser-sensitive media channels, and major institutions' broad-based legitimacy are key benefits of incumbency that can be mobilized to respond to challenges, even if key decision-making moments are difficult to identify. Individual incumbents are similarly explicable.

The same cannot be said about individual willingness to respond to challenges. By willingness I mean an attitudinal disposition toward a particular response. This factor is as analytically critical as it is empirically challenging. The social sciences, and none more so than sociology, are built on the observable and measurable. Behavior is easy to see, count, and test. It can be pinpointed and specified. It can be cross-tabbed and mapped. It can be presented with an arithmetic flourish that delights the eyes of the economist, the state, and the market. No such tools exist for attitudinal change. There is no protractor for measuring the subtle arc of a changed mind. Efforts exist. Interviewers, surveyors, and participant observers stand around people and groups with clipboards and digital recorders and keen observation skills. They extract sharp observations, cultural insights, key themes, and new questions. They describe, in the end, the wan arc of speech—the way people talk about the way that they think and feel. But how are we to measure what never gets said? And how are we to think about, ask about, talk about things that have no names? This is the realm of art, prophecy, and witchcraft. It is no wonder that we steer clear of motives. Yet surely social movements present changes at both the behavioral and attitudinal levels.

Otherwise, why are change agents in this racket, the business of changing hearts and minds? Counterinsurgencies win when they hold the land and the populace. Political campaigns win if their message resonates in the ballot box and the voters' narrative of the moment. If we really start to dig into attitudinal change, we are in much different territory from that traditionally trod in social movement scholarship. In fact, we are in the land of the missionary, the cult, the brainwasher, the military, and the church. We are in the land of the transformation of the mind, the conversion of the political self, and so forth. This is not a world easily mappable with the tools found in most movement scholars' toolkits.

Perhaps this terrain is not even mappable; it certainly proved too difficult to address in my own work. Nevertheless, there is always some fool willing to try. Movements change the cost-benefit analyses of incumbents. They also engage in broader debates that expand and transform the cultural and ideational space in which incumbents move. For example, consider a business that begins to feel uneasy about its manufacturing process but knows that doing the right thing will require increases in production costs that will raise the cost of a product above a certain threshold, beyond which consumer commitment is unmeasurable. In this case a social movement calling for a boycott will be met with a certain measure of appreciation, since the movement will have aggregated sentiment and demand and will have rallied public opinion around the possibility of a higher price point. The role of the social movement in this example is to help consumers overcome the hurdle represented by the higher costs, with the injustice frame serving as the key fulcrum in the process. The movement gains allow the incumbent institution to do the good it was originally hoping to do. Of course, this example presents a methodological challenge: Most corporations will cover a retreat with a vocal claim to a long-standing commitment to the issue at hand. Watching from the outside, from the movement's perspective, the movement scholar is unable to ascertain the true process. The solution here is methodological: More scholarship must be undertaken within a wider range of social actors. A current wave of mobilization intended to hold abusive police accountable will generate a solid wave of dissertations and subsequent monographs. Virtually every one will offer a new view from the blockade. Until that changes, incumbent motives will be heavily filtered, if they are explored at all.

TABLE 8.1 A PRIMITIVE TYPOLOGY OF INCUMBENT DECISION-MAKING

	High ability	Low ability
High willingness	Incumbent response (IR): Persist Outcome (O): Persistence	IR: Give up slowly O: Initial repression followed by resignation or adaptation
Low willingness	IR: Give up easily O: Adaptation (or quitting)	IR: Give up slowly O: Quitting (or adaptation)

In the anticipation of future research, I offer a hypothetical typology of individual movement targets' response (Table 8.1). I do so with an eye toward exploring the relationship between willingness and ability, between motive and capacity. This typology is premised on the assumption that not everyone is able to act as he or she pleases. Furthermore, it controls for variation in challenger attributes, especially worthiness, unity, numbers, and commitment. The punch line is that challengers are less likely to succeed should they go up against a challenger with deep pockets and an immunity or indifference to public opinion and market valuation (high ability) and with a core commitment to the status quo behavior targeted by the movement (high willingness). Of course, challenger-level and interaction-level factors matter tremendously, but these points are amply made by the lion's share of social movement scholarship.

Defiant Persistence: High Willingness and High Ability

In the "High ability" column of Table 8.1 are first the incumbents that are both willing and able to continue with the behavior that originally earned movement attention. This combination of capacity and commitment may deter movements from targeting such an actor in the first place, since it is unclear that collective action can raise the cost of persistence beyond what the incumbent can bear. Small-arms manufacturers in the United States, for example, appear determined to continue the mass production of the weapons used in mass killings. Although they face an incredibly charged political environment rather than a social movement, their incentive structures are biased away from public opinion and in favor of a better-mobilized set of institutional consumers (governments) and a formidable association (the National Rifle Association). This reality might lead movement advocates to direct their energies toward a softer target, such as elected representatives vulnerable to reelection challenges. Here the incumbent's initial response is to continue business as usual, and there may not appear be much that the movement itself can do to change this calculation as long as the target has strong commitments, has key resources, and lacks visible vulnerabilities.

Defiant Compromise: High Willingness and Low Ability

In the "Low ability" column are first the incumbents who would prefer to continue the status quo but may not necessarily be able to do so. This configuration represents ideal targeting conditions for a movement. The incumbent may assume it has capacities that it in fact lacks (i.e., both parties see an opportunity). Such a misperception may lead to a critical misstep should the incumbent choose to repress or countermobilize against the movement, only to find that a key source of legitimacy at the state or social level is no longer supportive. This possibility, too, was first identified by Goldstone and Tilly: The state may "overestimate its own support . . . [and] its own strength, and thus arrive at a different estimate of opportunity than that held by the protest group" (2001, 187). The result is that the state may face some difficulty in "picking the right level of concessions and repression to respond to a group" (187). Such conditions favor challengers who are willing to rapidly iterate tactics to find what works. In the postbellum American South, high willingness to continue slavery matched with a low ability to do so led to chain gangs, segregation, and poll taxes.

Compliant Adaptation: Low Willingness and High Ability

In the second row of the "High ability" column are incumbents who have the ability to continue engaging in status quo behavior but choose not to. This configuration also represents an ideal movement target as long as the movement is able to frame the issue in a way that resonates with the incumbent. Support for the status quo may be low for any number of reasons. It may have been eroded by broader social changes that shed new light on old practices. Legacy violators may recognize these changing times and perhaps even experience regret at some level (though regret rarely leads to sacrificial remuneration, such as reparations). Changes in the means of production may likewise undermine the long-term economic value of old practices. Movements may provide a rights-violating employer, for example, the opportunity to make a shift from manual labor to mechanized production and to do so in the name of enlightened humanitarianism. Here the outcome is likely to be either the adaptation of practices or simply quitting the targeted behavior altogether.

Compliant Resignation: Low Willingness and Low Ability

In the second row of the "Low ability" column are incumbents who find themselves targeted for actions that they do not support and cannot afford. This is quite similar to the preceding category, except incumbents here have no real choice in the matter, so they are perhaps less likely to pivot to other forms of exploitation. These are the incumbents that, if targeted, might most clearly represent what movements are talking about when they describe "success." The outcome is direct and it is final. It is direct because there is no iterative process as the unwilling incumbent struggles to come to terms with its more limited range of options. It is final because it is less likely that an incumbent will scramble to find an appropriate approximation for the targeted behavior. Here a note about willingness may be in order. Why would rights violators, for example, be actively engaged in activities they are unwilling to pursue? The puzzle is clear, yet this paradox is widespread in times of change, as incumbents profess sympathy for a particular claim but go on to state they "simply cannot afford it" or that "it's not the way things are done around here." Here we arrive at a sticky wicket—whether we believe such statements or dismiss them as false consciousness. My own position on this is informed by Elisabeth Noelle-Neumann's notion of the "spiral of silence," drawn directly from Alexis de Tocqueville: "More frightened of isolation than of committing an error, they joined the masses even though they did not agree with them" (quoted in Noelle-Neumann 1974, 43). In her empirical assessment, the simple reality of social life means that a person's "not isolating himself is more important than his own judgment" (43). The implication here is that an unknown number of social actors regularly engage in activities about which they harbor significant doubts and discomfort.

The key causal factor in the first row of the table is increased *cost*. In the second, it is changed *norms*. Perhaps here we find those moments in which targeted individuals operating on their own, or within institutions, see the rationale within a particular social change arguments but do not feel able to take the next step toward radical and costly action. If *incumbency* describes the worldview that accrues and accretes around patterned status, resources, and behavior, then what shall we call that moment when an individual sees beyond incumbency, outside the dominant frame? Might movements deliver moral shocks to incumbents (Jasper 1997)? Could collective action initiate cognitive liberation within a movement adversary (McAdam 1999)?

Conclusion

Contemporary social movement scholarship was conceived in the 1960s and born in the 1970s in the midst of an explosion of interest in "The People." This trend, and the sentiment that underpins it, is understandable. Who, after seeing gross injustice and then seeing the victims of injustice rise up against their oppressors, gives more credence to the powerful perpetrator of injustice, to the ones for whom histories have always been written? Since the

1960s, the answer has been clear: Very few are interested in the life and times of incumbents. As a result, case studies often present movement explanations of target motives and behavior as if they are the real thing.

As a result, incumbents are relegated to a residual category of the movement itself. They are rarely fully formed social actors with sociologically legible arguments. Incumbents' arguments are thought to come from an earlier era that is now contested, an era that is no longer right. As a result, their arguments, like the era they represent, are no longer relevant. It is easy to moralize in retrospect, once tactical victories give way to broader changes in the field itself. Once tactical victories enter the status quo, it is easy to forget how many movements have transformed social ills into positive social norms. It is important to recognize that many issues start out as acceptable and unremarkable yet end up being beyond the pale.

The novelty of this argument is empirical rather than theoretical. Definitions of social movements are politically neutral, emphasizing the process in a rather apolitical way. Protests are "the act of challenging, resisting, or making demands upon authorities, powerholders, and/or cultural beliefs and practices by some individual or group" (Goodwin and Jasper 2014, 3). Social movements are *contentious collective challenges, based on common purposes and social solidarities, in sustained interaction with elites, opponents, and authorities* (Tarrow 2011). Both approaches leave ample room for theorizing incumbent individuals, institutions, and ideas. If normative bias exists, it is to be found not in our definitions but in the assumptions that underpin our research designs and case selection. Movement-centric case studies relegate incumbents to a static role as a component of the opportunity structure.

Much more can be done if scholarship moves beyond structural assessments to incorporate more cultural and relational approaches to authorities, power holders, cultural beliefs, elites, opponents, and authorities. In this chapter, I attempt to suggest a number of possible paths for future research. At present, however, a few things can be said about incumbents: Their range of motion is shaped by their choice in tactics, their access to resources, their cultural position and capacity, the inertia of incumbency, and their perception of threats and opportunities. As a result, they play an important role in shaping the outcome of tactical struggles between incumbents and challengers. Unfortunately, our ability to test many of the hypotheses that emerge from these observations is limited by the fact that individual attitudinal change is difficult to measure. A series of movement successes may result in modified incumbent behavior, without ever addressing underlying attitudes. As a result, deep movement gains may be shown to have shallower roots in times of broad social, economic, and political transformation.

REFERENCES

Alexander, Michelle. 2012. *The New Jim Crow: Mass Incarceration in the Age of Color-blindness*. New York: New Press.

Andrews, Kenneth T. 2004. *Freedom Is a Constant Struggle: The Mississippi Civil Rights Movement and Its Legacy*. Chicago: University of Chicago Press.

Bales, Kevin. 2004. "Slavery and the Human Right to Evil." *Journal of Human Rights* 3 (1): 55–65.

Bartley, Tim, and Curtis Child. 2014. "Shaming the Corporation: The Social Production of Targets and the Anti-sweatshop Movement." *American Sociological Review* 79 (4): 653–679.

Blee, Kathleen. 2002. *Inside Organized Racism: Women in the Hate Movement*. Berkeley: University of California Press.

Buber, Martin. (1923) 1970. *I and Thou*. Translated by Walter Kaufmann. New York: Scribner.

Choi-Fitzpatrick, Austin. 2015. "From Rescue to Representation: A Human Rights Approach to the Contemporary Anti-slavery Movement." *Journal of Human Rights* 14 (4): 486–503.

———. 2016. "The Good, the Bad, the Ugly: Human Rights Violators in Comparative Perspective." *Journal of Human Trafficking* 2 (1): 1–14.

———. 2017. *What Slaveholders Think*. New York: Columbia University Press.

Davenport, Christian. 2007. "State Repression and Political Order." *Annual Review of Political Sociology* 10:1–23.

———. 2015. *How Social Movements Die: Repression and Demobilization of the Republic of New Africa*. New York: Cambridge University Press.

Duyvendak, Jan Willem, and James M. Jasper, eds. 2015. *Breaking Down the State: Protestors Engaged*. Amsterdam: Amsterdam University Press.

Earl, Jennifer. 2003. "Tanks, Tear Gas, and Taxes: Toward a Theory of Movement Repression." *Sociological Theory* 21 (1): 44–68.

Fischer, Eileen, and Rebecca Reuber. 2007. "The Good, the Bad, and the Unfamiliar: The Challenges of Reputation Formation Facing New Firms." *Entrepreneurship Theory and Practice* 31 (1): 53–75.

Fligstein, Neil, and Doug McAdam. 2012. *A Theory of Fields*. New York: Oxford University Press.

Freire, Paulo. 2018. *Pedagogy of the Oppressed*. Translated by Myra Bergman Ramos. New York: Bloomsbury Academic.

Gamson, William A. 1990. *The Strategy of Social Protest*. 2nd ed. Belmont, CA: Wadsworth.

Glymph, Thavolia. 2008. *Out of the House of Bondage: The Transformation of the Plantation Household*. New York: Cambridge University Press.

Goldstone, Jack, and Charles Tilly. 2001. "Threat (and Opportunity): Popular Action and State Response in the Dynamic of Contention Politics." In *Silence and Voice in the Study of Contentious Politics*, edited by Ronald Aminzade, Jack A. Goldstone, Doug McAdam, Elizabeth J. Perry, William H. Sewell, Sidney Tarrow, and Charles Tilly, 179–194. Cambridge: Cambridge University Press.

Goodwin, Jeff, and James M. Jasper. 1999. "Caught in a Winding, Snarling Vine: The Structural Bias of Political Process Theory." *Sociological Forum* 14:27–54.

———, eds. 2014. *The Social Movements Reader: Cases and Concepts*. New York: John Wiley.

Goodwin, Jeff, James M. Jasper, and Francesca Polletta, eds. 2009. *Passionate Politics: Emotions and Social Movements.* Chicago: University of Chicago Press.

Jackman, Mary. 1994. *The Velvet Glove: Paternalism and Conflict in Gender, Class, and Race Relations.* Berkeley: University of California Press.

Jasper, James M. 1997. *The Art of Moral Protest: Culture, Biography, and Creativity in Social Movements.* Chicago: University of Chicago Press.

Jasper, James M., and Jan Willem Duyvendak, eds. 2015. *Players and Arenas: The Interactive Dynamics of Protest.* Chicago: University of Chicago Press.

Jasper, James M., and Jane D. Poulsen. 1993. "Recruiting Strangers and Friends: Moral Shocks and Social Networks in Animal Rights and Anti-nuclear Protests." *Social Problems* 42:493–512.

King, Brayden G. 2008. "A Political Mediation Model of Corporate Response to Social Movement Activism." *Administrative Science Quarterly* 53:395–421.

Luders, Joseph E. 2010. *The Civil Rights Movement and the Logic of Social Change.* New York: Cambridge University Press.

Martin, Andrew, Clark McPhail, and John D. McCarthy. 2009. "Why Targets Matter: Toward a More Inclusive Model of Collective Violence." *American Sociological Review* 74:821–841.

Martin, Isaac. 2013. *Rich People's Movements: Grassroots Campaigns to Untax the One Percent.* Oxford: Oxford University Press.

McAdam, Doug. 1999. *Political Process and the Development of Black Insurgency, 1930–1970.* 2nd ed. Chicago: University of Chicago Press.

McCarthy, John D., and Mayer N. Zald. 1977. "Resource Mobilization and Social Movements: A Partial Theory." *American Journal of Sociology* 82:1212–1241.

McVeigh, Rory. 2009. *The Rise of the Ku Klux Klan: Right-Wing Movements and National Politics.* Minneapolis: University of Minnesota Press.

McVeigh, Rory, and Kevin Estep. 2019. *The Politics of Losing: Trump, the Klan, and the Mainstreaming of Resentment.* New York: Columbia University Press.

Noelle-Neumann, Elisabeth. 1974. *The Spiral of Silence: Public Opinion—Our Social Skin.* 2nd ed. Chicago: University of Chicago Press.

Piven, Frances Fox, and Richard A. Cloward. 1977. *Poor People's Movements: Why They Succeed, How They Fail.* New York: Vintage.

Rucht, Dieter. 2004. "Movement Allies, Adversaries, and Third Parties." In *The Blackwell Companion to Social Movements,* edited by David A. Snow, Sarah A. Soule, and Hanspeter Kriesi, 197–215. Malden, MA: Blackwell.

Sewell, William H. 1992. "A Theory of Structure: Duality, Agency, and Transformation." *American Journal of Sociology* 98:1–29.

Snow, David A., E. Burke Rockford Jr., Steven K. Worden, and Robert D. Benford. 1986. "Frame Alignment Processes, Micromobilization, and Movement Participation." *American Sociological Review* 51:464–481.

Statista. 2019. "Number of Employees at Goldman Sachs Worldwide from 2009 to 2018." Available at https://www.statista.com/statistics/250641/number-of-employees-at -goldman-sachs.

Tarrow, Sidney. 2011. *Power in Movement: Social Movements and Contentious Politics.* 3rd ed. Cambridge: Cambridge University Press.

Thompson, E. P. 1993. *Customs in Common: Studies in Traditional Popular Culture.* New York: New Press.

Tilly, Charles. 1998. *Durable Inequality.* Berkeley: University of California Press.

———. 1999. "From Interactions to Outcomes in Social Movements." In *How Social Movements Matter*, edited by Marco Giugni, Doug McAdam, and Charles Tilly, 253–270. Minneapolis: University of Minnesota Press.

Vasi, Ion Bogdan, and Brayden G King. 2012. "Social Movements, Risk Perceptions, and Economic Outcomes: The Effect of Primary and Secondary Stakeholder Activism on Firms' Perceived Environmental Risk and Financial Performance." *American Sociological Review* 77:573–596.

Walker, Edward T., Andrew W. Martin, and John D. McCarthy. 2008. "Confronting the State, the Corporation, and the Academy: The Influence of Institutional Targets on Social Movement Repertoires." *American Journal of Sociology* 114:35–76.

Weinstein, Jeremy. 2005. "Resources and the Information Problem in Rebel Recruitment." *Journal of Conflict Resolution* 49:598–624.

Contributors

Edwin Amenta is a professor of sociology and political science at the University of California, Irvine. He is the author of *Bold Relief: Institutional Politics and the Origins of Modern American Social Policy* (1998), *When Movements Matter: The Townsend Plan and the Rise of Social Security* (2006), and *Professor Baseball* (2007) and is a coeditor of the *Wiley-Blackwell Companion to Political Sociology* (2012). He is working with Neal Caren on a book about U.S. movements and the news media tentatively titled "The First Draft of Movement History."

Kenneth T. Andrews is Matthew Mason Professor of Sociology at the University of North Carolina at Chapel Hill. His work examines the dynamics and influence of protest, organizing, and civic associations on social and political change.

Austin Choi-Fitzpatrick is assistant professor of political sociology at the University of San Diego's Kroc School of Peace Studies and associate professor of social movements and human rights at the University of Nottingham's School of Sociology and Social Policy, where he is also a principal researcher at the Rights Lab. His work focuses on culture, politics, technology, and social change. His recent books include *What Slaveholders Think* (2017) and *Protest Tech* (forthcoming).

Sarah Gaby is a postdoctoral fellow at Washington University in St. Louis. She studies youth, social movements, organizations, and inequality. Her current project explores how organizations engage and politicize youth. Other current research analyzes the dynamics of social movements. She received her doctorate in sociology from the University of North Carolina at Chapel Hill.

Pablo Gastón is an assistant professor of sociology at the University of Michigan. A comparative historical sociologist, he studies historical changes in contentious practices in the American labor movement and the cultural and strategic imperatives that structure them. He is currently at work on a book project about how health-care workers' moral conceptions of caring shaped patterns of collective bargaining and economic conflict in the twentieth-century American hospital.

James M. Jasper writes about culture and politics. With Jan Willem Duyvendak he edited *Players and Arenas: The Interactive Dynamics of Protest* (2015) and *Breaking Down the State: Protestors Engaged* (2015). His most recent books are *The Emotions of Protest* (2018) and *Public Characters: The Politics of Reputation and Blame* (2019).

Brayden G King is the Max McGraw Chair of Management and the Environment at Northwestern University's Kellogg School of Management. He is a sociologist whose research examines the role of social movements in organizational, political, and social change.

Frances Fox Piven is the author or coauthor of a number of books on social movements, including *Poor People's Movements: Why They Succeed, How They Fail* (1977) and *Challenging Authority: How Ordinary People Change America* (2006). She recently retired from the faculty of the Graduate School of the City University of New York, where she was on the political science and sociology faculties.

Gay Seidman teaches sociology at the University of Wisconsin–Madison. Her research has focused on social movements in the Global South. In addition to two comparative-historical books on labor movements and transnational monitoring efforts, she has published research on women's movements; on boycotts and shaming movements, especially the antiapartheid divestment movement; and on the impact of social grants and minimum wage policies. She is currently doing research on the livelihood strategies of African refugees in South Africa's cities.

Nicole Shortt is a writer. She teaches writing and lives in Southern California with her dog.

Erica S. Simmons is an associate professor of political science and international studies at the University of Wisconsin–Madison, where she holds the Political Science Department Board of Visitors Professorship. She is the author of *Meaningful Resistance: Market Reforms and the Roots of Social Protest in Latin America* (2016), winner of the 2017 Charles Tilly award for distinguished contribution to scholarship on collective behavior and social movements. Her articles have appeared in *World Politics, Comparative Political Studies, Comparative Politics, PS: Political Science and Politics,* and *Theory and Society,* among others.

Katrin Uba is an associate professor in the Department of Government at Uppsala University and at the Skytte Institute, Tartu University. She has extensive experience in investigating protest behavior and the political impact of protests in Sweden. Her recent research focuses on social movement mobilization in a post-Soviet Estonia, the use of social media by the Swedish trade unions, and youth participation in the context of increasing inequalities.

Kim Voss is a professor of sociology and a scholar of labor, social movements, and inequality. Her current research investigates the resonance of frames used in the immigrant rights movement, examines dilemmas currently facing the U.S. labor movement, explores the ways in which worker identities in the United States are being reshaped by immigration, and analyzes the shifting terrain of U.S. higher education. In addition to publishing in academic journals in sociology, political science, and demography, she has written or edited six books: *Rallying for Immigrant Rights* (2011, with I. Bloemraad), *Hard Work: Remaking the American Labor Movement* (2006, with R. Fantasia), *Rebuilding Labor: Organizing and Organizers in the New Union Movement* (2004, with R. Milkman), *Des syndicats domestiques: Repression patronale et resistance syndicale aux Etas-Unis* (Domestic syndicates: Patronal repression and trade union resistance in the United States; 2003, with R. Fantasia), *Inequality by Design: Cracking the Bell Curve Myth* (1996, with five Berkeley colleagues), and *The Making of American Exceptionalism: The Knights of Labor and Class Formation in the Nineteenth Century* (1993).

Index

abortion, 148
activist identity, 50
actor-network theory, 11–12
adaptation, 207
Africa, 72
African National Congress (ANC), 79–81
American Federation of Labor and Congress
    of Industrial Organizations (AFL-CIO), 107
apartheid, 77–81
arenas, 11–14, 23–24, 150–152, 193–194;
    definition of, 126
attitudes, change in, 204–205
authority within movements, 91

Beirut, 86
Black Americans as voting bloc, 41–42. *See
    also* civil rights movement
Black Lives Matter, 45–46
Bolivia, water privatization in, 162, 166–176
bonded labor: definition of, 194; normalcy
    of, 199–201; as subject of mobilization,
    196–197
Bourdieu, Pierre, 8, 9
boycotts, 124, 198–199. *See also* unions
Brasilia, 71
Brazil, 73–74, 81–83, 85–86
Brown v. Board of Education, 129, 131–132
business: as political force, 42–44; as target,
    132–137, 149, 155–156

capitalism, 92
cash-transfer programs, 85–86

Chartist movement, 38
citizenship, 72; content of, 84–87; "insurgent,"
    74
civil rights movement, 35, 39–42, 124,
    128–129, 149; tactics of, 130–139; variety
    within, 125–127
Clinton, Bill, 43–44
coalitions: broad-based, 181, 182, 183; elec-
    toral, 37, 38, 41, 53, 57–60, 83, 153, 154;
    forming of, as union tactic, 97, 110; influ-
    ence of, 153, 154, 183; urban, 75, 86
collective action, 101–102
communities, imagined, 170
compromise, defiant, 207
consolidation of firms, 97
Copernican revolution, 148
corn, meanings of, 167, 176–183
corporate campaigns, 96–97, 104–105, 111,
    115
corporations, 5–6, 10, 12, 18–19, 92, 102;
    antiunion campaigns by, 96; vulnerabilities
    of, 97
costs, 202, 208
courts, 14
crowds, 1
culture, 2, 5, 21, 165–166; and targets, 163

democracy, 19, 37–39, 46; and associations,
    103; dilemmas of, 115–117; and power,
    100–102; in union governance, 113–117;
    and union revitalization, 106–107. *See also*
    politics: electoral

Democratic Party, 40–46. *See also* politics: partisan
democratization, 71–72
desegregation, 41, 124, 130, 132–139, 149; of schools, 129–132
development, inclusive, 75
developmentalism, 70–71
disruption, 20–21, 35–37; changing targets of, 99; as technique, 87
Durham, North Carolina, 124, 128–139

efficacy of protest, perceived, 49–50
election timing and controversies, 54
electoral politics, 135–136, 147, 149, 153–154; as protest opportunity, 53, 57, 59–61
emotion, 2
employment as movement goal, 133–137, 148. *See also* civil rights movement; desegregation
environmentalists, 15, 24
episodes, 19, 23–24; definition of, 125–126, 128–129; versus event, 128–129; relationship of, to movement, 127
event catalogs, 127–128
event size, 130

feminism, 201
field theory, 8, 9–11
financialization, 95, 97; of health care, 110; of real estate, 108–109
fracking, 148
French Revolution, 179–180

game theory, 2
gender, 200–201
geography and culture, 184
governance, 99–105, 184
government: local, 98; response of, to protests, 177–183
grievances: over inadequate public services, 74–87; as precondition for mobilization, 51–52, 56–59; regional differences in, 69–70; symbolic meanings of, 164–176

hierarchy, 36. *See also* inequality; power

identity, 50, 75, 97, 102, 174–176, 180–183; corporate, 110
identity movements, 22
imagined communities, 170
immigrant workers, 96
incumbents, 193–208. *See also* targets
India, 73

inequality, 69–72, 75, 77–87, 150–151. *See also* power
infrastructure, 71
innovation in contention, 115
institutional approach to targets, 21
institutional mediation models, 146, 152–157
institutions, 3–4, 6–8; as fields, 10; vulnerabilities of, 36–37
interactionism, 11, 23–25
internal movement dynamics, 18–19
isolation, 208

joint-effect mediation model, 153–156

labor, 6
leadership of movements, 137–139
Lebanon, 86
legislative bodies as targets, 20–21
living wage, 98

Marikana massacre, 80–81
markets, 169–173, 177–183
media, 14, 149–151, 156
methodology, 54–56
Mexico, 87, 167, 176–183; corn in, 162
military, 12
mobilization: of committed individuals, 152–153; innovation in, 107–111; motivation for, 49–50, 62
movements: as backfiring, 146; constraints on, 3–4; contexts of, 3–4; effectiveness of, 145–154; governance and organization of, 91; power of, 35–37, 145–146; success and failure of, 203–204; trajectories of, 164
movement-target dynamics, 17–19
Mumbai, 74

National Association for the Advancement of Colored People (NAACP), 124, 131, 133–138
National Labor Relations Act (NLRA), 93
National Labor Relations Board (NLRB), 95; circumvention of, 96–97
negotiation, 171–173, 175–176; as part of protest episodes, 133, 135–136, 138–139
neoliberalism, 83
networks, social, 52
normalcy, 199–201
norms, 208

Occupy Wall Street, 44, 84
opportunities: lack of, 49–50; for mobilization, 53–54, 58–61; political, 4–6. *See also* political opportunity theory

optimal size dilemma, 102, 104
organizational theory, 7–8
outcomes: complexity of, 24–25; mixed, 203–204; of social movements, 20–22

paternalism, 200
performance, 13–14
player-arena matrices, 23–24. *See also* arenas
players, 11–14, 150–152, 193–194
policing, 12, 156. *See also* repression
policy making, 153
political mediation models, 148, 152–156
political opportunity theory, 10, 151
political process theory, 1–2, 4–6
politics: electoral, 37–38, 40–45, 74, 80–81; interest group, 42, 42–45; partisan, 74, 154
poor communities, 73–74, 76–87
postcolonialism, 18, 69–70, 72, 77
postindustrial economy, 94–95
power, 150–151, 200–201; asymmetry in, 36; differentials in, 22; of movements, 36–37; of targets, 36–37
protests: forms of, 55–56; frequency of, 76–77, 83; ineffectiveness of, 149; scale of, 76–77, 79–83; for social services, 75; street, 171–176; suppression of, 51; trajectories of, 162

racism, 77–81. *See also* civil rights movement; desegregation
Red Scare, 15
referenda, 154–156. *See also* politics: electoral
relative deprivation, 56–59
repression, 6, 139, 200–204
Republican Party, 40–42, 45
reputation, 196, 198–199
resignation, 207–208
resource mobilization theory, 2, 147, 198–199
resources, 49–50, 52, 57–59, 199
right-wing parties, 83
right-wing politics, 43

São Paulo, 74
school desegregation, 129–132
secondary associations, 103
segregation. *See* desegregation
semiotic networks, 184
semiotics, 165–166
Service Employees International Union (SEIU), 93, 96, 105–115
service industries, 94–95
sexuality, 200–201

Shelby County v. Holder, 45
Shelley, Percy Bysse, 38
sit-ins, 132–137. *See also* civil rights movement
slavery, 39. *See also* bonded labor
social media, 70, 75
South Africa, 73–80, 85–87
stability, 9–11
state-level government, 44–45
states, 1–4, 9–10, 12, 37–39; as arenas, 151; as limiting powers of unions, 94
strategy, conditions influencing, 105–111
streets as site of protest, 70–71, 88
strikes, 36–37, 46; alternatives to, 92; changing targets of, 99; decline of, 92–95, 105; effects of, on governance, 103; rates of, 92; and wages, 94

tactics, choice of, 198–199. *See also* unions: tactics of
Taft-Hartley Act, 95
targets: ability of, to understand symbolic importance of movements, 167–168; choice of, 15–16, 197–199; motivations of, 20–21, 22; perceptions held by, 161, 163–164; as signaling broad support, 60–61; strategies of, 146–147; as unstudied, 191–192; vulnerabilities of, 116–117. *See also* incumbents
Truman, Harry, 40
Trump, Donald, 45

unions, 18–19, 43, 74, 80, 87, 92, 94–95; bureaucracy within, 102; centralization in, 111–117; democracy within, 100–105; dilemmas facing, 93; effects of size of, 102; governance of, 93, 106–107, 111–117; growth of, 104–105; non-strike tactics of, 95–99; revitalization of, 105–110; tactics of, 103–105, 108–110
universities as targets, 156
urbanism as goal, 84–86
urban movements, 18
U.S. Constitution, 38, 39

violence, 173–176
visibility, 195
voting rights, 15–16
Voting Rights Act of 1965, 39, 41, 45

Washington Consensus, 71
water, 166–176
workplace struggle, 114. *See also* strikes; unions

www.ingramcontent.com/pod-product-compliance
Lightning Source LLC
Chambersburg PA
CBHW020349270326
41926CB00007B/366